Oh My God!

A Fascinating Description Of God And The Divine System

Gurbux Kaur Kahlon

Dedication

This book is dedicated to my mother, Bibi Taro, who dared to dream a vision for my life under very challenging circumstances. With no schooling but feeling firmly that God was by her side, she was determined to make sure that her only daughter would get the education needed to be self-reliant in life and not live a life of helplessness and servitude that she found herself in. In addition to giving me the gift of life, she gave me an ever more precious gift of thinking beyond what we see.

Preface

I started my life's journey in India facing abandonment and adversity at a very young age. These experiences led my young mind to contemplate on whether there was God and if so, whether God had a system of justice. This introspective phase marked the beginning of my spiritual quest.

As I gained more control over my life with my education and career and immigrated to the United States in 1977, the issues about God and justice remained on my mind. However, they were now transcending my own life, seeing pervasive injustice in the world. I felt I had to resolve these issues for my own mind. As a follower of the Sikh religion, I decided to turn to the Sikh religious scripture Guru Granth Sahib for deeper understanding and guidance.

What I found blew my mind! What had so far consumed me as bad luck and adversity started to be visible as a chain of challenges and opportunities that were necessary to chart my journey through life. As I continued contemplating my newfound insights, the sense of peace, calm and optimism I felt was something I had never experienced before. Upon retiring from a long and busy career in the United States, I felt that sharing what I learned might do some good. So here is the book Oh My God!

Highlighting that we are all sparks of the same Divine and are here as part of the magnificent Divine Play, the Sikh scripture[1] describes the Divine and the Divine System as revealed to the Sikh Gurus and 15 non-Sikh saints through their personal experiences of the Divine. The descriptions are

---

[1] According to Britannica, there are 25-30 million followers of the Sikh religion.

in their own words with nothing added by anyone else. A key tenet of the scripture is that whoever has a longing to experience the Divine can explore and connect with the Divine regardless of the religion they are following and places no emphasis on religious conversion. The scripture does not focus on any history or personalities specific to Sikhism. and does not mandate any particular rituals or dogmas.

Written in verse more than 500 years ago, the scripture describes that there is indeed God who is superconscious and has designed a system that is automated to the hilt to run on its own. As per Divine design, we are all participants in the Magnificent Divine Play to live life fully and with purpose. To make the game of life challenging, we've been made to forget our true origin and the final destination. To make it even more interesting and challenging, some instincts have been made part of our minds that can lead us off course. The Divine system is designed such that we chart our own journey from life to life through our own actions or Karma. We go through the Karma-driven cycle of birth and death until we realize that there is God, and we develop a desire to go back to our Divine home. The fact that we do not see anybody running the system and the consequences of our actions are not dispensed immediately should not fool us into believing that there is no Divine justice and accountability. The playful God, being loving and forgiving, wants us to win the game of life and return home victorious.

The basic purpose of any religion is to provide answers to age-old questions such as whether there is a God and if so, what God is like, where we come from, and where we go after death. Prophets of various religions and sages and saints who experienced the Divine provided answers to many of these questions, which are remarkably similar. They all proclaimed that there is only One God for all of us who is conscious, compassionate, and in control and has a system which holds everyone accountable.

This leads one to wonder how hate, enmity and divisions among followers of various religions originated and why they keep on persisting. It seems that as each religion's establishment focused on expanding its own sphere of influence, the spiritual aspects of religions were pushed into the background.

Throughout history, as the expansionist interests of the religious establishments and the rulers coalesced, such monstrous atrocities were committed by rulers in the name of religion that they could never have done without it. Even in our time, religions have become a tool for pitting people against one another. People wishing to exert control over others have figured out that religion has the most sway over people, and in order to get them to do what works for their own self-interest, they cloak it in the garb of religion.

Drawing on the direct accounts of those who experienced the Divine, this book Oh My God! reminds us that there is only One God for all of us and lays bare the fallacy of thinking in terms of my God vs. their God. This God is the same conscious, compassionate, and in-control God that prophets of Christianity, Islam, Judaism, Sikh Gurus, and Hindu sages and saints described, even though to get more people into their tent, the religious establishments may have creatively added to the prophet's fundamental message.

The followers of every religion need to go back to the basics of their religion and examine whether what they are being told to believe and do is consistent with the depiction of the Divine and the Divine System their prophets laid out. Without this understanding, we can end up smearing our own prophets by distorting their messages and teachings, and by overlooking their emphasis on truth, compassion, kindness, and justice. In order to make this world a better place, followers of all religions must come together and stand firmly against those who use religion to divide people.

The purpose of this book is to help promote harmony, peace, and order in the world by re-focusing on the fundamental message of prophets of various religions that we all are children of the same God and that we need to conduct ourselves in this world with the awareness that God is conscious, compassionate and in control and the Divine system holds everyone accountable. Imagine a world where all of us acted with this awareness.

This book is also my humble attempt to caution the repressive rulers that there is a higher power above them. There will be a day of Divine justice when they will be held accountable, and none of the apparatus they have built around themselves here will enable them to hide their wrongdoings.

In presenting the detailed description of the Divine and the Divine System in this book from the Sikh scripture, I am by no means implying or claiming that the Sikh scripture is the only one to describe the Divine Reality and the Divine System. It is only because I am more familiar with the Sikh scripture and do not have deep knowledge about the scriptures of other religions.

Extensive quotations are provided to underscore that the statements made by those who experienced the Divine were not made in passing but reinforced by many of them multiple times.

I hope that practitioners of other faiths and seekers of the Divine who have had some experiential knowledge can critique or corroborate what is presented here so we can have a sincere and serious interfaith dialogue about the Divine and the Divine system. Such inter-religious collaboration is vital to begin the transformation of our understanding of the Divine and how we fit into the Divine system.

The time is now to dig into and reclaim your prophet's message of the Divine and to put an end to divisions, hatred, and enmity created by various religious and political establishments for their self-serving purposes.

Contents

Introduction

This book presents a description of the Divine and the Divine system provided by those who had personally experienced the Divine. The description is in their own words and is recorded in the scripture of the Sikh religion called Guru Granth Sahib. A key tenet of the scripture is that anyone can explore and connect with God if they have the curiosity and a longing to do so, regardless of which religion they are in. Therefore, it places no emphasis on conversion from one religion to another.

The scripture is a 1430-page compilation in verse and is wholly focused on God and the Divine System. It does not focus on history or personalities specific to the Sikh religion and does not mandate any rituals or dogmas.

Sikh religion or Sikhism is a monotheistic religion propounded by Guru Nanak Dev (1469-1539) in India in the fifteenth century. The literal meaning of the word Sikh is a student or a learner. The Sikh scripture was compiled by the Fifth Guru in the year 1604 from writings passed on by each Guru to the next and meticulously safeguarded by each subsequent Guru. In addition to the descriptions of the Divine by the Sikh Gurus in their own words, the scripture also includes descriptions of the Divine by 15 spiritually enlightened saints from other faiths who had personally experienced the Divine. Guru Nanak Dev and nine subsequent Sikh Gurus propagated the Sikh teachings as living Gurus until the tenth, and the last Guru decreed on October 6, 1708 that from there on out, Sikhs were to approach Guru Granth Sahib, the Sikh scripture as their eternal, living Guru, to seek support, inspiration, and guidance.

The Sikh Gurus and the 15 saints from other faiths whose descriptions of the Divine are included in Guru Granth Sahib were not philosophers or scholars who had rationally tried to come up with a paradigm or philosophy or a theoretical framework of how the world works or should work. Their descriptions are based on their own experiences of the Divine and the Divine system.

Key Tenets of the Sikh scripture

Similar to the Abrahamic religions (Christianity, Islam, and Judaism), the foundational concept of Sikhism is that there is only one God who is conscious, compassionate, and in control and has a system of Divine justice that holds us accountable. However, unlike Abrahamic religions, a key tenet of Sikhism is also that anyone can explore and connect with God regardless of their religion, as there can be many pathways to the Divine. The Sikh Gurus acknowledged that there have been enlightened people who had experienced the Divine Reality at other times and places and honored them by including some of their writings in the Sikh scripture along with their own. Instead of the emphasis on conversion from one religion to another, the scripture focuses on being aware of the Divine in everyday life, earning a livelihood in honest ways, and helping the needy.

As described in the Sikh scripture, there is only one God, even though we may give God various names. Everything and everyone emanates from that One God. God's consciousness and energy are the source of consciousness and life in all of us and everything, whether animate or inanimate. The intelligence and consciousness of God pervades and permeates everything and everyone. God is unaffected by time, so God does not get old and die like everyone and everything else.

2

God was there before the Creation, has always been there, and will always be there. God is not subject to birth and death.

We are sparks of the same Divine and are here as part of the grand Divine Play to live life to the fullest and to go back to our Divine home victorious by having overcome various challenges that are part of the Divine drama. The Divine system is designed such that we chart our own journey from one life to the next based on our own Karma and desires. So God has a built-in Karma-based justice system that holds everyone accountable, but God is also merciful and forgiving.

Death of the body is inevitable, but our true being or soul does not die. For the soul, this one life is just a short blip, even though it seems so long to us as we live through it. Upon death, it is only the body that dies. Because the soul, our real essence of life, does not die, we should be fearless about death and not hesitate to speak up against injustice and the tyranny of the rulers. The Sikh Gurus demonstrated this by giving their own life for justice. The 5th Sikh Guru was burned alive on May 30, 1606, on orders of the tyrannical Mughal ruler Jahangir by pouring hot sand on his body. He spoke of his execution as the will of God. The ninth Sikh Guru, Tegh Bahadur, was beheaded on November 24, 1675, in Delhi by the most tyrannical Mughal ruler, Aurangzeb, for challenging his order for Hindus to convert to Islam. Guru Tegh Bahadur stood up for freedom of religion for Hindus even though he was not a Hindu himself. The 10th Guru continued his fight for freedom of faith and justice, spending all his life resisting the Moghul army and losing all his four sons.

Written over 500 years ago, the scripture Guru Granth Sahib provides significant details about the universe's origin which is quite consistent with modern science. It describes that there are countless galaxies, suns, moons, and other planets and how they are held in place by Divine energy while orbiting tirelessly and precisely. The universe came into being with one Sound, which seems similar to the Big Bang theory. There was dense gaseous fog for a long time, and there was no visibility. Then came water, which is the source of all life. Everything and everyone has a beginning and an end. Suns, moons, and planetary bodies have a certain life. The process of Creation and Dissolution has been repeated many times. Creation happens when the Divine ordains it. All forms of life and matter are subsumed into One Divine when the Divine force draws it all in. All this was articulated in the scripture at a time when the prevailing wisdom was that the sun was revolving around the earth!

We are reminded to always remember God and the Divine system of accountability so we can be on the right path and avoid hurting others. Without being aware that indeed, there is God who is conscious and in charge and holds us accountable for our actions, it is difficult for us humans to tame our undesirable instincts.

There is reminder after reminder in the Sikh scripture that death is certain, and nobody gets to take any of their belongings or wealth with them. Given that no wealth can be taken with us after we leave the world, it does not make sense to accumulate ill-gotten wealth that we will leave behind. No offsprings, relatives, or friends that one might strive to leave any ill-gotten wealth to, can help come to the time of judgment.

To be born as a human is a great blessing and an opportunity to explore our inner selves as the human body is equipped with the unique intellect, intuition, and the ability to endeavor and control our environment that other species are not endowed with. This is a rare opportunity to understand that God pervades everywhere and the same Divine spark sustains all of us. We can make the most of it by always remembering God and by living in gratitude for the Creator, who has endowed us with so much in this world to enjoy. Becoming truly aware of how special our human life is and how much there is for us to enjoy, we will be living in awe and will develop a longing to see the Creator. Connecting back with the Creator and going to our eternal Divine abode upon completing our journey is the purpose of human life.

Brief Historical Context

Before Guru Nanak Dev propounded the Sikh religion in India in the fifteenth century, knowledge of the Divine and the Divine System existed in India as part of the Hindu religion because India had a long and rich tradition of pursuit of the Divine. Most serious followers of the Hindu religion used to renounce the world and go to the mountains to engage in this pursuit. However, all that knowledge was not made accessible to people as the Hindu religious scriptures were written in Sanskrit, which was not a spoken language of the people. It was an academic language exclusively reserved for the priestly class. At the level of the masses, Hindu religion was practiced as various rituals to appease a number of deities and gods and goddesses to be spared from their wrath.

Ten Sikh Gurus, over time, propagated the fundamental tenets of the Sikh faith one after the other. On October 6, 1708, the tenth (the last) Sikh Guru, Gobind Singh, ordained that Sikhs are to regard the scripture as their living Guru, thereby ending the guruship of a person. Since then, the scripture has been revered as Guru Granth Sahib. A Sikh is advised to approach Guru Granth Sahib on any issue, where they will find valuable advice, encouragement, guidance, and support. Every Sikh temple (called Gurdwara) has the seat of Guru Granth Sahib adorned as the seat of a living Guru.

The Sikh scripture does not include any of the writings of the tenth (the last) Guru, Guru Gobind Singh. Most of his own writings were lost as he was always under attack by the Moghul rulers and did not have any safe place to preserve them. The Sikhs found some of that lost literature years later but had a hard time figuring out which ones were exactly the tenth Guru's own writings. Analyzing the content for conformity with how he lived his life and for consistency with the previous nine Gurus' writings, scholars tasked by the Sikh religious establishment determined which ones were most likely his writings[2]. The writings they determined as his are part of the daily Sikh religious routine. In this book, in addition to quotations from the Sikh scripture Guru Granth Sahib, quotations are also presented from those writings of the tenth Guru that have been determined to be his.

The tenth Guru created the Sikh order of the Khalsa in the year 1699 on the first day of the second month in the Indian calendar. Sikhs celebrate the Khalsa creation day on this day each year. The Khalsa is the culmination of a Sikh's practice and faith in the Almighty God, where a Sikh becomes fearless and without enmity toward anyone and stands up to

---

[2] The confusion arose because, as a connoisseur of literature, the tenth Guru had encouraged poets and writers in his attendance to translate Hindu religious literature into the common language for people. Some of this translated literature presented to him may have mentioned the Guru's name when he annotated those texts with his own comments to set the record straight about the subject.

6

repression and injustice faced by anyone regardless of the religion, caste, and creed of those repressed.

The 10th Guru laid down specific code of conduct for how Sikhs who evolve into Khalsa must conduct themselves and how they should be recognizable by their distinct appearance. A Sikh's appearance with a turban and beard represents a deep respect and reverence for the Divine's design of the human body. To maintain the universality of the Sikh scripture for all, the 10th Guru did not include in the scripture any of the edicts that he laid down for Khalsa as the distinct Sikh religious order.

All concepts and descriptions in this book are presented with extensive quotations from the Sikh scripture, citing pages and line numbers for easy reference. All are strongly encouraged to read these actual statements by those who experienced the Divine on each subject as they are so very fascinating.

Chapter 1: First things first

First Things First

This book presents a description of the Divine and the Divine system using statements of those who said that they have described what they had actually witnessed and experienced.

But one might ask why should we believe that they truly experienced and witnessed the Divine and its system? It's only natural for us to be skeptical unless they could take us along for a ride and show us firsthand what they saw.

Unfortunately, to the great dismay of our scientifically trained and evidence-based mindset, we have to rely on secondary evidence and logic to have faith in their statements. There is no medium to transport us to the realm of the Divine simply because we are skeptical. They laid out a path for us to follow to see the Divine System ourselves but it is definitely not a quick trip to the Divine realm and back for any of us.

So, what secondary evidence should we look for to believe that their statements are authentic depictions of the Divine? A commonsense and simple approach would be to start with the search for the motive behind their statements. Did any of these people make things up because they wanted to get rich off of other people? Were they lying to get big followings of people? Did they make false promises to people to help them get a seat in heaven or get a pass and not go to hell? Were their own actions consistent with the values that they were preaching to other people? Were their statements about the Divine and the Divine system contradictory to each other? Have any of their statements proven to be untrue as we have learned more through science?

Of what is known about them, they were from very humble backgrounds and led simple and frugal lives. They had no schooling to be able to go through other religions' scriptures and borrow ideas and concepts. Among the 15 saints featured in the descriptions, one was a weaver from a village, another working with hyde and making shoes, and yet another earned a living by stitching and washing clothes for others. They were from the lowest caste in the Hindu caste hierarchy. The Sikh Gurus, likewise, were from ordinary families living in villages with no formal schooling.

We cannot test the validity of their assertions about the Divine and the Divine system as it is not visible to us for verification. However, when you go over their statements about the nature of the universe in Chapter 10, you will be astounded to find that many of their statements have been proven by science to be true. These people, with no schooling and no telescopes and other observatory instruments, stated that there were countless planets precisely orbiting on their own. This was the time when the prevailing wisdom in the Western world was that the Sun was revolving around the earth.

These people did not claim themselves to be God, nor did they say they had special access to God to make people follow them. They did not engage in any miracles to impress people. Instead, their whole emphasis was to make people aware that there is God who is conscious and in control and will hold each of us accountable for how we lead our lives.

None of them tried to get a following or tried to get rich by promising people heaven after death. Instead, in their statements, they cautioned people that it is their own deeds that will decide their destiny after death. They told people not to waste their time and money by engaging in meaningless rituals and exhorted them to contemplate on God and do good deeds. These were the people whose lives reflected what they were preaching. There is remarkable consistency between their descriptions of the Divine.

In their writings, they presented themselves as the lowest of the lowly and humble servants of God. The tenth and the last Guru of the Sikh religion, in fact, warned his followers never to consider him as God. He had a dire warning for those who might think of him as God, stating that anyone who does so would be doomed to the fires of hell. Here is what he said in his own words:

Guru Gobind Singh, Bachitar Natak
ਜੋ ਹਮ ਕੋ ਪਰਮੇਸਰ ਉਚਰਿ ਹੈਂ ॥ ਤੇ ਸਭ ਨਰਕਿ ਕੁੰਡ ਮਹਿ ਪਰਿਹੈਂ ॥
ਮੋ ਕੋ ਦਾਸ ਤਵਨ ਕਾ ਜਾਨੋ ॥ ਯਾ ਮੈ ਭੇਦ ਨ ਰੰਚ ਪਛਾਨੋ ॥੩੨॥
Those who call me God shall be condemned to the fire of hell. Consider me a humble servant of God. Have no doubt about the authenticity of this statement whatsoever.

All the concepts, principles, and conclusions presented here are based on their statements as recorded in the Sikh scripture, providing detailed quotations by page and line number. This book is not about biographical accounts of their lives but what they said about the Divine and the Divine system. The reason to provide quotations extensively is to show that these subjects were not addressed by them in passing but laid out in detail for us to understand and to incorporate that understanding in our lives.

Hopefully, this is enough for you to take a leap of faith and see what those who experienced the Divine want us to know.

Chapter 2: There is only One God—Our God

> *One God permeating everything and everyone*

There is only One God - our God.

As we go to our respective religious places to remember and worship God, how many of us can ever visualize that people going to another religious worship place on the other side of the street are trying to connect to the same God? I'm sure none of us can truly relate to the God we think resides in the other building. This question isn't meant to make us feel guilty; rather, we need to explore why this disconnect exists and why we think in terms of our God vs. their God.

God sends prophets from time to time in various corners of the world to speak to us in our own language about the Divine Reality and deliver a message of hope and redemption. The prophets tell us about the existence of God and how we are all children of the same God. They show us how to chart our journey in this world with God in our hearts and minds, for joy, peace, and comfort for ourselves and those around us, and to witness the great Divine after we exit this life.

So, what happened to the prophets' messages that all of us belong to the same God. How did followers of various religions come to have so much hate and enmity towards one another? The reason is that, over time, some power-hungry individuals have distorted the prophets' messages to manipulate people. Instead of focusing on the message of their prophet about the One Divine, they have used the names of different prophets to divide people for their self-interest. To solidify their own following and power, they use the prophets' names to force or promote religious conversions while engendering hate and bigotry against others. It is conceivable that the religious establishments may have creatively added to their prophet's fundamental message to claim exclusive access to the Divine.

Those who experienced the Divine testify that there is only One God - our God. There is no other. God is indivisible and equally accessible to all of us. This God is the same conscious, compassionate, and in-control God that the Prophets of Christianity, Islam, Judaism, Sikh Gurus, and Hindu sages and saints described. All prophets said that God holds us accountable but is kind and merciful and forgives us when we reach out to Him. The same God provides for all beings regardless of their race, ethnicity, language, and color of skin.

The very first page of the Sikh scripture starts with the number 1 (Ik Onkar) and goes on to highlight the salient attributes of the One and Only God. It is the One from whom everything emanates. There is only One Creator, Divine Being, or God who has ordained an order or system (referred to as Hukam in Guru Granth Sahib) that governs the beginning of life, sustenance of life, and the end of life. There is No Other. The creative power of this Divine Being is unimaginable and magnificent. He is the Creator of all life and matter, animate and inanimate, and everything with or without form. He is without fear and has no enmity towards anyone. Time does not affect Him and His appearance. He is self-existent. He never dies and is never born and is beyond the cycle of birth and death. Only He is the One whose existence or Name is forever. He is only accessible through His remembrance and His Grace.

India had a long and rich tradition of pursuit of the Divine. People used to renounce the world and go to the mountains to engage in this pursuit. Before Sikhism emerged, some Hindu scriptures did mention there being One God along the lines of what Guru Nanak, the founder of the Sikh religion, proclaimed. However, the knowledge accumulated from the experiences of enlightened sages and saints was not made accessible to people as the Hindu scriptures were written in Sanskrit, which was not a spoken language of the people. It was an academic language exclusively reserved for the priestly class. At the level of the masses, Hindu religion continued to be practiced as various rituals to appease a number of deities and gods and goddesses to be spared from their wrath and to please certain other deities to have a good life.

The founder of the Sikh religion, Guru Nanak Dev, was born in a Hindu family in India. Hinduism was the dominant religion at the time. As most of his audience were Hindus worshipping various gods and goddesses, he meticulously used the names of various gods and goddesses that they were worshipping to help them understand that there is only one God. He explained that if there were any deities, gods, or goddesses, they were under the command of the One God. He exhorted them to remember and revere One God instead of a multitude of gods, goddesses, and deities.

The Sikh Gurus went to great lengths to explain to their Hindu audience that One God is the Creator, and instead of worshipping the mythical deity Brahma as the creator, they should use the word Brahma for God. They clarified that it is One God who sustains life, not the mythical deity Vishnu. They suggested using the name Vishnu to refer to God as the sustainer. Similarly, they emphasized that it is this same One God who creates and sustains that ultimately ends life, not the deity Shiva whose mythical stories they were used to and that they should use the name Shiva for God. To the Hindus, who following the epic book Ramayana (believed to be written in approx. 200 BCE by sage Valmik), were worshipping Ram (the once exiled son of King Dashrath and husband of Sita) as God, they explained that they should use the word Ram to remember God who is pervading everywhere (in Hindi and

15

Punjabi language in India, Ram also means Ramya or pervading everywhere).

The Sikh scripture freely uses names for God that were being used in both Hinduism and Islam to teach their followers that they all have the same God and to inspire them to be a true follower of own religion to be on the path to the Divine. Because Hindus were used to names of deities such as Brahma, Vishnu, Shiva, Ram and others, the scripture uses many of these familiar names to illustrate that the powers associated by people with these deities are, in fact, powers of God and exhorts them to rise above deities and connect with God instead. Similarly, the scripture uses the Muslim name for God Allah in some places to stress that it is the same God regardless of which religion one associates with.

In their own words:

First Sikh Guru, Nanak Dev-Guru Granth Sahib (GGS) Page 1, line 1

ੴ ਸਤਿ ਨਾਮੁ ਕਰਤਾ ਪੁਰਖੁ ਨਿਰਭਉ ਨਿਰਵੈਰੁ ਅਕਾਲ ਮੂਰਤਿ ਅਜੂਨੀ ਸੈਭੰ ਗੁਰ ਪ੍ਰਸਾਦਿ ॥

ONE the Source of everything that ever exists. Whose Existence/Name is forever. The Creator Being. Without fear. Without enmity. His image (appearance) is not affected by time. Beyond Birth, Self-Existent. Accessible only By His Grace.

First Sikh Guru, GGS p.57, line 5

ਨਾਨਕ ਏਕੋ ਰਵਿ ਰਹਿਆ ਦੂਜਾ ਅਵਰੁ ਨ ਕੋਇ ॥੮॥੬॥

Says Nanak, the One is pervading everywhere; there is no other at all.

Fifth Sikh Guru, Guru Arjan Dev, GGS p.192, line 2

ਮਾਰੈ ਰਾਖੈ ਏਕੋ ਸੋਇ ॥੧॥

He alone sustains and destroys.

Third Sikh Guru, Guru Amar Das, GGS p.37, line 9
ਸਭ ਏਕੋ ਇਕੁ ਵਰਤਦਾ ਅਲਖੁ ਨ ਲਖਿਆ ਜਾਇ ॥

The One and Only Divine is (invisibly) pervading and permeating all; hard to fathom and articulate.

Third Guru, GGS p.113, line 17
ਏਕੋ ਵੇਖਾ ਅਵਰੁ ਨ ਬੀਆ ॥

I see only the One and no other.

First Guru GGS p. 350, line 4
ਸਾਹਿਬੁ ਮੇਰਾ ਏਕੋ ਹੈ ॥ ਏਕੋ ਹੈ ਭਾਈ ਏਕੋ ਹੈ ॥੧॥

The Divine Ruler is One; My Brethren, One and only One.

Third Guru GGS p. 947, line 10
ਨਾਨਕ ਏਕੋ ਨਦਰੀ ਆਇਆ ਜਹ ਦੇਖਾ ਤਹ ਸੋਇ ॥੩॥

Says Nanak, I see the One Divine wherever I look.

Fifth Guru (Guru Arjan Dev), GGS p. 821, line 14
ਏਕੰਕਾਰੁ ਏਕੁ ਪਾਸਾਰਾ ਏਕੈ ਅਪਰ ਅਪਾਰਾ ॥

The whole Creation is the Expanse of One Creator who is Infinite and Unfathomable.

Fifth Guru GGS p. 884, line 8
ਏਕੈ ਏਕੈ ਏਕ ਤੂਹੀ ॥ ਏਕੈ ਏਕੈ ਤੂ ਰਾਇਆ ॥

You alone are the One and the only God. You alone are the ruler.

Fifth Guru GGS p. 821, line 14
ਏਕੁ ਬਿਸਥੀਰਨੁ ਏਕੁ ਸੰਪੂਰਨੁ ਏਕੈ ਪ੍ਰਾਨ ਅਧਾਰਾ ॥੩॥

All (that we see) is the manifestation of the One, Perfect One who is the support of the breath of life.

Fourth Guru, GGS p. 980, line 13

ਸਹਸ ਨੇਤ੍ਰ ਨੇਤ੍ਰ ਹੈ ਪ੍ਰਭ ਕਉ ਪ੍ਰਭ ਏਕੋ ਪੁਰਖੁ ਨਿਰਾਰੇ ॥

The thousands of eyes are the eyes of God-the One God, the Unique Primal Being.

Fifth Guru GGS p.897, line 6

ਏਕੋ ਅਲਹੁ ਪਾਰਬ੍ਰਹਮ ॥੫॥੩੪॥੪੫॥

Call Him Allah (as Muslims do) or Parbraham (as Hindus do), He is one and the same.

First Guru GGS p. 358, line 14

ਤੇਰੇ ਨਾਮ ਅਨੇਕਾ ਰੂਪ ਅਨੰਤਾ ਕਹਣੁ ਨ ਜਾਹੀ ਤੇਰੇ ਗੁਣ ਕੇਤੇ ॥੧॥

Your Names are so many, and Your Forms are endless. No one can describe how many glorious attributes You have.

Fourth Guru GGS p. 1319, line 5

ਹਰਿ ਕੇ ਨਾਮ ਅਸੰਖ ਅਗਮ ਹਹਿ ਅਗਮ ਅਗਮ ਹਰਿ ਰਾਇਆ ॥

The Divine has countless Names and is unfathomable. The Sovereign Divine is just unfathomable.

Fifth Guru GGS p. 986, line 12

ਅਗਮ ਰੂਪ ਗੋਬਿੰਦ ਕਾ ਅਨਿਕ ਨਾਮ ਅਪਾਰ ॥

The beauty of the Master of the Universe is profound and unfathomable; His Names are innumerable.

Tenth Guru, Jaap Sahib Stanza 9

ਨਮਸਤੰ ਸੁ ਏਕੈ ॥

Salutation to You, the ONLY ONE God.

Tenth Guru, Jaap sahib Stanza 43

ਅਨੇਕ ਹੈਂ ॥ ਫਿਰਿ ਏਕ ਹੈਂ ॥੪੩॥

You manifest in countless forms, but you are One.

Tenth Guru, Benti Chaupai stanza 385

18

ਆਦਿ ਅੰਤਿ ਏਕੈ ਅਵਤਾਰਾ ॥ ਸੋਈ ਗੁਰੂ ਸਮਝਿਯਹੁ ਹਮਾਰਾ ॥੩੮੫॥

The One Divine who is in-charge of the Creation from beginning to the end. Know that that is my Guru.

Tenth Guru, Jaap Sahib stanza 1
ਤੂ ਸਰਬ ਨਾਮ ਕਥੈ ਕਵਨ ਕਰਮ ਨਾਮ ਬਰਣਤ ਸੁਮਤਿ ॥੧॥

Who can enumerate all your names- the wise ones describe You by Your actions or attributes.

One God permeating everything and everyone

Those who experienced the Divine state that the Divine energy emanating from the One God permeates everyone and everything and is at the same time within each of us (immanent) and outside of us (transcendent).

Imagine explaining to people in the fifteenth or sixteenth century that humans could communicate and even see each other from continents apart without any visible cables or connections. They would think you were crazy, or you might go insane trying to convince them that it's possible. We are in a similar state of ignorance about the Divine and its system today. We remain skeptical about God's existence and unsure if God is intelligent, conscious, and in control because it is not visible to us.

God is not contained in a particular location or form. God is distinct but, at the same time, infused in the entire creation. God is everywhere, within us, around us, and beyond us, and watching the Divine System play out. It is His Divine spark that sustains all. God is our life force. Without the Divine spark, nothing would exist. We are all manifestations of this Divine presence. Those who experienced the Divine say that the biggest wonder is that even though God is watching everything, we remain unaware of it. Since God's Energy is within us, He even knows every thought that passes through our hearts and minds. The One and Only Creator who created all the forms (animate and inanimate) is pervading everywhere. All will one day merge back into the One. He resides within each and every being and is always with us. It is futile to look for God elsewhere.

God is at the same time within each of us (immanent) and outside of us (transcendent). Everyone and everything is a microcosm of the universe. To explain this, Guru Nanak gives an example of a droplet of water and the ocean and says that just like the droplet of water is in the ocean, the ocean is in the droplet of water. In the same vein, the fifth Guru describes that God is within us, and we are within God. Whatever physical phenomena is around us is also within us.[3] According to the Sikh scripture, the Whole contains all the information about its parts or the particles, and the particles contain all the information about the Whole.

Without actually experiencing the Divine Reality, it is difficult for us to logically comprehend how God can be at the same time within each of us (immanent) and outside of us (transcendent). At the time the Sikh scripture was written and compiled in the fifteenth and sixteenth century trying to explain this, the state of science was such that it was being debated in the Western world whether the Sun revolves around the Earth or the Earth revolves around the Sun.

However, it is possible that someday, knowing more about the nature of matter and energy, physicists may be able to help us understand these descriptions in Guru Granth Sahib of the Divine energy pervading and permeating everything, animate

---

[3] Luke 17:21 "The Kingdom of God is Within You" (Bible KGV)

and inanimate. It seems that some of it is already being indicated by the postulates of the Particle Theory of Physics, which suggests that all matter is composed of particles, and these particles are kinesthetic and move around and are attracted to each other. The explanation in Guru Granth Sahib that seemingly inanimate things also have Divine Energy pervading in them also seems to be similar to the Unified Field Theory, which describes all particles as vibrating strings with different modes of vibration producing different particles.

In their own words:

Fifth Guru GGS p. 276, line 5
ਸਭ ਤੇ ਨੇਰੈ ਸਭਹੂ ਤੇ ਦੂਰਿ ॥ ਨਾਨਕ ਆਪਿ ਅਲਿਪਤੁ ਰਹਿਆ ਭਰਪੂਰਿ ॥੪॥

He is near to all, and yet far from all; Says Nanak, He Himself remains distinct, while yet pervading all.

First Guru GGS p. 7, line 3
ਓਹੁ ਵੇਖੈ ਓਨਾ ਨਦਰਿ ਨ ਆਵੈ ਬਹੁਤਾ ਏਹੁ ਵਿਡਾਣੁ ॥

The biggest wonder is that He sees us all but we do not see Him.

First Guru GGS p. 433, line 17
ਦੇਖੈ ਬੂਝੈ ਸਭੁ ਕਿਛੁ ਜਾਣੈ ਅੰਤਰਿ ਬਾਹਰਿ ਰਵਿ ਰਹਿਆ ॥੨੪॥

He sees, understands, and knows everything; He is within us and outside of us.

First Guru GGS p. 728, line 13
ਜਲਿ ਥਲਿ ਮਹੀਅਲਿ ਰਵਿ ਰਹਿਆ ਸੋਇ ॥੩॥

Almighty God is pervading and permeating the waters, the lands and the skies.

Third Guru GGS p. 956, line 11
ਰਵਿ ਰਹਿਆ ਸਰਬਤਿ ਨਾਨਕੁ ਬਲਿ ਜਾਈ ॥੨੦॥

He is pervading everywhere. Says Nanak, I so revel in His presence that I can offer to die for Him.

Fourth Guru GGS p. 174, line 15
ਆਪੇ ਜਲਿ ਥਲਿ ਵਰਤਦਾ ਮੇਰੇ ਗੋਵਿੰਦਾ ਰਵਿ ਰਹਿਆ ਨਹੀ ਦੂਰੀ ਜੀਉ ॥

Almighty God Himself is permeating and pervading the waters and the lands. He is All-pervading — is not far away.

Fourth Guru GGS p. 1310, line 8
ਓਅੰਕਾਰਿ ਏਕੋ ਰਵਿ ਰਹਿਆ ਸਭੁ ਏਕਸ ਮਾਹਿ ਸਮਾਵੈਗੋ ॥

The One and Only Creator who created all the forms (animate and inanimate) is pervading everywhere. All shall one day merge back into the One.

Fourth Guru GGS p. 775, line 12
ਸਭ ਮਹਿ ਰਵਿ ਰਹਿਆ ਸੋ ਪ੍ਰਭੁ ਅੰਤਰਜਾਮੀ ਰਾਮ ॥

The Almighty God who even knows what goes on in our hearts and minds resides in all.

Saint Kabir GGS p. 1350, line 1
ਖਾਲਿਕੁ ਖਲਕ ਖਲਕ ਮਹਿ ਖਾਲਿਕੁ ਪੂਰਿ ਰਹਿਓ ਸ੍ਰਬ ਠਾਂਈ ॥੧॥ ਰਹਾਉ ॥

The Creator is in the Creation and the Creation is in the Creator, with the Creator pervading and permeating all places.

Fifth Guru GGS p. 102, line 19
ਤੂੰ ਗੁਪਤੁ ਪਰਗਟੁ ਪ੍ਰਭ ਆਪੇ ॥

O' God, You Yourself are the Manifest and the Unmanifest.

Third Guru GGS p. 124, line 16
ਗੁਪਤੁ ਪਰਗਟੁ ਤੂੰ ਸਭਨੀ ਥਾਈ ॥

You are everywhere, (in some) visibly and (in others) invisibly.

Third Guru GGS p. 126, line 10
ਅੰਤਰਿ ਜੋਤਿ ਪਰਗਟੁ ਪਾਸਾਰਾ ॥
Within each is the Light of God; the expanse of His creation is the manifest form of it.

Saint Kabir GGS p.331, line 8
ਜਤ ਪੇਖਉ ਤਤ ਅੰਤਰਜਾਮੀ ॥੩॥
Wherever I look, I see the all-knowing who knows whatever goes on in every heart and mind.

Fifth Guru, GGS p. 45, line 17
ਥਾਨ ਥਨੰਤਰਿ ਰਵਿ ਰਹਿਆ ਪਾਰਬ੍ਰਹਮੁ ਪ੍ਰਭੁ ਸੋਇ ॥
The Almighty God is pervading all places and interspaces.

Fifth Guru GGS p. 47, line 11
ਅੰਤਰਿ ਬਾਹਰਿ ਰਵਿ ਰਹਿਆ ਤਿਸ ਨੋ ਜਾਣੈ ਦੂਰਿ ॥
Almighty God is pervading within us and outside of us, and yet people think that He is far away.

Fifth Guru GGS p. 48, line 18
ਘਟ ਘਟ ਅੰਤਰਿ ਰਵਿ ਰਹਿਆ ਸਦਾ ਸਹਾਈ ਸੰਗਿ ॥੧॥
He resides within each and every being- always with us and supporting us.

Fifth Guru GGS p. 775, line 12
ਰਵਿ ਰਹਿਆ ਪ੍ਰਭੁ ਸਭ ਮਹਿ ਆਪੇ ॥
God Himself is pervading, and permeating all.

Third Guru GGS p. 1052, line 8
ਆਪੇ ਗੁਪਤੁ ਵਰਤੈ ਸਭ ਅੰਤਰਿ ਗੁਰ ਕੈ ਸਬਦਿ ਪਛਾਤਾ ਹੇ ॥੧॥

The Divine Shabad reveals that the Divine Himself invisibly is pervading within all.

First Guru GGS p. 878, line 18
ਸਾਗਰ ਮਹਿ ਬੂੰਦ ਬੂੰਦ ਮਹਿ ਸਾਗਰੁ ਕਵਣੁ ਬੁਝੈ ਬਿਧਿ ਜਾਣੈ ॥
The droplet of water is in the ocean, and the ocean is in the droplet of water, whoever can unravel this mystery and comprehend.

Fifth Guru GGS p. 287, line 3
ਬ੍ਰਹਮ ਮਹਿ ਜਨੁ ਜਨ ਮਹਿ ਪਾਰਬ੍ਰਹਮੁ ॥
God is in His created beings and the created beings are in God.

Fifth Guru GGS p. 293, line 18
ਸੋ ਅੰਤਰਿ ਸੋ ਬਾਹਰਿ ਅਨੰਤ ॥ ਘਟਿ ਘਟਿ ਬਿਆਪਿ ਰਹਿਆ ਭਗਵੰਤ ॥
ਧਰਨਿ ਮਾਹਿ ਆਕਾਸ ਪਇਆਲ ॥ ਸਰਬ ਲੋਕ ਪੂਰਨ ਪ੍ਰਤਿਪਾਲ ॥
The Infinite Creator is inside, and also outside. Deep within each and every heart, the Almighty God is pervading. He is everywhere-the earth, Akash (the empty gravitational space over the earth) and in the worlds below our world. He, the Perfect One, provides for people in all the worlds.

Tenth Guru, Jaap Sahib stanza 77
ਸਰਬੰ ਪ੍ਰਾਣੰ ॥
You are the life of all.

Tenth Guru Jaap Sahib Stanza 22
ਨਮੋ ਸਰਬ ਗਾਉਨੇ ॥ ਨਮੋ ਸਰਬ ਭਉਨੇ ॥
Salutation to You, O' All-pervasive. Salutation to You, Permeating Everywhere.

Saint Pipa GGS p. 695, line 15

24

ਜੋ ਬ੍ਰਹਮੰਡੇ ਸੋਈ ਪਿੰਡੇ ਜੋ ਖੋਜੈ ਸੋ ਪਾਵੈ ॥

All that is in the universe is also in the body. Whoever explores it, will find out.

Chapter 3: Is God intelligent and conscious?

➢ *Does God have a physical form?*
➢ *Playful and Blissful God, really?*
➢ *Does God have a life span and does He die?*
➢ *God's parents and lineage?*
➢ *Is God loving, merciful or forgiving?*
➢ *Does God act out of vengeance or invoke His wrath?*

Is God intelligent and conscious, and in charge of our messy world?

Imagine a future where human look-alikes generated by artificial intelligence start asserting that they came into existence on their own and all of their extraordinary abilities to perceive things and respond to them have evolved on their own. Does that sound like us?

Seeing the dysfunctional world around us, all of us have at times felt that maybe humans have invented the concept of God just to make sense of the world. Nobody seems to be in charge, and nobody seems to be making sure there is order, justice, and accountability.

However, those who have experienced the Divine affirm that there is a Creator or God who embodies supreme consciousness. This Creator is the source of the consciousness and intelligence present in every being. We are intelligent and conscious because our Creator, the designer of the world, is intelligent and conscious. His intelligence and consciousness are behind the design and operation of the whole universe. God is formless and is neither male nor female even though, as the authority controlling everything, we may conveniently use adjectives such as He, Him, or His. He is pure Conscious Energy, which can manifest in any form but is formless in essence.

The Super-Conscious God even knows every thought that goes on in our hearts and minds. It is His spark in all beings that imparts consciousness to them. Through the Divine Order or system that God has laid out, He is in charge of all Creation, its maintenance, and ultimate dismantling of everything. When He so wishes, He sets in motion the cycle of Creation with His Energy manifesting in countless forms, live and inert.

When He so wishes, and the grand scheme laid out by Him runs out, He draws it all in and subsumes all manifest forms back into His fold so there is only the Formless Divine. The Super-Conscious God pervades everything and everyone. His Infinite Energy and magnificent creativity manifests in limitless diversity of forms, life, materials, heavenly bodies, and the natural beauty of His creation.

Because His Super-Conscious Energy, Intelligence, and Creativity have created a magnificent system that runs on its own, it appears to our senses that there is no intelligence or consciousness behind it. But just because our senses cannot comprehend how the system is running and there is nobody running things for us to see, it is foolish to assume that there is no intelligence or consciousness behind it.

We see humans and animals creating their own kind; trees and plants duplicating themselves on their own, and sun, moon and other heavenly bodies precisely orbiting every day in their pre-determined cycles and conclude that there is no Conscious Energy or Intelligence behind it. For us to think that would be like robots, artificial intelligence systems, and other automated systems to think that they came into being on their own without being created by another intelligent source. If humans, with their minuscule intelligence, can create such wondrous automation systems and processes, just think about the super-conscious Divine's creativity and capacity to create all we see and what is beyond our sight and perception[4]. The enlightened ones who had the opportunity to experience the Divine at various times and places describe that God is Superconscious and the source of all Intelligence throughout the Creation[5].

For us to start developing curiosity about whether there is Divine Intelligence behind all that we see, we can start with our own bodies and the natural environment around us. There are trillions of cells in our bodies that are working around the clock, without us giving them any direction on how to run our bodies in order to keep us well. Think about how wonderfully intricate and precise parts of our body are and how automated their functioning is. Food is digested without us doing anything. Heart and respiration work around the clock. Check out the intricate anatomical details of your ears, eyes, and nose and how they function. Reflect on the intelligence of your immune system, which identifies and combats countless viruses without you instructing it to do anything[6]. Your body knows of any invader before you have any knowledge of the infection or inflammation. Think about the sun rising and setting on its own so precisely that you can calculate the length of days and nights years in advance. Be curious about how air pressures and wind movements function such that one can calculate the timing of rain and

---

[4] Isaac Newton: "This most beautiful system of the sun, planets, and comets could only proceed from the counsel and dominion of an intelligent and powerful Being."

[5] Albert Einstein: Everyone who is seriously committed to the cultivation of science becomes convinced that in all the laws of the universe is manifest a spirit vastly superior to man, and to which we with our powers must feel humble."

[6] Thomas A. Edison: "My utmost respect and admiration to all the engineers, especially the greatest of them all: God."

storms. And then think about how all of this could have happened randomly on its own without a source of intelligence behind it!

In their own words:

Fifth Guru GGS p. 743, line 3
ਸਰਬ ਨਿਰੰਤਰਿ ਏਕੋ ਜਾਗੈ ॥
The One Conscious permeates within everyone.

Saint Kabir GGS p. 479, line 6
ਸਤਿਗੁਰੁ ਜਾਗਤਾ ਹੈ ਦੇਉ ॥
The Great Guru, the Creator is awake (conscious).

Fifth Sikh Guru GGS p. 300 line 7
ਪਾਰਬ੍ਰਹਮੁ ਪਰਮੇਸਰੋ ਸਭ ਬਿਧਿ ਜਾਨਣਹਾਰ ॥
The Supreme God, the Transcendent Master, is the Knower of all the ways everything happens.

Fifth Guru GGS p. 1230, line 17
ਜਾਨਤੇ ਦਇਆਰ ॥੧॥
Merciful God knows it all.

Fifth Guru, GGS p. 892 line 8
ਜਾਨਣਹਾਰੁ ਰਹਿਆ ਪ੍ਰਭੁ ਜਾਨਿ ॥
God, the Knower, knows all.

Fifth Guru, GGS p, 269, line 8
ਜਾਨਨਹਾਰ ਪ੍ਰਭੁ ਪਰਬੀਨ ॥
The Omniscient God is the Knower of everything.

First Guru GGS p. 1021, line 1
ਆਪੇ ਸੁਘਤੁ ਸਰੂਪੁ ਸਿਆਣਾ ॥
He Himself is all-wise, magnificent and all-knowing.

30

First Guru GGS p. 1040, line 1

ਸਰਬ ਨਿਰੰਜਨ ਪੁਰਖੁ ਸੁਜਾਨਾ ॥

The Primal Being is everywhere, immaculate and all-knowing.

First Guru GGS p. 936, line 2

ਆਪੇ ਚਤੁਰੁ ਸਰੂਪੁ ਹੈ ਆਪੇ ਜਾਣੁ ਸੁਜਾਣੁ ॥੪੨॥

He Himself is so smart and so very beautiful; He Himself is wise and all-knowing.

Fifth Guru GGS p. 462, line 10

ਸੁੰਦਰੁ ਚਤੁਰੁ ਸੁਜਾਨ ਸੁਆਮੀ ਕਵਨ ਰਸਨਾ ਗੁਣ ਭਨਾ ॥

My beautiful, astute and all-knowing Master, with which tongue can I describe your attributes?

Fourth Guru GGS p. 854, line 1

ਜਨ ਨਾਨਕ ਕੈ ਵਲਿ ਹੋਆ ਮੇਰਾ ਸੁਆਮੀ ਹਰਿ ਸਜਣ ਪੁਰਖੁ ਸੁਜਾਨੁ ॥

My Master, the All-knowing friend has come to my aid -to the aid of humble Nanak.

Saint Kabir GGS p. 1376, line 5

ਕਬੀਰ ਲਾਗੀ ਪ੍ਰੀਤਿ ਸੁਜਾਨ ਸਿਉ ਬਰਜੈ ਲੋਗੁ ਅਜਾਨੁ ॥

Says Kabir, I am now in love with the All-knowing Divine; the ignorant ones try to hold me back.

Fifth Guru, GGS p. 300, line 7

ਅੰਤਰਜਾਮੀ ਪ੍ਰਭੁ ਸੁਜਾਨੁ ਅਲਖ ਨਿਰੰਜਨ ਸੋਇ ॥

God, the knower of whatever goes on in every heart and mind, is all-knowing, indescribable and immaculate.

Fifth Guru, GGS p. 216, line 2
ਅਪਨੇ ਕਰਤਬ ਆਪੇ ਜਾਨੈ ਜਿਨਿ ਇਹੁ ਰਚਨੁ ਰਚਾਇਆ ॥

He alone who created the Creation, knows about His wondrous actions.

Tenth Guru Jaap Sahib, stanza 52
ਨਮੋ ਪਰਮ ਗਿਆਤਾ ॥

Salutation to You, the Supreme Knower of everything.

Tenth Guru Jaap Sahib stanza 70
ਨਮੋ ਸਰਬ ਗਿਆਨੰ ॥

Salutation to You, the Omniscient One!

Fifth Guru GGS p. 1356, line 4
ਸ੍ਰਿਜੰਤ ਰਤਨ ਜਨਮ ਚਤੁਰ ਚੇਤਨਹ ॥

He created the jewel of human life, with all its cleverness and intelligence.

Fifth Guru GGS p. 288. Line 1
ਰਚਿ ਰਚਨਾ ਅਪਨੀ ਕਲ ਧਾਰੀ ॥

Having created the Creation, He infused His own Conscious Energy into it.

Fourth Guru, Guru Ram Das GGS p. 507, line 2
ਅਲਖ ਨਿਰੰਜਨੁ ਏਕੋ ਵਰਤੈ ਏਕਾ ਜੋਤਿ ਮੁਰਾਰੀ ॥

Invisible to us, the One immaculate Divine is pervading everywhere with the sparkling light of His Energy.

Tenth Guru, Benti Chaupai stanza 388
ਏਕ ਏਕ ਕੀ ਪੀਰ ਪਛਾਨੈ ॥ ਘਟ ਘਟ ਕੇ ਪਟ ਪਟ ਕੀ ਜਾਨੈ ॥੩੮੮॥

He recognizes the agony of everyone. He knows what goes on in every heart and mind.

Does God have a physical form?

Those of us who are believers associate a physical appearance with God. Haven't we all fantasized about a God in a human physical form that we can run to and offload all of our fears and worries and be replenished with unconditionally loving energy? Well, we might find comfort in the words of those who have encountered the Divine. According to them, the One God or the Divine Being who has created everything has kind of Super-Human-like attributes but does not have a physical form that we can describe using our vocabulary or comprehend intellectually.

God is pure consciousness and has a subtle visual image that is nothing like you have ever seen before. We cannot intellectually or rationally come up with a conception of God as He is inconceivable. They all say that describing God's image in our vocabulary is difficult, but they claim to have witnessed the Divine and found Him absolutely enthralling and mesmerizing. This Super-Human like God knows everything and does indeed speak to us in ways that we fail to notice because we are not plugged into His Energy. He is pervading everywhere in all directions and corners as pure love.

The Sikh Gurus and non-Sikh saints whose descriptions of the Divine are included in Guru Granth Sahib have used the word Purkh many times to describe God while at the same time saying that He is formless. The literal meaning of the word Purkh is a Living Conscious Being with personality. The very first sentence of the scripture Guru Granth Sahib describes God as Karta Purkh which literally means Creator Being with Consciousness but says this Creator is formless (Nirankar) and does not have a physical form.

In describing God as Purkh, they say that this Primal Divine Being has no specific physical form and has no limbs, such as arms and legs, to do things and to go places as we do. God in no way looks like a human being or an angelic being with wings. He is neither male nor female even though in order to make a connection with the Divine using familiar human relationships, initially we may use words such as He/She. However, God does have a subtle image which is nothing like you have ever seen before. The image and personality of the Primal Being is unique and cannot be described. He is pure Intelligence. His image is all light and He is radiantly effulgent. No one can find the limits of this Supreme Being. Nobody can put in words what God looks like.

Various verses describe God as Karta Purkh (the Creator Being), Akal Purkh (The Being unaffected by Time), Aad Purkh (the Primal Being), Purkh Niranjan (the Immaculate Being), Purkh Bhagwan (God Being), Pooran Purkh (the Perfect Being) while at the same time saying he is formless with a subtle image that can take any form(s). They say that God has Akal Moorat which means God has a subtle image or look which does not change over time. He is unaffected by Time. He is Self-existent (Sabhoun) and was never born and never dies. He is never young and never old.

While God is formless, all the countless forms and manifested images are His images as well, as they are all manifestations of Him. No one can fully describe the Supreme Being who is all-wise, magnificent and all-knowing. It is His boundless intelligence and creativity that has designed the whole Creation, sustains it, and ultimately concludes a phase of Creation by drawing it all unto Himself where nothing in any form remains. The image and personality of the Primal

Being is unique. He has an image, and yet has countless forms. He has no eyes or ears but then has countless eyes and ears he created, which are His eyes and ears. He has countless forms while still being formless.

Perhaps He has entered our life and the lives of countless other people as a teacher who imparted precious advice to navigate life, a loving pet who consoled in moments of loneliness or alerted to an impending emergency or a stranger looking at whom opened up your mind's eye! Perhaps the key to feel Him is to maintain curiosity and an open mind so He could surprise us with His presence.

In their own words:

First Guru, GGS p. 686, line 3
ਸੂਰਤਿ ਮੂਰਤਿ ਆਦਿ ਅਨੂਪੁ ॥
The image and personality of the Primal Being is unique.

First Guru GGS p. 685, line 17
ਨਾਰਿ ਨ ਪੁਰਖੁ ਕਹਹੁ ਕੋਉ ਕੈਸੇ ॥
He is not male, and He is not female; how can anyone describe Him?

First Guru GGS p. 1034, line 19
ਰੂਪੁ ਨ ਰੇਖਿਆ ਮਿਤਿ ਨਹੀ ਕੀਮਤਿ ਸਬਦਿ ਭੇਦਿ ਪਤੀਆਇਦਾ ॥੯॥
Through the Divine Shabad, one unlocks the mystery of the Divine-that He has no form or shape or bounds and is immeasurable.

First Guru GGS p. 907, line 10
ਜਿਨਿ ਕੀਏ ਖੰਡ ਮੰਡਲ ਬ੍ਰਹਮੰਡਾ ਸੋ ਪ੍ਰਭੁ ਲਖਣ ਨ ਜਾਈ ॥੬॥
The Divine who created the worlds, solar systems and galaxies cannot be described (in words).

First Guru GGS p. 1010, line 14

ਨਾਰਿ ਨ ਪੁਰਖੁ ਨ ਪੰਖਣੂ ਸਾਚਉ ਚਤੁਰੁ ਸਰੂਪੁ ॥

He is neither a woman, nor a man, nor an angelic being with wings; the Divine Being is so very smart and so beautiful.

First Guru GGS p. 1020, line 15

ਆਪੇ ਪੁਰਖੁ ਆਪੇ ਹੀ ਨਾਰੀ ॥

He Himself is the male, and He Himself is the female.

First Guru GGS p. 1021, line 15

ਆਪੇ ਜੋਤਿ ਸਰੂਪੀ ਬਾਲਾ ॥

He is the embodiment of light, forever young.

First Guru, GGS, p. 1168, line 11

ਤੇਰੀ ਮੂਰਤਿ ਏਕਾ ਬਹੁਤੁ ਰੂਪ ॥

You have one image, and yet You have countless forms.

Tenth Guru, Benti Chaupai stanza 394

ਏਕੈ ਰੂਪ ਅਨੂਪ ਸਰੂਪਾ ॥

His One Image manifested in many forms in a unique way.

Guru Gobind Singh, Jaap Sahib stanza 11

ਨਮਸਤੰ ਨ੍ਰਿਧਾਤੇ ॥

Salutation to You, the One not made of the (five) elements.

First Guru, GGS p. 663, line 7

ਸਹਸ ਤਵ ਨੈਨ ਨਨ ਨੈਨ ਹੈ ਤੋਹਿ ਕਉ ਸਹਸ ਮੂਰਤਿ ਨਨਾ ਏਕ ਤੋਹੀ ॥

Thousands are Your eyes, and yet You have no eyes. Thousands are Your forms, and yet You have not even one form.

First Guru, GGS, p. 13, line 4

ਸਹਸ ਪਦ ਬਿਮਲ ਨਨ ਏਕ ਪਦ ਗੰਧ ਬਿਨੁ ਸਹਸ ਤਵ ਗੰਧ ਇਵ ਚਲਤ
ਮੋਹੀ ॥੨॥

You have thousands of feet, and yet You do not have even
one foot. You have no nose, but you have thousands of
noses. I am entranced by this Play of Yours.

First Guru GGS p. 1021, line 1
ਆਪੇ ਸੁਘੜੁ ਸਰੂਪੁ ਸਿਆਣਾ ॥

He Himself is all-wise, magnificent and all-knowing.

Saint Kabir, GGS p. 870, line 15
ਇਆ ਮੂਰਤਿ ਕੈ ਹਉ ਬਲਿਹਾਰੈ ॥੧॥

(I am so mesmerized looking at His image), I can sacrifice
my life for this image of the Divine.

Saint Kabir, GGS p. 727, line 10
ਹਕੁ ਸਚੁ ਖਾਲਕੁ ਖਲਕ ਮਿਆਨੇ ਸਿਆਮ ਮੂਰਤਿ ਨਾਹਿ ॥੨॥

The True Creator is diffused into His creation; He is not
the dark-skinned Krishna (worshipped in India).

Saint Kabir GGS p. 344, line 1
ਜੋਤਿ ਸਰੂਪੀ ਤਤ ਅਨੂਪ ॥

Embodiment of light and of incomparable essence.

Fourth Guru, GGS p. 10, line 17
ਸੋ ਪੁਰਖੁ ਨਿਰੰਜਨੁ ਹਰਿ ਪੁਰਖੁ ਨਿਰੰਜਨੁ ਹਰਿ ਅਗਮਾ ਅਗਮ ਅਪਾਰਾ ॥

God, the Primal Being, the Divine Being is Immaculate.
He is boundless and beyond intellectual comprehension.

Fifth Guru GGS p. 717, line 18
ਦੇਖਿ ਸਰੂਪੁ ਪੂਰਨੁ ਭਈ ਆਸਾ ਦਰਸਨੁ ਭੇਟਤ ਉਤਰੀ ਭੁਖ ॥੧॥

Gazing upon the Divine's image, my desires have been
fulfilled; Having had this visual experience has satiated all
my desires.

Fifth Guru GGS p. 187, line 15

ਆਦਿ ਪੁਰਖ ਅਪਰੰਪਰ ਦੇਵ ॥੨॥

The Primal Being, the Infinite Divine Master. ||2||

Fifth Guru GGS p. 240, line 11

ਦਇਆਲ ਪੁਰਖ ਪੂਰਨ ਪ੍ਰਤਿਪਾਲੈ ॥੧॥ ਰਹਾਉ ॥

The Perfect and Merciful Being provides sustenance to all.

Fifth Guru GGS p. 259, line 3

ਪੂਰਨ ਘਟ ਘਟ ਪੁਰਖ ਬਿਸੇਖਾ ॥

The Unique Primal Being pervading each and every heart.

Fifth Guru GGS, p. 284, line 4

ਨਾਨਕ ਤਿਸੁ ਪੁਰਖ ਕਾ ਕਿਨੈ ਅੰਤੁ ਨ ਪਾਇਆ ॥੨॥

Says Nanak, no one can fully describe that Supreme Being.

Saint Kabir GGS p. 1194, line 12

ਓਇ ਪਰਮ ਪੁਰਖ ਦੇਵਾਧਿ ਦੇਵ ॥

The Supreme Being, God of the gods.

Fifth Guru GGS p. 628, line 2

ਦਇਆਲ ਪੁਰਖ ਮਿਹਰਵਾਨਾ ॥

The Merciful and Compassionate Primal Being.

Fifth Guru GGS p. 102, line 10

ਨੈਨ ਨਿਹਾਲੀ ਤਿਸੁ ਪੁਰਖ ਦਇਆਲੈ ॥

With my eyes, I behold the Compassionate Primal Being.

Fifth Guru GGS p. 187, line 15

ਆਦਿ ਪੁਰਖ ਅਪਰੰਪਰ ਦੇਵ ॥੨॥

He is the Primal Being, the Infinite Divine.

Fifth Guru GGS p. 240, line 11

ਦਇਆਲ ਪੁਰਖ ਪੂਰਨ ਪ੍ਰਤਿਪਾਲੈ ॥੧॥

The Perfect and Merciful Primal Being provides sustenance to all.

Fifth Guru GGS p. 1362, line 16
ਸੁੰਦਰ ਪੁਰਖ ਬਿਰਾਜਿਤ ਪੇਖਿ ਮਨੁ ਬੰਚਲਾ ॥
Beholding the Beautiful Primal Being, my mind is fascinated.

Fifth Guru GGS p. 1385, line 4
ਆਦਿ ਪੁਰਖ ਕਰਤਾਰ ਕਰਣ ਕਾਰਣ ਸਭ ਆਪੇ ॥
The Primal Being, the Creator is the Cause of all causes.

Saint Kabir GGS p. 343, line 8
ਆਦਿ ਪੁਰਖ ਮਹਿ ਰਹੈ ਸਮਾਇ ॥੨॥
One who remains absorbed in the Primal Being. ||2||

Fifth Guru GGS p. 1077, line 14
ਪ੍ਰਗਟ ਭਏ ਪ੍ਰਭ ਪੁਰਖ ਨਿਰਾਰੇ ॥
The Unique Primal Being has revealed Himself.

Fifth Guru GGS p. 1148, line 9
ਪੁਰਖ ਨਿਰੰਜਨ ਸਿਰਜਨਹਾਰ ॥
The Immaculate Primal Being, the Creator of all.

Ninth Guru GGS p. 1186, line 10
ਜਨ ਨਾਨਕ ਸਭ ਹੀ ਮੈ ਪੂਰਨ ਏਕ ਪੁਰਖ ਭਗਵਾਨੇ ॥੨॥੧॥
Says servant Nanak, the One Primal Being, God, is permeating everywhere.

Saint Naam Dev GGS p. 1351, line 7
ਅਕੁਲ ਪੁਰਖ ਇਕੁ ਚਲਿਤੁ ਉਪਾਇਆ ॥
The Primal Being who has no ancestry has staged this play.

Saint Kabir GGS p. 343, line 8

ਘਟ ਮਹਿ ਖੇਲੈ ਅਘਟ ਅਪਾਰ ॥

He is playing within the hearts without the body – He is Infinite.

Fifth Guru GGS p. 613, line 19
ਖਿਨ ਮਹਿ ਅਵਰੁ ਖਿਨੈ ਮਹਿ ਅਵਰਾ ਅਚਰਜ ਚਲਤ ਤੁਮਾਰੇ ॥ ਰੂੜੋ ਗੂੜੋ ਗਹਿਰ ਗੰਭੀਰੋ ਊਚੌ ਅਗਮ ਅਪਾਰੇ ॥੩॥

In an instant, You are one thing, and in another instant, You are another. Wondrous are Your ways! You are beautiful, mysterious, profound, unfathomable, lofty, inaccessible and infinite.

Tenth Guru Jaap Sahib, stanza 79
ਆਦਿ ਰੂਪ ਅਨਾਦਿ ਮੂਰਤਿ ਅਜੋਨਿ ਪੁਰਖ ਅਪਾਰ ॥

Always with the same Primal Eternal Image, He is Self-Existent and Unfathomable Primal Being.

Tenth Guru, Jaap Sahib Stanza 3
ਨਮਸਤੰ ਅਕਾਏ ॥

Salutation to you, who has no physical body.

Tenth Guru Jaap Sahib Stanza 81
ਏਕ ਮੂਰਤਿ ਅਨੇਕ ਦਰਸਨ ਕੀਨ ਰੂਪ ਅਨੇਕ ॥ ਖੇਲ ਖੇਲ ਅਖੇਲ ਖੇਲਨ ਅੰਤ ਕੋ ਫਿਰਿ ਏਕ ॥੮੧॥

Though He has One Image, He manifests in countless forms. After He winds up His Worldly Drama, He alone is there.

Tenth Guru Jaap Sahib, Stanza 83
ਪਰਮ ਰੂਪ ਪੁਨੀਤ ਮੂਰਤਿ ਪੂਰਨ ਪੁਰਖ ਅਪਾਰ ॥ ਸਰਬ ਬਿਸ੍ਵ ਰਚਿਓ ਸੁਯੰਭਵ ਗੜਨ ਭੰਜਨਹਾਰ ॥੮੩॥

You, the Divine are Supreme-looking with the holiest image, the Perfect Primal Being who is beyond description.

You are the Self-existent Creator who has created everything; You are also the One who ends it all.

Tenth Guru Jaap Sahib, stanza 85
ਅੰਗ ਹੀਨ ਅਭੰਗ ਅਨਾਤਮ ਏਕ ਪੁਰਖ ਅਪਾਰ ॥ ਸਰਬ ਲਾਇਕ ਸਰਬ ਘਾਇਕ ਸਰਬ ਕੋ ਪ੍ਰਿਤਿਪਾਰ ॥੮੫॥

He is without physical limbs, indestructible, unfathomable Primal Being. He is all-capable who sustains all and who ultimately winds it all up.

Tenth Guru Jaap Sahib stanza 137
ਪ੍ਰਕਾਸ ਹੈਂ ॥੧੩੭॥

You are all Effulgence.

Tenth Guru, Jaap Sahib stanza 1
ਚਕ੍ਰ ਚਿਹਨ ਅਰੁ ਬਰਨ ਜਾਤਿ ਅਰੁ ਪਾਤਿ ਨਹਿਨ ਜਿਹ ॥
ਰੂਪ ਰੰਗ ਅਰੁ ਰੇਖ ਭੇਖ ਕੋਊ ਕਹਿ ਨ ਸਕਤਿ ਕਿਹ ॥
ਅਚਲ ਮੂਰਤਿ ਅਨਭਵ ਪ੍ਰਕਾਸ ਅਮਿਤੋਜ ਕਹਿਜੈ ॥

He who is without form or a recognizable profile, without any caste or lineage. Nobody can describe His look, color, form or garb. With His never changing image, He is all Effulgence and Unfathomable like an ocean.

Tenth Guru, Jaap Sahib stanza 150
ਕਿ ਜਾਹਰ ਜਹੂਰ ਹੈਂ ॥ ਕਿ ਹਾਜਰ ਹਜੂਰ ਹੈਂ ॥

(O' Almighty God) You can be clearly witnessed. You are present everywhere.

Tenth Guru, Jaap Sahib stanza 151
ਕਿ ਸਾਹਿਬ ਦਿਮਾਗ ਹੈਂ ॥ ਕਿ ਹੁਸਨਲ ਚਰਾਗ ਹੈਂ ॥
ਕਿ ਕਾਮਲ ਕਰੀਮ ਹੈਂ ॥ ਕਿ ਰਾਜਕ ਰਹੀਮ ਹੈਂ ॥

(O' God) You are pure Intelligence. You shine as the most Handsome. You are the most forgiving. You provide sustenance to all.

Tenth Guru Jaap Sahib stanza 152
ਕਿ ਹੁਸਨਲ ਜਮਾਲ ਹੈਂ ॥੧੫੨॥
You are the epitome of Beauty (most Handsome).

Tenth Guru, Jaap Sahib stanza 159
ਕਿ ਅਚਲੰ ਪ੍ਰਕਾਸ ਹੈਂ ॥
You are in perpetual illumination.

Tenth Guru; Jaap Sahib stanza 17
ਨਮਸਤਸਤੁ ਅਜਬੈ ॥੧੭॥
Salutation to You, O' One with Unique Wondrous look.

Tenth Guru Jaap Sahib stanza 80
ਨਾਮ ਠਾਮ ਨ ਜਾਤਿ ਜਾ ਕਰ ਰੂਪ ਰੰਗ ਨ ਰੇਖ ॥ ਆਦਿ ਪੁਰਖ ਉਦਾਰ ਮੂਰਤਿ ਅਜੋਨਿ ਆਦਿ ਅਸੇਖ ॥
ਦੇਸ ਅੰੋਰ ਨ ਭੇਸ ਜਾ ਕਰ ਰੂਪ ਰੇਖ ਨ ਰਾਗ ॥ ਜਤੁ ਤਤੁ ਦਿਸਾ ਵਿਸਾ ਹੁਇ ਫੈਲਿਓ ਅਨੁਰਾਗ ॥੮੦॥
You, the Divine do not have a particular name, place of residence, caste, color or form. You are the Self-existent Primal Being, benevolent, beyond birth or beginning. You do not belong to a particular country (location) and have no particular garb or form. You are pervading everywhere in all directions and corners as pure love.

Playful and Blissful God, really?

Many of us are used to thinking of God as an older father figure who provides for us but someone who we need to be fearful of. Have you ever imagined God as playful?

Those who have experienced the Divine describe God as playful and blissful and full of joy and unimaginable creativity. The whole Creation is a reflection of the playful nature of the Divine. As manifestations of the Divine, our essence or soul is also naturally playful and blissful. However, as we move through cycles of birth and death influenced by our Karma, and get farther and farther from our origin and source-the Creator, we encounter suffering and sorrow. We get out of touch with our original playful and blissful nature by being caught in the rat race of the world. Even though we cannot take anything with us when we depart the world, we spend our lives striving and stressing to accumulate more instead of enjoying. We need to look at the world through the eyes of a child and experience the wonder, beauty, and playfulness of the world.

In their own words:

First Guru, GGS p. 685, line 18

ਆਨੰਦ ਮੂਲੁ ਅਨਾਥ ਅਧਾਰੀ ॥

He is blissful in essence-the support of those without support.

First Guru, GGS p. 1041, line 16

ਆਨੰਦ ਰੂਪੁ ਅਨੂਪੁ ਸਰੂਪਾ ਗੁਰਿ ਪੂਰੈ ਦੇਖਾਇਆ ॥੨॥

The perfect Master has shown me -He is a personification of bliss with a uniquely beautiful image.

Fifth Guru GGS p. 395, line 9

ਸਦਾ ਅਨੰਦ ਅਨੰਦੀ ਸਾਹਿਬੁ ਗੁਨ ਨਿਧਾਨ ਨਿਤ ਨਿਤ ਜਾਪੀਐ ॥

My Playful Master is forever in ecstatic bliss; meditate continually and forever on Him, the source of all excellence.

Fifth Guru GGS p. 409, line 3

ਹਰਖ ਸੋਗ ਬੈਰਾਗ ਅਨੰਦੀ ਖੇਲੁ ਰੀ ਦਿਖਾਇਓ ॥੧॥ ਰਹਾਉ ॥

As the Blissful God has revealed to me, pleasure, sorrow and (finally) the longing to go back home are all part of His Play.

Fifth Guru GGS p. 1073, line 16

ਕਰੈ ਅਨੰਦੁ ਅਨੰਦੀ ਮੇਰਾ ॥

My Blissful God is forever in blissful play.

Fifth Guru GGS p. 1096, line 2

ਤੂ ਪੁਰਖੁ ਅਨੰਦੀ ਅਨੰਤ ਸਭ ਜੋਤਿ ਸਮਾਹਰਾ ॥

You are the blissful and infinite Primal Being; Your Light is all-pervading.

Tenth Guru, Jaap Sahib stanza 64

ਅਨੰਦੀ ਸਰੂਪੇ ॥

You, the ever Blissful.

Does God have a life span and does He die?

Growing up, finding solace and comfort in thinking there is God, one of my worries used to be what would happen if God died. I vividly remember a few days when I felt so hopeless and depressed over this thought that I could see no ray of hope.

However, those who experienced the Divine tell us that God does not age, get old, and die. Unaffected by Time, God is forever young. God does not diminish over time. He was there before the Creation, throughout time, and will always be there after everything runs its course. There will come a time when God will subsume the whole Creation unto Himself, and only the formless God will remain. The cycle of

Creation and its ultimate absorption into God has happened many times.

In their own words:

First Guru, GGS p. 1038, line 15
ਤੂ ਅਕਾਲ ਪੁਰਖੁ ਨਾਹੀ ਸਿਰਿ ਕਾਲਾ ॥
You are the Primal Being unaffected by Time and will never die.

First Guru GGS p. 223, line 5
ਸਰਬ ਨਿਰੰਤਰਿ ਪ੍ਰੀਤਮੁ ਬਾਲਾ ॥੪॥
Dwelling constantly among all is my ever-youthful Beloved Divine.

Fifth Guru GGS p. 1354, line 15
ਨਹ ਘਟੰਤ ਕੇਵਲ ਗੋਪਾਲ ਅਚੁਤ ॥
Only the Eternal, Unchanging God does not wane over time.

Saint Kabir GGS p. 343, line 9
ਨਾ ਓਹੁ ਬਢੈ ਨ ਘਟਤਾ ਜਾਇ ॥
God does not increase or decrease.

Fifth Guru GGS p. 240, line 14
ਪੂਰਨ ਪੁਰਖੁ ਨਵਤਨੁ ਨਿਤ ਬਾਲਾ ॥
The Perfect Being is ever-fresh and ever-young.

Fifth Guru GGS p. 1006, line 18
ਨਵਲ ਨਵਤਨ ਚਤੁਰ ਸੁੰਦਰ ਮਨੁ ਨਾਨਕ ਤਿਸੁ ਸੰਗਿ ਬੀਧਿ ॥੨॥੩॥੨੬॥
Says Nanak, my mind is pierced (lovingly engrossed) by the always new, fresh and young, clever and beautiful Divine.

Tenth Guru, Jaap Sahib stanza 2

ਨਮਸਤੂੰ ਅਕਾਲੇ ॥

Salutation to You, the One unaffected by Time.

God's parents and lineage?

Those who experienced the Divine say that God is self-existent and was not created by anyone. He had no parents who gave birth to Him. He is not from any one family or clan. He is pure consciousness and light.

He was never born and will never die. He was there before the outset of the creation, has always been there, and will always be there. God does not age and die like us. He is beyond the cycle of birth and death.

In their own words:

First Guru, GGS, p. 597, line 5
ਜਾਤਿ ਅਜਾਤਿ ਅਜੋਨੀ ਸੰਭਉ ਨਾ ਤਿਸੁ ਭਾਉ ਨ ਭਰਮਾ ॥੧॥

God is casteless with no caste; He was not born to any one, is self-illumined, and free of delusion and desire.

First Guru, GGS p. 597, line 19
ਸੋ ਬ੍ਰਹਮੁ ਅਜੋਨੀ ਹੈ ਭੀ ਹੋਨੀ ਘਟ ਭੀਤਰਿ ਦੇਖੁ ਮੁਰਾਰੀ ਜੀਉ ॥੨॥

Not born to anyone, He is, and shall ever be. Behold Him deep within your heart.

First Guru, GGS p. 838, line 19
ਅਮਰੁ ਅਜੋਨੀ ਜਾਤਿ ਨ ਜਾਲਾ ॥

Immortal, not born to anyone, beyond social class or involvement.

Tenth Guru Jaap Sahib stanza 21
ਨਮਸਤੰ ਅਜਨਮੇ ॥

Salutation to You, who is not subject to birth.

46

Tenth Guru, Jaap Sahib stanza 23

ਨਮਸਤੰ ਅਮਰਨੇ ॥੨੩॥

Salutation to You who is not subject to death.

Is God loving, merciful or forgiving?

Do you know the name of a prophet or saint who declared that God has a lot of anger and is looking for opportunities to punish us?

I don't know of any prophet who said anything like that. Instead, every prophet, saint, and enlightened person speaks about God as being very loving, compassionate, merciful, and forgiving.[7] In the Sikh scripture, the Sikh Gurus and saints testify to His immense love for His Creation and refer to Him as father, mother, dear friend, partner in romantic love, etc.

Given the widespread suffering and misery in the world, it can be difficult to comprehend and believe that God is loving and merciful in the face of such experiences. Since we know so little about the design and workings of the Divine system, we should turn to the words of our own prophets about God and the Divine system. No prophet has said that God is not kind, compassionate, and not in charge of the system. Jesus Christ did not proclaim that God was unjust and unaware when he was crucified[8]. In Sikhism, Islam and Hinduism, likewise, God is described as kind, merciful, and conscious of what is happening.

---

[7] Psalm 145:8-9 "The Lord is gracious and compassionate, slow to anger and rich in love. The Lord is good to all; he has compassion on all he has made" (Bible NIV)

[8] Luke 23:46 "Jesus called out with a loud voice, Father, into your hands I commit my spirit. When he had said this, he breathed his last." (Bible NIV)

The Sikh Gurus, who proclaimed that God is kind, merciful, forgiving, and loving, themselves faced the wrath of the mighty Moghul emperors who were forcing conversions into Islam, and endured indescribable tyranny. The Moghul emperor Jahangir persecuted the fifth Sikh Guru, Guru Arjun Dev, by slowly burning his body by pouring hot sand while alive. The ninth Sikh Guru, Guru Teg Bahadur, was beheaded by the Moghul emperor Aurangzeb. The tenth Guru, Guru Gobind Singh's young sons (aged 13 and 17 years) were killed fighting the Moghuls while his two 6 and 9-year-old sons were executed by the Mughal ruler on December 26, 1705, by burying them alive in a brick wall. In the face of such horrific tyranny and suffering, the fifth Guru, the ninth Guru, and the tenth Guru, while speaking against the unjust rulers, always proclaimed that God and the Divine system are just and everything that was happening was consistent with the Divine System they called Hukam. They never blamed God for being unjust or not being in charge. A letter (known as Zafarnama or declaration of victory) that the tenth Guru, Gobind Singh wrote to the mighty Moghul emperor Aurangzeb after losing all his family proclaims many times that God is the perfect Being, merciful, loving, and sovereign of the sovereigns.

So, when seeing suffering and misery in the world and having doubts about the Divine's awareness and ability to run the system, we need to go back to our prophets' proclamations that God is loving, just, merciful, and forgiving.

We should be more aware of the fact that what we see is not all and that a lot more of why things happen is not visible to us. Per Divine design, there is a veil of ignorance around us such that we are not privy to the whole story of why things are happening[9].

When we see pain and suffering around us, instead of concluding that God is not kind or not in control, we should do our part in mitigating such suffering. We are God's eyes, ears, and hands. We are best served by doing our part in making the world a better place instead of complaining about God's system. When we help others, it helps us the most in the end.

In their own words:

Third Guru GGS, p. 27, line 11
ਨਿਰਭਉ ਸਦਾ ਦਇਆਲੁ ਹੈ ਸਭਨਾ ਕਰਦਾ ਸਾਰ ॥
The Fearless God is forever Merciful; He takes care of all.

Fifth Guru GGS p. 249, line 3
ਕਰੁਣਾ ਮੈ ਸਮਰਥੁ ਸੁਆਮੀ ਘਟ ਘਟ ਪ੍ਰਾਣ ਅਧਾਰੀ ॥
The Embodiment of compassion and all-powerful Master sustains each and every one.

Fifth Guru, GGS p. 294, line 15
ਇਸ ਤੇ ਹੋਇ ਸੁ ਨਾਹੀ ਬੁਰਾ॥
He never does anything bad to us.

Fourth Guru, GGS p. 130, line 1
ਤੂ ਦਇਆਲੁ ਕਿਰਪਾਲੁ ਪ੍ਰਭੁ ਸੋਈ ॥
You God, the Kind and the Merciful.

Fifth Guru, GGS p. 184, line 5

---

[9] Corinthians 4:18 "We look not to the things that are seen but to the things that are unseen. For the things that are seen are transient, but the things that are unseen are eternal".(Bible KGV)

ਕਰਣ ਕਰਾਵਨਹਾਰ ਦਇਆਲ ॥

The Merciful Divine is the Doer, the Cause of causes.

Fifth Guru GGS p. 290, line 9
ਪ੍ਰਭ ਬਖਸੰਦ ਦੀਨ ਦਇਆਲ ॥

God is forgiving and kind.

Fifth Guru GGS p. 105, line 4
ਜਲਿ ਥਲਿ ਪੂਰਿ ਰਹਿਆ ਮਿਹਰਵਾਨਾ ॥

The Merciful Divine is pervading and permeating the waters and the lands.

First Guru GGS p.722, line 1
ਹਉ ਕੁਰਬਾਨੈ ਜਾਉ ਮਿਹਰਵਾਨਾ ਹਉ ਕੁਰਬਾਨੈ ਜਾਉ ॥

I can sacrifice my life for you, O' Dear Merciful Divine; I can sacrifice my life for you.

Fifth Guru, GGS, p. 724, line 5
ਮਿਹਰਵਾਨੁ ਸਾਹਿਬੁ ਮਿਹਰਵਾਨੁ ॥

Merciful, the Master is Merciful.

Tenth Guru, Jaap Sahib, stanza 28
ਨਮੋ ਸਰਬ ਦਿਆਲੇ ॥

Salutation to you, the Kind One!

Tenth Guru Jaap Sahib, stanza 23
ਨਮਸਤਸਤੁ ਦਿਆਲੇ ॥

Salutation to You, the Benevolent One.

Saint Sheikh Farid GGS p. 488, line 11
ਤੇਰੀ ਪਨਹ ਖੁਦਾਇ ਤੂ ਬਖਸੰਦਗੀ ॥

You, Almighty God, are my sanctuary. You are forgiving.

Saint Naam Dev GGS p. 727, line 15
ਨਾਮੇ ਚੇ ਸੁਆਮੀ ਬਖਸੰਦ ਤੂੰ ਹਰੀ ॥੩॥੧॥੨॥

O' Master of (me) Naam Dev, you are the merciful God of forgiveness.

Fifth Guru GGS p. 866, line 9

ਪਾਰਬ੍ਰਹਮ ਪੂਰਨ ਬਖਸੰਦ ॥

The Perfect Almighty God forgives.

Tenth Guru Jaap Sahib, stanza 8

ਨਮਸਤੰ ਉਦਾਰੇ ॥

Salutation to you, O' Benevolent One!

Tenth Guru Jaap Sahib stanza 25

ਨਮਸਤੰ ਕਰੀਮੇ ॥੨੫॥

Salutation to You, O' the Merciful One.

Tenth Guru Jaap Sahib stanza 73

ਕ੍ਰਿਪਾਲੰ ਸਰੂਪੇ ਕੁਕਰਮੰ ਪ੍ਰਣਾਸੀ ॥

You, the Embodiment of Mercy and a Destroyer of Sins.

Does God act out of vengeance or invoke His wrath?

There are times in everybody's life when life seems to be out of control, nothing seems to work, and we feel that God is upset and out to punish us. It seems that storms, floods, famines, droughts, and diseases are indicative of divine wrath and vengeance. However, those who have experienced the Divine declare that God does not have enmity towards anyone and never acts out of vengeance. He is pervading everywhere in all directions and corners as pure love.

Per Divine Design, unless we are plugged into God's energy, our Karma or actions over many lifetimes beget reactions and counter-reactions, which can take us downhill and create chaos in our lives. God does not act out of fear or insecurity because there is no Other. God is never angry. Instead, God is always blissful and playful. Some natural calamities like droughts, flooding, and fires happen when we do not take good care of ourselves and our environment. Events that seem disastrous to us are actually part of a grand Divine order that we may not fully understand. These events can't be explained completely because we do not know the whole story. The rules of the Divine Order that govern us and the rest of the natural environment are precise and cannot be circumvented. Any wrong actions on our part that upset the natural balance are bound to have consequences per the rules of the Divine Order, as the Divine System is automated to the hilt with actions resulting in reactions.

In their own words:

First Guru, GGS, p. 596, line 11
ਨਿਰਭਉ ਨਿਰੰਕਾਰੁ ਨਿਰਵੈਰੁ ਪੂਰਨ ਜੋਤਿ ਸਮਾਈ ॥
Fearless, Formless and absolutely without vengeance; His Light permeates all.

Fourth Guru, Guru Ram Das, GGS, p. 1201, line 16
ਨਿਰਵੈਰੁ ਅਕਾਲ ਮੂਰਤਿ ॥
He has no vengeance, His appearance is not affected by time.

Fifth Guru GGS p. 99 line 6
ਨਿਰਭਉ ਨਿਰਵੈਰ ਅਥਾਹ ਅਤੋਲੇ ॥
Fearless,   without   vengeance,   Unfathomable, Immeasurable,

Fourth Guru, GGS p. 302, line 9
ਹਰਿ ਸਤਿ ਨਿਰੰਜਨ ਅਮਰੁ ਹੈ ਨਿਰਭਉ ਨਿਰਵੈਰੁ ਨਿਰੰਕਾਰੁ ॥
The Ever-existent God is immaculate and eternal; Has no fear, enmity or form.

Tenth Guru Jaap Sahib stanza 6
ਨਮਸਤੰ ਅਭੀਤੇ ॥

Salutation to You, the Fearless One.

Chapter 4: Is there a Divine system or is it all random?

> *Everyone and everything is subject to the Divine Order or System*

Everyone and everything is subject to the Divine Order or System.

Those who experienced the Divine testify that God has set up a Divine system that runs on its own according to the rules of the Divine Order. Nothing happens outside of the rules of the Divine Order. The Divine System is so automated that we see nobody running the system and mistakenly believe that there is no God or anybody running the system.

Everything happens according to the rules of the Divine Order. Actions have reactions, and causes have effects. Chemicals have distinct properties determined by the Divine System. Planets have their orbits and schedules. All physical matter is governed by the laws of the Divine Order. The fact that we do not see anybody running the System does not mean that the System evolved on its own without anybody having designed and created it[10].

The Divine System is the product of the Divine Being's super-consciousness, intelligence, creativity, masterful designing, and has around-the-clock operation and maintenance on its own as it is automated to the hilt. For us to assert that there is no Creator or operator behind the vast natural phenomena and all kinds of life that we see, would be like robots and all artificial intelligence-controlled equipment and communication systems to assert that they evolved on their own without having been created in the first place by intelligent creators!

---

[10] Charles Darwin: "I think the greatest argument for the existence of God is the impossibility of demonstrating and understanding that the immense universe, sublime above all measure, and man were the result of chance."

Everyone and everything is subject to the Divine Order or System; nothing is beyond the Divine Order. However, that does not mean that we have no free will at all. It simply means that our actions are bound by the rules of the Divine Order, and they cause reactions and chain reactions according to these rules. The Divine Order cannot be fully described in words using our vocabulary. All the worlds or realms are subject to the One God's Divine Order. The rules of the Divine Order are precise and cannot be circumvented.

All life is created according to the Divine Order and acts subject to the rules of the system. The Creation in different forms and colors is per His Divine Order. Humans and other life forms have been designed to reproduce themselves according to the Divine Order. A union of the sperm and egg starts a life that grows according to the process created by the Divine system. Trees and all kinds of vegetation have the capability to reproduce per the Divine Order. Additionally, all life has a life span limited by the rules of the Divine order. One's good or bad actions are subject to the Divine order.

The planetary bodies stay suspended and keep orbiting precisely supported by His Divine Order. Even Suns, moons, and all other planetary bodies have a life span per the Divine Order. Everything and everyone is created per His Divine Order and shall merge again into Him. The winds, fire, rains, and all other physical phenomena that we see are created with certain properties per the Divine Order and behave according to the rules of the Divine Order. In short, all the natural rules that physical Sciences such as Physics, Chemistry, and

Astronomy address are the product of the Creator's Design and Divine Order[11].

As part of the Divine design, God has provided us enough in one fell swoop for everybody including for all kinds of life below and above the earth. We have the ability to create and recreate using the resources available to us for as long as there is life. God does not need to intervene and replenish what He gave to us from time to time because He also built-in the capacity for the system to replenish itself.

In their own words:

First Guru, GGS p. 1, line 9
ਹੁਕਮੈ ਅੰਦਰਿ ਸਭੁ ਕੋ ਬਾਹਰਿ ਹੁਕਮ ਨ ਕੋਇ ॥
Everyone, everything is subject to the Divine Order or System; nothing is beyond the Divine Order.

First Guru, GGS p. 1, line 7
ਹੁਕਮੀ ਹੋਵਨਿ ਆਕਾਰ ਹੁਕਮੁ ਨ ਕਹਿਆ ਜਾਈ ॥
Forms/bodies are created per Divine Order; The Divine Order or System cannot be described in words.

First Guru, GGS p. 4, line 14
ਨਾਨਕ ਹੁਕਮੀ ਆਵਹੁ ਜਾਹੁ ॥੨੦॥
Says Nanak, we come to this world and depart it according to the Divine order or System.

First Guru, GGS p. 55, line 17
ਹੁਕਮੀ ਸਭੇ ਉਪਜਹਿ ਹੁਕਮੀ ਕਾਰ ਕਮਾਹਿ ॥

---

[11] Louis Pasteur: "The more I study nature, the more I stand amazed at the work of the Creator. Science brings men nearer to God."

Everyone is created according to Divine Order or System and acts under the rules of the System.

First Guru, GGS p. 1412, line 18
ਪੂਰੇ ਕਾ ਕੀਆ ਸਭ ਕਿਛੁ ਪੂਰਾ ਘਟਿ ਵਧਿ ਕਿਛੁ ਨਾਹੀ ॥
The Perfect Almighty God has designed a perfect system- nothing needs to be added to or taken out of it.

First Guru GGS p. 7, line 5
ਜੋ ਕਿਛੁ ਪਾਇਆ ਸੁ ਏਕਾ ਵਾਰ ॥
He has provided what is needed (to sustain life) in one fell swoop.

First Guru, GGS p. 223, line 7
ਏਕੋ ਹੁਕਮੁ ਵਰਤੈ ਸਭ ਲੋਈ ॥
All the worlds or realms are subject to the One God's Divine Order.

Fifth Guru, GGS p. 277, line 1
ਹੁਕਮੇ ਧਾਰਿ ਅਧਰ ਰਹਾਵੈ ॥ ਹੁਕਮੇ ਉਪਜੈ ਹੁਕਮਿ ਸਮਾਵੈ ॥
ਹੁਕਮੇ ਊਚ ਨੀਚ ਬਿਉਹਾਰ ॥ ਹੁਕਮੇ ਅਨਿਕ ਰੰਗ ਪਰਕਾਰ ॥
(Planets) are created and maintained unsupported per His Divine Order. Everything and everyone is created per His Divine Order and shall merge again into Him. One's good or bad actions are subject to the Divine order. The Creation in different forms and colors is per His Divine order.

Fifth Guru, GGS p. 390, line 18
ਹੁਕਮੇ ਬਾਧਾ ਕਾਰ ਕਮਾਇ ॥
One's actions are governed by the Divine System or order.

Fourth Guru GGS, p. 723, line 6

ਸਭਿ ਆਏ ਹੁਕਮਿ ਖਸਮਾਹੁ ਹੁਕਮਿ ਸਭ ਵਰਤਨੀ ॥

Everyone comes here according to the Divine System. All are subject to the Divine order.

Fifth Guru, GGS p. 1071, 11

ਗਗਨੁ ਰਹਾਇਆ ਹੁਕਮੇ ਚਰਣਾ ॥

He has spread Akash or Gagan (empty gravitational space) over the earth supported by His Command.

First Guru, GGS p. 1037, line 4

ਹੁਕਮੇ ਆਡਾਣੇ ਆਗਾਸੀ ॥ ਹੁਕਮੇ ਜਲ ਥਲ ਤ੍ਰਿਭਵਣ ਵਾਸੀ॥

Per His Order, Akash (the empty gravitational space) is spread over the earth. Per His Order, there are lands and water and the creatures that dwell in there.

First Guru GGS p. 355, line 13

ਮੰਨੇ ਹੁਕਮੁ ਸੁ ਪਰਗਟੁ ਜਾਇ ॥

One who acknowledges the Divine's System or Order, gets to see how it works.

Chapter 5: Buckle up now -you are on a wild ride here!

- ➤ *We are all actors in the magnificent Divine Play.*
- ➤ *The Divine system filming our lives?*
- ➤ *Why do people have greed, ego and other undesirable instincts, if God created them?*
- ➤ *If we came to the world as part of God's creation, why don't we have any memory of it?*
- ➤ *Is the veil of ignorance ever lifted?*
- ➤ *Am I doomed due to my failure to avoid bad Karma?*

We are all actors in the magnificent Divine Play.

The Sikh scripture highlights a central theme that this world is designed as a grand Divine Play or a challenge for us by the playful, blissful, merciful, all-pervading, all-knowing Primal Being. The challenge is about winning the game of life and taking right actions, despite many hurdles and the built-in instincts that make it hard for us to stay on track. So, welcome to the wild ride here in this world!

This was intended to be a fun game where God wants us to live life to the fullest and to win the game of life by getting over the built-in challenges. We are all here acting in the Divine play or game, with the formless Creator manifesting in various forms and having those various forms play certain roles. The Divine Play is created to have us enjoy having body forms and minds, creating and recreating, using the height of our imagination.

The drama begins with us, the actors, purposely made to forget our origin (which is Divine and immortal, blissful and playful) as we enter this world. We do not know who we actually are and where we came from. We are kept in the dark about the existence of the Creator or God and our destination. We get entrenched in our roles such that we forget that we are actors in a play, and after our role ends, we must leave everything behind.

It seems somewhat like the TV show Survivor with many challenges built in as part of the game. However, unlike the Survivor show participants, we have been made to forget our origin and our ultimate destination and have come to believe that this world is all there is. Our challenge is so much more difficult to overcome and go back as winners because of the veil of ignorance. We have no idea that someone is keeping a record of our actions and we will be judged after life.

As part of the grand play or scheme of Creation, we are intentionally subjected to some built-in perverse instincts and traits like ego, pride, attachment to family and worldly possessions, greed, anger, lust, and aggressiveness. The challenge for us is to navigate our roles in the Divine drama and overcome the hurdles presented to us. Natural forces and phenomena and impediments (like wild cards or random factors) beyond our control add to the intensity of the drama.

In this Divine Drama, suspense is maintained to the very end of life as nobody has knowledge of when it will be their time to leave this world. Not knowing that there is the Divine and the Divine justice system, people do bad things and hurt others. Because of our ignorance of our origin and destination and not knowing about the Divine and the Divine System, this world is a very difficult place to navigate and to stay on the right path. But all this is part of the challenge that has been set up for us to see how well we overcome the hurdles and go back home victorious.

The drama is about who wins the game of life and does the right actions in spite of the built-in perverse instincts, hurdles, and challenges. So, the challenge is to keep these instincts in check and take the right actions. Failure to keep these instincts under check and hurting others with our excessive ego, attachment to family and worldly things, greed, anger, and lust is bad Karma for which we will be answerable.

Per Divine design, we, the actors, do not get punished or rewarded by God immediately for our actions because then everybody would do the right actions, and the drama would not be able to go on. Everybody's life is constantly filmed and there is a review of good or bad actions (Karma) after this life is over.

There is a lot of pleasure and pain to the actors but they remain firmly attached to this world, not knowing their origin and the ultimate destination. The veil of ignorance, or Maya, keeps them in the dark about the Reality. They think this world is the be-all and end-all and do not know that it is a Divine drama and that this world is not their permanent home. Driven by Karma, the actors go through the cycle of birth and death. Good Karma leads to a good next life after death. Good and bad Karma and their desires lead the way for them after they leave the body.

The actors in the Divine Play are always on a slippery slope of committing bad Karma due to the built-in undesirable instincts as part of the challenge. They are unaware that there will be a review of how they conducted themselves through their life-time. Additionally, they do not know that they can end the cycle of birth and death and pain and suffering by realizing that it is a drama created by their Creator and by connecting with the Creator. They are ignorant about a very important feature of the Divine Drama, which is that they can opt out of the drama and its automated Karma-driven cycle of birth and death upon leaving the body at death.

It is not a drama or play in the usual sense of the word and cannot be taken lightly because there are serious consequences of our actions as we play our roles. It is a drama only in the sense that the Creator created it, and all actors come from the Creator and are part of the Creator. While playing our roles, every bit of it is real because it results in real pain, suffering, or pleasure. It also determines the kind of life we will have next and how long we will stay separated from the Creator and suffer. After our role ends, we are judged by how well we managed various perverse instincts and how much we hurt or helped others.

Through people who have experienced the Divine (saints, prophets, gurus, rishis), God gives us clues as to the nature and working of the Divine Order or System. Only those who wake up to the fact that it is a Divine drama and there is a Creator and they have an eternal home to return to, get out of the Karma-driven cycle of birth and death. They are freed and get salvation from the Karma-driven cycle of birth and death. They do not incarnate in body again unless they are tasked by the Divine to bring us the message of His existence or to turn things around when tyranny and chaos prevail.

When over time, due to the lack of awareness about the Divine Order, conditions devolve to an extent that there is more pain and suffering caused by the Drama rather than pleasure, God ends the drama by subsuming all of His Creation back into Himself.

In their own words:

First Guru GGS p.946, line 18
ਅਬਿਨਾਸੀ ਪੁਭਿ ਖੇਲੁ ਰਚਾਇਆ ਗੁਰਮੁਖਿ ਸੋਝੀ ਹੋਈ ॥
The imperishable God has staged this Play; only the enlightened ones understand it.

Third Guru, GGS p. 117, line 12
ਤਿਨਿ ਕਰਤੈ ਇਕੁ ਖੇਲੁ ਰਚਾਇਆ ॥
The Creator set this Play in motion.

Fifth Guru GGS p. 1185, line 12
ਕਾਮੁ ਕ੍ਰੋਧੁ ਲੋਭੁ ਮੋਹੁ ਜੀਤਹੁ ਐਸੀ ਖੇਲ ਹਰਿ ਪਿਆਰੀ ॥੨॥

Conquer lust, anger, greed, and worldly attachment.
(Having thrown these instincts into the game), conquering
these instincts is a game dear to God.

Fifth Guru GGS p. 209 line 11
ਨਾ ਕਿਛੁ ਆਵਤ ਨਾ ਕਿਛੁ ਜਾਵਤ ਸਭੁ ਖੇਲੁ ਕੀਓ ਹਰਿ ਰਾਇਓ ॥
Nobody comes and leaves the world (as we see it); It is all
a Play set in motion by God, the Sovereign ruler.

Fifth Guru GGS p. 1074, line 12
ਨਾ ਕੋ ਆਵੈ ਨਾ ਕੋ ਜਾਵੈ ਗੁਰਿ ਦੂਰਿ ਕੀਆ ਭਰਮੀਜਾ ਹੇ ॥੧੪॥
Nobody comes (to this world) and nobody leaves (as we see
it). The Guru has driven out my ignorance.

Fifth Guru GGS p. 281, line 18
ਨਹ ਕਿਛੁ ਜਨਮੈ ਨਹ ਕਿਛੁ ਮਰੈ ॥ ਆਪਨ ਚਲਿਤੁ ਆਪ ਹੀ ਕਰੈ ॥
Nothing is born (as we see it), and nothing dies (as we see
it). It is all His Divine Play.

Fourth Guru GGS p. 174, line 9
ਚੋਜੀ ਮੇਰੇ ਗੋਵਿੰਦਾ ਚੋਜੀ ਮੇਰੇ ਪਿਆਰਿਆ ਹਰਿ ਪ੍ਰਭੁ ਮੇਰਾ ਚੋਜੀ ਜੀਉ ॥
Playful is my Master of the Universe; Playful is my
Beloved. My Master God is wondrous and Playful.

First Guru GGS p. 1031, line 6
ਤੇਰੇ ਚੋਜ ਨ ਜਾਣੈ ਕੋਈ ਤੂ ਪੂਰਾ ਪੁਰਖੁ ਬਿਧਾਤਾ ਹੇ ॥੧॥
No one knows Your wondrous Plays; You are the perfect
designer of this Play.

Fifth Guru GGS p. 1095, line 15
ਇਹੁ ਆਵਾ ਗਵਣੁ ਰਚਾਇਓ ਕਰਿ ਚੋਜ ਦੇਖੰਤਾ ॥
He created the cycle of coming ang going (birth and death)
as part of this wondrous Play and watches it play out.

First Guru GGS p.1033, line 12

ਪਉਣੁ ਪਾਣੀ ਅਗਨੀ ਇਕ ਵਾਸਾ ॥ ਆਪੇ ਕੀਤੋ ਖੇਲੁ ਤਮਾਸਾ ॥

By making air, water and fire coexist, he himself staged His wondrous Play.

Fourth Guru GGS p. 1320, line 17

ਹਰਿ ਕੇ ਚੋਜ ਵਿਡਾਨ ਦੇਖੁ ਜਨ ਜੋ ਖੋਟਾ ਖਰਾ ਇਕ ਨਿਮਖ ਪਛਾਨੈ ॥

Behold the wondrous and amazing Play of the Divine. In an instant, He distinguishes the genuine from the counterfeit.

Third Guru GGS p. 786, line 17

ਇਹੁ ਜਗੁ ਆਪਿ ਉਪਾਇਓਨੁ ਕਰਿ ਚੋਜ ਵਿਡਾਨੁ ॥

He Himself created this world as part of the wondrous Play.

Fifth Guru GGS p. 963, line 17

ਸਭਿ ਤੇਰੇ ਚੋਜ ਵਿਡਾਣ ਸਭੁ ਤੇਰਾ ਕਾਰਣੈ ॥੧੩॥

Everything is Your wondrous Play; You are the cause of the whole creation.

Fifth Guru GGS p. 253, line 14

ਆਪਨ ਖੇਲੁ ਆਪ ਹੀ ਕੀਨੋ ॥

He Himself set His own Play in motion.

Fifth Guru GGS p. 280, line 19

ਅਪਨਾ ਖੇਲੁ ਆਪਿ ਕਰਨੈਹਾਰੁ ॥

He Himself has created this Drama.

Fifth Guru, GGS p. 292, line 2

ਆਪਨ ਖੇਲੁ ਆਪਿ ਕਰਿ ਦੇਖੈ ॥

He Himself is beholding the Drama He created.

Fifth Guru GGS p. 292. Line 2

ਖੇਲੁ ਸੰਕੋਚੈ ਤਉ ਨਾਨਕ ਏਕੈ ॥੭॥

When He winds up the Drama, says Nanak, then He alone remains.

Fifth Guru, GGS p. 294, line 13
ਆਵਨ ਜਾਨੁ ਇਕੁ ਖੇਲੁ ਬਨਾਇਆ ॥
Coming to and going out of this world is a Drama that He created.

Fifth Guru, GGS p.409, line 3
ਹਰਖ ਸੋਗ ਬੈਰਾਗ ਅਨੰਦੀ ਖੇਲੁ ਰੀ ਦਿਖਾਇਓ ॥੧॥ ਰਹਾਉ ॥
As the Blissful God has revealed to me, pleasure, sorrow and (finally) the longing to go back home are all part of His Play.

Fourth Guru GGS p. 507, line 7
ਏਹੁ ਪਰਪੰਚੁ ਖੇਲੁ ਕੀਆ ਸਭੁ ਕਰਤੈ ਹਰਿ ਕਰਤੈ ਸਭ ਕਲ ਧਾਰੀ ॥
All this worldly Drama is set in motion by the Creator; He has infused His Divine Energy into it.

Third Guru, GGS p. 513, line 19
ਹਰਿ ਭਾਣਾ ਤਾ ਭਰਮਾਇਅਨੁ ਕਰਿ ਪਰਪੰਚੁ ਖੇਲੁ ਉਪਾਇ ॥
It is part of the grand design of the Divine Play that actors are not aware that it is a Drama.

Fourth Guru, GGS p. 723, line 7
ਸਚੁ ਸਾਹਿਬੁ ਸਾਚਾ ਖੇਲੁ ਸਭੁ ਹਰਿ ਧਨੀ ॥੧॥
It is really a Play or Drama by the Real Master. All of it is Him.

Fifth Guru, GGS p. 746, line 10
ਕਹਨੁ ਨ ਜਾਈ ਖੇਲੁ ਤੁਹਾਰਾ ॥
Your Play cannot be fully described.

Third Guru, GGS p. 754, line 17

ਸਚੈ ਆਪਣਾ ਖੇਲੁ ਰਚਾਇਆ ਆਵਾ ਗਉਣੁ ਪਾਸਾਰਾ ॥

The True Master has created and staged His own Play where actors are coming and going.

First Guru, GGS p. 764, line 14

ਸਾਚਾ ਖੇਲੁ ਤੁਮ੍ਹਾਰਾ ॥

It is a real Play by You.

First Guru, GGS p. 903, line 13

ਝੂਠੇ ਖੇਲੁ ਖੇਲੈ ਬਹੁ ਨਟੂਆ ॥

You play all sorts of clever tricks, like a juggler.

Third Guru, GGS, p. 948, line 15

ਸਭੁ ਕਿਛੁ ਤੇਰਾ ਖੇਲੁ ਹੈ ਸਚੁ ਸਿਰਜਣਹਾਰਾ ॥

Everything is Your play, O' Eternal Creator.

Third Guru, GGS, p. 953, line 18

ਸਭੁ ਕਿਛੁ ਹਰਿ ਕਾ ਖੇਲੁ ਹੈ ਗੁਰਮੁਖਿ ਕਿਸੈ ਬੁਝਾਈ ॥੧੩॥

Everything is the Play of God. The Gurmukh (those pursuing the Divine) come to understand this.

Fifth Guru GGS p. 999, line 19

ਭਣਤਿ ਨਾਨਕੁ ਜਬ ਖੇਲੁ ਉਝਾਰੈ ਤਬ ਏਕੈ ਏਕੰਕਾਰਾ ॥੪॥੪॥

Says Nanak, when He brings His Play to its close, then only the One, the One Creator remains.

First Guru, GGS p. 1020, line 16

ਆਪੇ ਪਿੜ ਬਾਧੀ ਜਗੁ ਖੇਲੈ ਆਪੇ ਕੀਮਤਿ ਪਾਈ ਹੇ ॥੫॥

He Himself created the world arena to stage the Drama and He Himself evaluates the actors' performance.

Third Guru, GGS, p. 1044, line 4

ਆਪੇ ਖੇਲ ਕਰੇ ਸਭਿ ਕਰਤਾ ਆਪੇ ਦੇਇ ਬੁਝਾਈ ਹੇ ॥੫॥

The Creator Himself stages all His Plays; He Himself gives clues to understand it.

Third Guru, GGS p. 1056, line 10
ਮੇਰੈ ਪ੍ਰਭਿ ਸਾਚੈ ਇਕੁ ਖੇਲੁ ਰਚਾਇਆ ॥
My eternal God has staged a Play.

Fifth Guru, GGS p. 1095, line 14
ਸਭੁ ਬ੍ਰਹਮ ਪਸਾਰੁ ਪਸਾਰਿਓ ਆਪੇ ਖੇਲੰਤਾ ॥
The Creator spread out to create the expanse for the entire universe, and He Himself plays in it.

Third Guru GGS p. 1128 line 11
ਕਰਿ ਪ੍ਰਸਾਦੁ ਇਕੁ ਖੇਲੁ ਦਿਖਾਇਆ ॥
By His Grace, He has shown me that it is all a Play.

Fifth Guru, GGS p. 1181, line 6
ਸਭੁ ਤੇਰੋ ਖੇਲੁ ਤੁਝ ਮਹਿ ਸਮਾਹਿ ॥
Everything is Your play; it all merges back into You.

Fourth Guru GGS p. 1311, line 2
ਸੁਪਨੰਤਰੁ ਸੰਸਾਰੁ ਸਭੁ ਬਾਜੀ ਸਭੁ ਬਾਜੀ ਖੇਲੁ ਖਿਲਾਵੈਗੋ ॥
The whole world is a game like in a dream, all a game. God plays and causes the game to be played.

First Guru GGS p. 1330, line 1
ਆਪੇ ਖੇਲ ਕਰੇ ਸਭ ਕਰਤਾ ਐਸਾ ਬੂਝੈ ਕੋਈ ॥੩॥
It is all a Play by the Creator Himself; only a few understand this.

Third Guru GGS p. 1334, line 12
ਆਪੇ ਭਾਂਤਿ ਬਣਾਏ ਬਹੁ ਰੰਗੀ ਸਿਸਟਿ ਉਪਾਇ ਪ੍ਰਭਿ ਖੇਲੁ ਕੀਆ ॥
God Himself fashioned the many forms and colors; He created the Universe and staged the Play.

Fifth Guru GGS p. 247, line 10
ਮੇਰਾ ਮਨੁ ਤਨੁ ਮੋਹਿ ਲੀਆ ਜੀਉ ਦੇਖਿ ਚਲਤ ਤੁਮਾਰੇ ॥

My mind and body are mesmerized beholding Your
wondrous Play.

Fourth Guru GGS p. 303, line 3
ਨਾਨਕ ਦੁਹੀ ਸਿਰੀ ਖਸਮੁ ਆਪੇ ਵਰਤੈ ਨਿਤ ਕਰਿ ਕਰਿ ਦੇਖੈ ਚਲਤ
ਸਬਾਏ ॥੧॥

Says Nanak, God the Master is the One at both ends (at
the doing and the receiving end); Day in and day out, He
acts and beholds His own Play.

Fifth Guru GGS p. 205, line 10
ਖੰਡ ਬ੍ਰਹਮੰਡ ਕਾ ਏਕੋ ਠਾਣਾ ਗੁਰਿ ਪਰਦਾ ਖੋਲਿ ਦਿਖਾਇਓ ॥

One Creator holds the continents and the solar systems in
place. The Guru has lifted the veil of ignorance and shown
this to me.

Fifth Guru GGS p. 673, line 17
ਹਉ ਬਲਿਹਾਰੀ ਸਤਿਗੁਰ ਅਪੁਨੇ ਜਿਨਿ ਇਹੁ ਚਲਤੁ ਦਿਖਾਇਆ ॥

I can sacrifice my life for the Ever-existent Divine, who has
shown me this wondrous play.

Fifth Guru GGS p. 885, line 14
ਕਉਨੁ ਮੂਆ ਰੇ ਕਉਨੁ ਮੂਆ ॥ ਬ੍ਰਹਮ ਗਿਆਨੀ ਮਿਲਿ ਕਰਹੁ ਬੀਚਾਰਾ
ਇਹੁ ਤਉ ਚਲਤੁ ਭਇਆ ॥੧॥

Who has died? O' who has died? O' people with Divine
knowledge, think about what a wondrous drama this
world is.

Third Guru GGS p. 921, line 16
ਗੁਰ ਪਰਸਾਦੀ ਬੁਝਿਆ ਤਾ ਚਲਤੁ ਹੋਆ ਚਲਤੁ ਨਦਰੀ ਆਇਆ ॥

By the Divine's Grace, I have understood that it is a show;
I have seen that it is a show.

Fifth Guru GGS p. 1018, line 19

ਕਹੁ ਨਾਨਕ ਗੁਰਿ ਚਲਤੁ ਦਿਖਾਇਆ ਮਨ ਮਧੇ ਹਰਿ ਹਰਿ ਰਾਵਨਾ ॥੮॥੨॥੫॥

Says Nanak, the Divine has revealed His Play to me; I relish my mind absorbed in His Name.

First Guru GGS p. 1037, line 18

ਉਤਭੁਜੁ ਚਲਤੁ ਕੀਆ ਸਿਰਿ ਕਰਤੈ ਬਿਸਮਾਦੁ ਸਬਦਿ ਦੇਖਾਇਦਾ ॥੭॥

The Supreme Creator has created this grand play with life sprouting everywhere. Through the Shabad (Divine Sound energy), He reveals His Wonderous Show.

Fifth Guru GGS p. 1291, line 10

ਸਭੇ ਵਰਤੈ ਚਲਤੁ ਚਲਤੁ ਵਖਾਣਿਆ ॥

Everything and everyone is a participant in the Divine Play, so has been revealed to me.

Fifth Guru GGS p. 1077, line 7

ਆਵਣੁ ਜਾਣਾ ਸਭੁ ਚਲਤੁ ਤੁਮਾਰਾ ॥

Coming to and going out of this world is all part of Your wondrous play.

First Guru GGS p. 1033, line 12

ਆਪੇ ਕੀਤੋ ਖੇਲੁ ਤਮਾਸਾ ॥

He Himself stages His wondrous drama or play.

Fourth Guru GGS p. 314, line 2

ਤੂ ਘਟਿ ਘਟਿ ਇਕੁ ਵਰਤਦਾ ਸਚੁ ਸਾਹਿਬ ਚਲਤੈ ॥

You are the One, pervading within everyone; O' True Master, this is part of Your Play.

Tenth Guru Jaap Sahib stanza 81

ਏਕ ਮੂਰਤਿ ਅਨੇਕ ਦਰਸਨ ਕੀਨ ਰੂਪ ਅਨੇਕ ॥ ਖੇਲ ਖੇਲ ਅਖੇਲ ਖੇਲਨ ਅੰਤ ਕੋ ਫਿਰਿ ਏਕ ॥੮੧॥

71

You have One Image, but You manifest yourself in countless forms. After You wind up your Worldly Drama, You are One again.

The Divine system filming our lives?

According to those who experienced the Divine, there is a review of all of our good/bad actions or Karma after we leave the body upon death. Everybody is shown their life's film, which had been invisibly recorded all along. The Divine system dispenses justice based on this review.[12]

Are you starting to panic about what happened to the God you were told would shower you with unconditional love and forgiveness? How can a loving God constantly monitor what we do and hold us accountable?

However, we also know that the society we live in would fall apart in chaos and misery if anybody could do whatever they liked with no consequences. Anybody with parental experience can tell you that a parent's love for their children is abundant and always there, but that does not mean that a parent should not discipline their children when love alone does not seem to keep them on right track. Accountability and discipline are essential elements of everyday life. God, as the super parent, knows this better than any of us parents and has set up a system of accountability. Does this start to make sense?

Also, take heart. Those who experienced the Divine tell us that the merciful, forgiving God knows that because of the design of the Divine Drama being such and the challenging

---

[12] Hebrews 4:13: "Nothing in all creation is hidden from God's sight. Everything is uncovered and laid bare before the eyes of him to whom we must give account".(Bible NIV)

instincts we are afflicted with, we are always susceptible to making mistakes and being on a slippery slope of bad Karma.

Because we have a tough task of navigating life properly in the face of so many challenges and limitations, as part of the Divine Play, God has created a system in which those who become aware of the existence of God and realize the error of their ways are exempted from judgment. They qualify for emancipation or salvation from the Karma-driven cycle of birth and death and live in blissful Divine existence[13] until they are tasked to come into a life form to perform some Divine duty.

Because our actions are not punished/rewarded by God promptly, we should not be fooled into thinking that there is nobody watching and keeping account. As per Divine Order, everybody is judged by their Karma at the end of life.

Even though we are not aware of God, there is His voice in our heads that alerts us when we are about to do something we should not do. A thief hears the voice telling him not to steal, but he chooses to ignore it or rationalizes it by convincing himself that the person he is stealing from did not obtain the item honestly either. Even a murderer hears that voice before committing the horrible act but somehow rationalizes that the person does not deserve to live.

At the review or judgment time, there is no hiding behind any lies because the Divine System records everything, good or bad, all the time. There is no way to game the system or subvert it to escape accountability. The only way to get out of the Karma-driven cycle of birth and death is to realize that there is God and cultivate a desire to connect with Him.

---

[13] John 6:47- "Very truly I tell you, the one who believes has eternal life." (Bible NIV)

Our actions or Karma determine the quality of life we will be ordained to next, per Divine Design[14]. The cycle of birth and death driven by Karma continues, sometimes rewarding good actions and sometimes punishing for bad ones. Actions cause reactions per Divine design, and people get caught up in a Karma-driven cycle. Continued evil or bad actions devolve the mind and can make it difficult to get out of the cycle of birth and death. The Karma-driven cycle of birth and death goes on until one becomes aware of the existence of God and develops a longing to go back home to the Divine.

The playful God, being loving and forgiving, wants us to win the game of life and go back home victorious. The Divine drama is about who wins the game of life and does the right actions in spite of various instincts, hurdles, and challenges.

While in power, kings and rulers keep repressing people, thinking that they are here forever and they will be wielding the power forever, but they forget that the real ruler of the world is Almighty God, who will hold them to account for their actions. Those who experienced the Divine tell us that everybody's record of actions is naked in the Divine Court with nowhere to hide. Upon leaving the body, everyone is shown a record of their life as direct evidence and there can be no denials for any wrongdoing. There are no powerful people, family members, advocates, or allies you had when living who can help. Those in power should remember that they were rewarded with precious human life and a powerful role (such as being an emperor or ruler) based on their previous good Karma. Their repressive and unjust actions can roll them off the cliff.

---

[14] Job 4:8 - "As I have seen, those who plow iniquity and sow trouble reap the same." (Bible ESV)

In their own words:

First Guru GGS p. 1110, line 15
ਘੜੀ ਚਸੇ ਕਾ ਲੇਖਾ ਲੀਜੈ ਬੁਰਾ ਭਲਾ ਸਹੁ ਜੀਆ ॥

There is accounting for every second, every instant; one is accountable both for the bad and the good.

Fifth Guru, GGS p. 393, line 15
ਚਿਤੁ ਗੁਪਤੁ ਸਭ ਲਿਖਤੇ ਲੇਖਾ ॥

All of our actions are being recorded (Chitr Gupt) invisibly and an account of everything is being created.

Third Guru, GGS p. 127, line 2
ਘੜੀ ਮੁਹਤ ਕਾ ਲੇਖਾ ਲੇਵੈ ਰਤੀਅਹੁ ਮਾਸਾ ਤੋਲ ਕਢਾਵਣਿਆ ॥੫॥

Each instant and each moment is accounted for. Every little thing is weighed and counted.

First Guru, GGS p. 952, line 4
ਸਭਨਾ ਕਾ ਦਰਿ ਲੇਖਾ ਹੋਇ ॥

Everyone's actions are reviewed and judged in the Divine court.

First Guru, GGS p. 7, line 13
ਕਰਮੀ ਕਰਮੀ ਹੋਇ ਵੀਚਾਰੁ ॥

The deeds and actions are reviewed and judged.

First Guru, GGS p. 953, line 13
ਲੇਖਾ ਰਬੁ ਮੰਗੇਸੀਆ ਬੈਠਾ ਕਢਿ ਵਹੀ ॥

Opening His ledger, God will call you to account.

First Guru GGS p. 1342, line 6
ਜੈਸੀ ਮਨਸਾ ਤੈਸੀ ਦਸਾ ॥

One's desires shape one's life's direction.

Third Guru GGS p. 918, line 11

ਐਸਾ ਕੰਮੁ ਮੂਲੇ ਨ ਕੀਚੈ ਜਿਤੁ ਅੰਤਿ ਪਛੋਤਾਈਐ ॥

Don't do anything that you will regret in the end.

Second Guru GGS p. 146, line 15

ਚੰਗਿਆਈਆ ਬੁਰਿਆਈਆ ਵਾਚੈ ਧਰਮੁ ਹਦੂਰਿ ॥

Good deeds and bad deeds-the record is scrutinized by the Divine Judge.

Third Guru GGS p. 112, line 1

ਦੇਹੀ ਜਾਤਿ ਨ ਆਗੈ ਜਾਏ ॥

The body (with all its beauty) and (the high) status shall not accompany you to the world hereafter.

Fifth Guru, GGS p. 134, line 18

ਜੇਹਾ ਬੀਜੈ ਸੋ ਲੁਣੈ ਕਰਮਾ ਸੰਦੜਾ ਖੇਤੁ ॥

As you sow, so shall you reap in the field of Karma.

Fifth Guru GGS p. 1356, line 5

ਦਾਨੰ ਪਰਾ ਪੂਰਬੇਣ ਭੁੰਚੰਤੇ ਮਹੀਪਤੇ ॥

Kings (having gotten their position because of good deeds of the past life) are eating up the blessings of the charitable actions of their past lives.

Saint Ravidas GGS p. 486, line 8

ਜੀਅ ਜੰਤ ਜਹਾ ਜਹਾ ਲਗੁ ਕਰਮ ਕੇ ਬਸਿ ਜਾਇ ॥

Wherever the beings and creatures are, they are there according to the Karma (their past actions).

Saint Tirlochan GGS p. 695, line 2

ਦੁਕ੍ਰਿਤ ਸੁਕ੍ਰਿਤ ਬਾਰੋ ਕਰਮੁ ਰੀ ॥੧॥ ਰਹਾਉ ॥

Hey, pain and pleasure are the result of your own actions.

Saint Kabir, GGS, p. 792, line 13

ਅਮਲੁ ਸਿਰਾਨੇ ਲੇਖਾ ਦੇਨਾ ॥

One has to account for actions.

Third Guru, GGS p. 111, line 2
ਲੇਖਾ ਮਾਗੈ ਤਾ ਕਿਨਿ ਦੀਐ ॥

When called to account for actions, who will answer then?

Fourth Guru, GGS p. 317, line 5
ਜੇਵੇਹੇ ਕਰਮ ਕਮਾਵਦਾ ਤੇਵੇਹੇ ਫਲਤੇ ॥

Whatever we receive is the fruit of our deeds.

Third Guru, GGS p. 363, line 11
ਤੇਹਾ ਹੋਵੈ ਜੇਹੇ ਕਰਮ ਕਮਾਇ ॥

As are the deeds done, so does one become.

Third Guru GGS p. 1128, line 3
ਕਹਤੁ ਨਾਨਕ ਇਹੁ ਜੀਉ ਕਰਮ ਬੰਧੁ ਹੋਈ ॥

Says Nanak, the beings are shackled by their actions.

First Guru GGS, p. 473, line 19
ਦਰਿ ਲਏ ਲੇਖਾ ਪੀੜਿ ਛੁਟੈ ਨਾਨਕਾ ਜਿਉ ਤੇਲ ॥੨॥

Says Nanak, in the Divine court, where accounts are examined, one feels such pain as if being crushed in a press like oil seeds.

Fifth Guru GGS p. 546, line 11
ਲੇਖਾ ਧਰਮ ਭਇਆ ਤਿਲ ਪੀੜੇ ਘਾਣੀ ਰਾਮ ॥

Going through the Divine accounting system is (painful) and it feels like sesame seeds being pressed in the oil-press.

First Guru GGS p. 1028, line 8
ਲੇਖਾ ਲੀਜੈ ਤਿਲ ਜਿਉ ਪੀੜੀ ॥

Going through the accounting process is (painful) like sesame seeds going through the oil press.

First Guru GGS, p. 1090, line 9

ਸਾਹਿਬੁ ਲੇਖਾ ਮੰਗਾਸੀ ਦੁਨੀਆ ਦੇਖਿ ਨ ਭੂਲੁ ॥

The Divine Master shall call you to account; watching this world, do not forget that.

Third Guru GGS p. 1417, line 19

ਖੇਤਿ ਸਰੀਰਿ ਜੋ ਬੀਜੀਐ ਸੋ ਅੰਤਿ ਖਲੋਆ ਆਇ ॥

The human body is like a farm; whatever you plant in this farm, will be standing in front of you after this life.

Fifth Guru, GGS p. 717, line 3

ਨਿਰਮਲ ਰੂਪ ਅਨੂਪ ਸੁਆਮੀ ਕਰਮ ਭੂਮਿ ਬੀਜਨ ਸੋ ਖਾਵਨ ॥੧॥

The Divine image is immaculate and pure; He is the incomparable Divine Master. Whatever we sow in the field of actions /Karma, that is what we harvest and eat.

Saint Kabir GGS p. 856, line 9

ਕੋਊ ਹਰਿ ਸਮਾਨਿ ਨਹੀ ਰਾਜਾ ॥ ਏ ਭੂਪਤਿ ਸਭ ਦਿਵਸ ਚਾਰਿ ਕੇ ਝੂਠੇ ਕਰਤ ਦਿਵਾਜਾ ॥੧॥ ਰਹਾਉ ॥

There is no king equal to the Almighty God. All these worldly kings last for only a short while, putting on their false displays.

Fourth Guru GGS p. 645, line 3

ਏਹ ਭੂਪਤਿ ਰਾਣੇ ਰੰਗ ਦਿਨ ਚਾਰਿ ਸੁਹਾਵਣਾ ॥

The kings and emperors have pleasures of the world, but only for a short while.

Why do people have greed, ego and other undesirable instincts, if God created them?

Going to churches, temples and mosques, all of us have heard since our very childhoods about how perfect God is. As we grow up, get schooling, are equipped with reasoning abilities, and experience the world, that view of God becomes hard to hang on to. We begin to ask: if God is so perfect, how come his prized creation, the humans behave so badly? A perfect God could not have created such an imperfect product!

Hang tight! Those who have experienced the Divine claim that as part of the Grand Divine Play, certain instincts were intentionally built into us to make it challenging.

Instincts and traits such as ego and pride, attachment to family and to worldly things, greed, anger, lust, and aggressiveness were built-in for us to enact roles in the Divine drama. All these instincts are necessary to a certain extent to live life in this world. These instincts become a problem when we are not able to manage them.

As with other plays, movies, or thrillers we watch, perverse instincts and suspense are an integral part of its design. If everyone behaved properly, remembered God, and did everything right, the drama would cease, and all would return to the Creator. So, to keep it challenging and going, everybody has been purposely afflicted with selfish instincts and greed. Everybody thinks they are the real doers and in-charge of their life and have a distinct sense of the self and ego. They are unaware that all of their actions are being monitored, and there will be a review of how they conducted themselves living this life. Even though they know they will not be able to take anything with them when they depart the world, they stay defiant and keep accumulating. Even though they think they are in charge of their life, nobody knows what tomorrow is going to be like.

In their own words:

First Guru GGS p. 138, line 17
ਮੋਹ ਠਗਉਲੀ ਪਾਇ ਕੈ ਤੁਧੁ ਆਪਹੁ ਜਗਤੁ ਖੁਆਇਆ ॥

You Yourself tricked the world with attachments so they would forget who they really are.

First Guru GGS p. 139, line 6
ਹਉਮੈ ਗਰਬੁ ਉਪਾਇ ਕੈ ਲੋਭੁ ਅੰਤਰਿ ਜੰਤਾ ਪਾਇਆ ॥

The Divine afflicted humans with egotism and arrogant pride, and engendered greed in them.

Third Guru GGS p. 1066 line 1
ਮਾਇਆ ਮੋਹੁ ਹੁਕਮਿ ਬਣਾਇਆ ॥

Illusion or ignorance about the nature of our existence and, attachments (that entrench us into this world) are part of the Divine Design, (Divine Order or System).

Fifth Guru GGS p. 394, line 17
ਮਾਇਆ ਮੋਹਿ ਸਭੋ ਜਗੁ ਬਾਧਾ ॥

The whole world is in bondage of delusion and attachment.

First Guru GGS p. 439, line 7
ਸੰਸਾਰੁ ਮਾਇਆ ਮੋਹੁ ਮੀਠਾ ਅੰਤਿ ਭਰਮੁ ਚੁਕਾਇਆ ॥

In delusion, all are sweetly attached to the world, but in the end, this delusion is dispelled.

Third Guru GGS p. 918, line 8
ਕੁਰਬਾਣੁ ਕੀਤਾ ਤਿਸੈ ਵਿਟਹੁ ਜਿਨਿ ਮੋਹੁ ਮੀਠਾ ਲਾਇਆ ॥

I am willing to sacrifice my life for the One God who afflicted the world with sweet emotional attachment.

First Guru GGS p. 937, line 4
ਮਾਇਆ ਮਮਤਾ ਮੋਹਣੀ ਜਿਨਿ ਕੀਤੀ ਸੋ ਜਾਣੁ ॥

Know the One who created delusion and the enticing attachments.

First Guru GGS p. 229, line 9
ਸਭੁ ਆਪੇ ਆਪਿ ਵਰਤਦਾ ਆਪੇ ਭਰਮਾਇਆ ॥

It is He Himself operating while keeping everybody in the dark.

Fifth Guru, GGS p. 1096, line 8
ਤੁਧੁ ਜਗ ਮਹਿ ਖੇਲੁ ਰਚਾਇਆ ਵਿਚਿ ਹਉਮੈ ਪਾਈਆ ॥

You have staged this play in the world, and infused egotism into all beings.

Third Guru GGS p. 67, line 9
ਮਾਇਆ ਮੋਹੁ ਮੇਰੈ ਪ੍ਰਭਿ ਕੀਨਾ ਆਪੇ ਭਰਮਿ ਭੁਲਾਏ ॥

My Master God Himself used delusion and attachment (as part of the design of the Play) so actors would not know who they are.

If we came to the world as part of God's creation, why don't we have any memory of it?

Think of the physical and mind games that we humans have designed for us to enjoy, with more and more difficult hurdles to overcome. And then think of the Creator who has designed the Grand Divine Play and the intricacies of it! A key element of enacting the Grand Divine Play is that we would not remember our origin and our essential nature, which is Divine, eternal, playful, and blissful. As part of the Grand Divine Play, we are purposely made to forget our origin, which is Divine.

There is a veil of ignorance referred to as Maya, which keeps us in the dark. This veil of ignorance, coupled with various kinds of alluring attachments to this world, to ourselves, and to our families, makes us think that this world is our true home. We forget all about our eternal abode. Ego, attachments, greed, anger, the desire to control everyone else, and other desires take over us in this world, not knowing our origin and destination. These difficult challenges fail us over and over in the game of life and subject us to the Karma-driven cycle of birth and death. The key is to unlock the mystery of our existence and realize that we are all actors in the great Divine drama. The only way to go back home is to recognize and connect with God.

In their own words:

First Guru GGS p. 229, line 9
ਸਭੁ ਆਪੇ ਆਪਿ ਵਰਤਦਾ ਆਪੇ ਭਰਮਾਇਆ ॥
It is He Himself operating while keeping everybody in the dark.

Third Guru GGS p. 441, line 19
ਇਉ ਕਹੈ ਨਾਨਕੁ ਕਿਆ ਜੰਤ ਵਿਚਾਰੇ ਜਾ ਤੁਧੁ ਭਰਮਿ ਭੁਲਾਏ ॥੯॥
Thus says Nanak: what can the poor creatures do, when You Yourself purposely keep them in the dark.

Third Guru GGS p. 513, line 19
ਹਰਿ ਭਾਵਾ ਤਾ ਭਰਮਾਇਅਨੁ ਕਰਿ ਪਰਪੰਚੁ ਖੇਲੁ ਉਪਾਇ ॥
It is part of the grand design of the Divine Play that actors are not aware that it is a Drama.

Fifth Guru GGS p. 812, line 11
ਮਤ ਭੁਲਹੁ ਮਾਨੁਖ ਜਨ ਮਾਇਆ ਭਰਮਾਇਆ ॥
Don't be fooled, O' mortal beings that you have been placed under the spell of Maya (illusion or ignorance).

Saint Naam Dev GGS p. 525, line 3

ਸਭ ਤੇ ਉਪਾਈ ਭਰਮ ਭੁਲਾਈ ॥

You created all and keep all in the dark (about the Reality that it is all a Divine drama).

Fifth Guru GGS p. 258, line 14

ਭਰਮੇ ਸੁਰਿ ਨਰ ਦੇਵੀ ਦੇਵਾ ॥

The angelic beings, goddesses and gods are in delusion too (not knowing their origin and destination).

Saint Kabir GGS p. 330, line 10

ਜਿਸ ਕਾ ਭਰਮੁ ਗਇਆ ਤਿਨਿ ਸਾਚੁ ਪਛਾਨਾ ॥੬॥

One whose delusion is dispelled, comes to know what the Reality is.

First Guru GGS p. 439, line 7

ਸੰਸਾਰੁ ਮਾਇਆ ਮੋਹੁ ਮੀਠਾ ਅੰਤਿ ਭਰਮੁ ਚੁਕਾਇਆ ॥

Due to the veil of ignorance, we are sweetly attached to this world, but in the end, this delusion is dispelled.

Ninth Guru GGS p. 537, line 11

ਅਗਨਤ ਅਪਾਰੁ ਅਲਖ ਨਿਰੰਜਨ ਜਿਹ ਸਭ ਜਗੁ ਭਰਮਾਇਓ ॥

The Immeasurable, Infinite, Incomprehensible and Immaculate Divine has kept the entire world in the dark.

Third Guru GGS p. 558, line 10

ਇਹ ਜਗਤੁ ਭਰਮਿ ਭੁਲਾਇਆ ਵਿਰਲਾ ਬੂਝੈ ਕੋਇ ॥੧॥

Rarely somebody understands that the world is in the dark (about the fact that we are part of the Divine drama).

First Guru GGS p. 581, line 15

ਜਿਉ ਬਾਜੀਗਰੁ ਭਰਮੇ ਭੂਲੈ ਝੂਠਿ ਮੁਠੀ ਅਹੰਕਾਰੇ ॥

Like the juggler tricks people, we are tricked by Him using egotism, and illusion.

Saint Kabir GGS p. 655, line 3

ਹਮਰਾ ਭਰਮੁ ਗਇਆ ਭਉ ਭਾਗਾ ॥

With my ignorance of the Reality gone, my fears ran away,

Fifth Guru GGS p. 700, line 17

ਨਾਮੁ ਜਪਤ ਕੋਟਿ ਸੂਰ ਉਜਾਰਾ ਬਿਨਸੈ ਭਰਮੁ ਅੰਧੇਰਾ ॥੧॥

Chanting the Naam, (the Name of the Divine), the darkness from ignorance and skepticism is dispelled as if by the light of millions of suns.

Third Guru GGS p. 880, line 5

ਭਰਮਿ ਭੁਲਾਨੇ ਜਾਇਹ ਦੋਇ ॥

Deluded by ignorance, they think they exist separately and on their own (in duality).

Third Guru GGS p. 1016, line 7

ਦਿਬ ਦ੍ਰਿਸਟਿ ਜਾਗੈ ਭਰਮੁ ਚੁਕਾਏ ॥

The illusion or ignorance is driven out when spiritual vision is awakened

First Guru GGS p. 1042, line 18

ਆਨਦ ਰੂਪ ਅਨੂਪ ਅਗੋਚਰ ਗੁਰ ਮਿਲਿਐ ਭਰਮੁ ਜਾਇਆ ॥੩॥

The Divine is the embodiment of bliss, incomparably beautiful and unfathomable; meeting the Divine, doubt is dispelled.

Third Guru GGS p. 1061, line 11

ਆਪੇ ਕਰੇ ਕਰਾਏ ਕਰਤਾ ਆਪੇ ਭਰਮਿ ਭੁਲਾਇਦਾ ॥੧੩॥

The Creator Himself acts and causes others to act; He Himself keeps all in dark (about the Divine Play).

Fifth Guru GGS p. 1074, line 12

ਨਾ ਕੋ ਆਵੈ ਨਾ ਕੋ ਜਾਵੈ ਗੁਰਿ ਦੂਰਿ ਕੀਆ ਭਰਮੀਜਾ ਹੇ ॥੧੪॥

Nobody comes (to this world) and nobody leaves (as we see it). The Guru has driven out my ignorance.

Third Guru GGS p. 1128, line 18
ਮਮਤਾ ਲਾਇ ਭਰਮਿ ਭੋਲਾਇਆ ॥੨॥

He has afflicted us with (maternal and paternal) attachments to keep us from seeing the Reality.

Fifth Guru GGS p. 1302, line 18
ਆਗੈ ਦ੍ਰਿਸਟਿ ਆਵਤ ਸਭ ਪਰਗਟ ਈਹਾ ਮੋਹਿਓ ਭਰਮ ਅੰਧੇਰੋ ॥੧॥

Hereafter (when you leave the body), everything is revealed for you to see; but the darkness of ignorance keeps all enticed here in this world.

Third Guru GGS p. 67, line 9
ਮਾਇਆ ਮੋਹੁ ਮੇਰੈ ਪ੍ਰਭਿ ਕੀਨਾ ਆਪੇ ਭਰਮਿ ਭੁਲਾਏ ॥

My Master God Himself used delusion and attachment (as part of the design of the Play) so actors would not know who they are.

First Guru GGS p. 72, line 2
ਇਹੁ ਜਗਤੁ ਭਰਮਿ ਭੁਲਾਇਆ ॥

This world has been deluded because of ignorance.

Fourth Guru GGS p. 82, line 9
ਹਰਿ ਆਪੇ ਭਰਮਿ ਭੁਲਾਇਦਾ ਹਰਿ ਆਪੇ ਹੀ ਮਤਿ ਦੇਇ ॥

The Almighty God Himself keeps us in the dark and He Himself imparts understanding (per the Divine System).

Saint Kabir GGS p. 92, line 1
ਐਸਾ ਤੈਂ ਜਗੁ ਭਰਮਿ ਲਾਇਆ ॥

You have kept the world in the dark in such a way.

Third Guru GGS p. 114, line 3

ਭਰਮੇ ਭੂਲਾ ਤਤੁ ਨ ਜਾਣੈ ॥

Lost due to ignorance, they do not understand the essence of Reality.

Third Guru GGS p. 233, line 17
ਇਹੁ ਜਗੁ ਭਰਮਿ ਭੁਲਾਇਆ ਮੋਹ ਠਗਉਲੀ ਪਾਇ ॥

You have kept the world in the dark (about their existence) by tricking them with emotional attachments.

Is the veil of ignorance ever lifted?

As per Divine design, in this life, we are not privy to any information about where we came from and where we go from here. The veil of ignorance around us makes us forget who we are and why we came here and attaches us to this world that we see. We are unaware that our whole life is being filmed to be reviewed after the end of life. In this magnificent Divine play, we are kept in the dark about everything beyond this world.

Our life does not end with the death of the body. The veil of ignorance is lifted upon leaving the body at death. Everybody gets a glimpse of God's Divine Energy and system as it actually is, after leaving the body upon death. After we die, we are no longer bound by the limitations of our physical body.

Those who experienced the Divine say that one can pierce through the veil of ignorance and experience the Reality of the Divine Order while living this life through meditation and His Grace. God sends His messengers in the form of prophets, gurus and saints over time here and there to give us clues to the rest of the story and to remind us of the Reality.

In our own time, we sometimes come across stories of people who had clinically died but came back to life. Many of those people have shared vivid memories of what they saw after leaving the body. Invariably, they speak of witnessing powerful, compassionate energy and the dispelling of darkness, which sheds their fear of dying. This could very well be another type of messaging from the Divine that what we see here is not all and to give us pointers as to what is beyond our veil of ignorance.

In their own words:

First Guru GGS p. 439, line 7

ਸੰਸਾਰੁ ਮਾਇਆ ਮੋਹੁ ਮੀਠਾ ਅੰਤਿ ਭਰਮੁ ਚੁਕਾਇਆ ॥

In delusion, all are sweetly attached to the world, but in the end, this delusion is dispelled.

Fifth Guru GGS p. 1302, line 18

ਆਗੈ ਦ੍ਰਿਸਟਿ ਆਵਤ ਸਭ ਪਰਗਟ ਈਹਾ ਮੋਹਿਓ ਭਰਮ ਅੰਧੇਰੋ ॥੧॥

Hereafter (when you leave the body), everything is revealed for you to see; but the darkness of ignorance keeps all enticed here in this world.

Am I doomed due to my failure to avoid bad Karma?

Years ago, I used to listen to a radio talk show hosted by a well-known psychotherapist where people would call in and seek advice on their parenting issues. One day, a father called in and asked the talk show host if he should agree to financially support his son, who had gone off track for some time and now wanted to go back to college. The psychotherapist said that he should absolutely not agree to support his son because he had erred. I don't know if that father followed her advice, but what I do remember is that I was so disgusted by that advice that I never watched that show again. That was the time when I had a similar issue and had decided to support my own child who had strayed. The end result, in my own case, was stellar, where my child worked really hard and graduated from a top law school in the country.

God is a merciful, forgiving parent who is always waiting for us to unlock the mystery that He is there for us. God does not simmer anger inside and is not looking for a chance to get us.

Per Divine design, those who become aware of the existence of God and develop a longing to connect with Him do not face the Divine Judge, and their record of Karma is set aside.[15] However, that is not because God is arbitrary and capricious in dispensing justice or is narcissistic and loves flattery and sycophancy. Remembrance of God means to be aware that there is God who has created us all and we have a home to go back to. Remembrance of God acts as a reminder that we should avoid hurting others.

We are here as part of the grand Divine Play. The Creator unconditionally loves us and forgives us when we reach out to Him. Per Divine design, at the end of our life, we can choose to leave the Divine Play and return to our Divine home, thereby ending the cycle of birth and death driven by Karma.

---

[15] This revelation about being forgiven and the setting aside of the Karma record in the Sikh scripture is similar to the forgiveness of sins in Christianity as seen in John 5:24. The difference seems to be that the Sikh scripture states that you have to cultivate remembrance of God to get Karma record set aside whereas the Bible recognizes Christ as the savior from record of sins.

John 5:24 "Very truly I tell you, whoever hears my word and believes him who sent me has eternal life and will not be judged but has crossed over from death to life". (Bible NIV)

Only those who cultivated remembrance of God are able to exercise that option. Those who do not acknowledge the existence of God and keep on in their ways continue through the Karma-driven cycle. According to the Sikh scripture, remembrance and awareness of God are the keys to getting out of the Karma-driven cycle of birth and death and going back home.

So, we need to cultivate remembrance of God for at least two reasons. One reason is that those who realize that there is one Divine Creator who is omnipotent, omniscient, kind, super-conscious, and forgiving are more likely to refrain from engaging in bad actions and hurting others. They are always aware that they will be judged for how they played their role in the grand Divine Play. Constant remembrance of God reminds a person about the transient nature of life and leads a person to earn livelihood in honest ways. They are more likely to help those in need while avoiding actions that cause harm to others. Such people become acutely aware that we are here only for a short while and will not be able to take any of our possessions and relationships with us after death.

Secondly, those who acknowledge the existence of God and remember God during this life will have that remembrance at the time of death as well. Deep faith, remembrance, and longing for the Creator will help them get their Karma record set aside.[16] These people with God in their mind at the transitional time of death are exempted from going to the Divine Court, where all the Karma is judged and are thus forgiven. They are liberated from the automated Karma-driven cycle. This is why the Sikh scripture exhorts people to remember God.

---

[16] John 10:28: "I give them eternal life, and they shall never perish; no one will snatch them out of my hand" (Bible NIV).

People who, even in their final days of life, develop that awareness and longing will carry that awareness with them after death, which will help them get out of the Karma-driven cycle of birth and death. However, nobody can game this and plan on remembering God at the end of life while continuing to do bad things while living. Nobody knows when death will knock on the door, and nobody can turn on the switch of remembrance of God at death.

Those who do not become aware of the Creator continue through the cycle of birth and death. They take on lives to get rewarded for their good deeds and punishment for their evil deeds and do not get liberated from the cycle of birth and death. However, as God is merciful and is the Creator of the drama, even people who have done terrible things can have forgiveness and liberation by praying to God. For bad actions and sins to be written off, one's mind has to be transformed such that they cannot do harm again.

In their own words:

Fourth Guru GGS p. 235, line 3
ਹਰਿ ਹਰਿ ਨਾਮੁ ਸਮਾਲਿ ਤੂੰ ਹਰਿ ਮੁਕਤਿ ਕਰੇ ਅੰਤ ਕਾਲਿ ॥੬॥

Remember and be aware of the Name (existence) of the Divine which will liberate you (from the cycle of birth and death) in the end.

Third Guru GGS p. 601, line 12
ਮਨ ਮੇਰੇ ਹਰਿ ਜੀਉ ਸਦਾ ਸਮਾਲਿ ॥ ਅੰਤ ਕਾਲਿ ਤੇਰਾ ਬੇਲੀ ਹੋਵੈ ਸਦਾ ਨਿਬਹੈ ਤੇਰੈ ਨਾਲਿ ॥

O' my mind, always remember and be aware of God. At the end of life, He alone shall be your support and shall always stand by you.

Ninth Guru GGS p. 902, line 1

ਅਜਾਮਲ ਕਉ ਅੰਤ ਕਾਲ ਮਹਿ ਨਾਰਾਇਨ ਸੁਧਿ ਆਈ ॥
ਜਾਂ ਗਤਿ ਕਉ ਜੋਗੀਸੁਰ ਬਾਛਤ ਸੋ ਗਤਿ ਛਿਨ ਮਹਿ ਪਾਈ ॥੨॥

(As a famous story of a sinner named Ajamal in the Hindu Puranic literature illustrates), Ajamal at the very end of his life became aware of God and was in an instant able to attain a spiritual state that even the supreme Yogis endeavor to attain.

First Guru GGS p. 1030, line 8

ਅੰਤ ਕਾਲਿ ਜਮੁ ਜੋਹਿ ਨ ਸਾਕੈ ਹਰਿ ਬੋਲਹੁ ਰਾਮੁ ਪਿਆਰਾ ਹੋ ॥੫॥

If you (think and) remember all-pervading God, at the time of death, the Messenger of Death (who takes you to where judgment is delivered based on Karma) will not be able to touch you.

First Guru GGS p. 1153, line 16

ਨਾਮੁ ਵਿਸਾਰਿ ਚਲਹਿ ਅਨ ਮਾਰਗਿ ਅੰਤ ਕਾਲਿ ਪਛੁਤਾਹੀ ॥੭॥

Forgetting the Naam (Existence of God), they go astray and at the very last moment, regret and repent.

First Guru GGS p. 1189, line 15

ਮੂਰੇ ਕਾਹੇ ਬਿਸਾਰਿਓ ਤੈ ਰਾਮ ਨਾਮ ॥ ਅੰਤ ਕਾਲਿ ਤੇਰੈ ਆਵੈ ਕਾਮ ॥੧॥

O' fool, why have you forgotten the all-pervading Divine. At the very last moment, it and it alone shall be of any use to you.

First Guru GGS p. 1189, line 19

ਅੰਤ ਕਾਲਿ ਮੂਰੇ ਚੋਟ ਖਾਹਿ ॥੭॥

At that very last moment, you fool, you shall be punished.

First Guru GGS p. 55, line 5

ਪਤਿ ਸਿਉ ਲੇਖਾ ਨਿਬੜੈ ਰਾਮ ਨਾਮੁ ਪਰਗਾਸਿ ॥੭॥

Your account shall be settled honorably, if the awareness (Name) of the all-pervading Divine has illuminated you.

First Guru GGS p. 109, line 12
ਸਭਨਾ ਕਾ ਦਰਿ ਲੇਖਾ ਸਚੈ ਛੂਟਸਿ ਨਾਮਿ ਸੁਹਾਵਣਿਆ ॥੩॥

Everyone's account is reviewed in the Real Court; those who revel in the Name of God are exonerated.

Third Guru GGS p. 112, line 2
ਜਿਥੈ ਲੇਖਾ ਮੰਗੀਐ ਤਿਥੈ ਛੁਟੈ ਸਚੁ ਕਮਾਏ ॥

Where the accounting is done, one is emancipated only by laboring for the Divine.

Fourth Guru GGS p. 165, line 17
ਜਨ ਨਾਨਕ ਸਾਹੁ ਹਰਿ ਸੇਵਿਆ ਫਿਰਿ ਲੇਖਾ ਮੂਲਿ ਨ ਲੇਈ
॥੪॥੧॥੭॥੪੫॥

Says Servant Nanak, those who served the ultimate accounts keeper, God, are exonerated from the review of the account.

Fourth Guru GGS p. 170, line 11
ਮੇਰੇ ਮਨ ਸੇਵਹੁ ਅਲਖ ਨਿਰੰਜਨ ਨਰਹਰਿ ਜਿਤੁ ਸੇਵਿਐ ਲੇਖਾ ਛੁਟੀਐ ॥

O' my mind, serve the Indescribable, Immaculate, All-Powerful Divine- serving Him, your account will be cleared.

Fourth Guru GGS p. 234, line 6
ਜਿਥੈ ਲੇਖਾ ਮੰਗੀਐ ਹਰਿ ਆਪੇ ਲਏ ਛਡਾਇ ॥੨॥

When you are called to answer for your account, the Divine Himself shall get you released.

Third Guru GGS p. 435, line 17
ਨਾਨਕ ਜਿਨ੍ ਕਉ ਸਤਿਗੁਰੁ ਮਿਲਿਆ ਤਿਨ੍ ਕਾ ਲੇਖਾ ਨਿਬੜਿਆ

Says Nanak, those who have met (the Divine), the Eternal Guru, they are exonerated from review.

Fifth Guru GGS p. 614, line 6

ਧਰਮ ਰਾਇ ਅਬ ਕਹਾ ਕਰੈਗੋ ਜਉ ਫਾਟਿਓ ਸਗਲੋ ਲੇਖਾ ॥੩॥

What can the Dharamraj (the Divine court judge) do now, since all my accounts have been torn up.

Fourth Guru GGS p. 643, line 16

ਵਿਚਿ ਹਉਮੈ ਲੇਖਾ ਮੰਗੀਐ ਫਿਰਿ ਆਵੈ ਜਾਇਆ ॥

Actions done in egotism (as the doer, not realizing the Grand Play), are called to account and result in going through birth and death.

Fourth Guru GGS p. 668, line 11

ਲੇਖਾ ਚਿਤੂ ਗੁਪਤਿ ਜੋ ਲਿਖਿਆ ਸਭ ਛੂਟੀ ਜਮ ਕੀ ਬਾਕੀ ॥੨॥

The account created by the invisible recording, Chitr Gupt is erased so there is nothing left for Jam, the Messenger of Death.

Ninth Guru GGS p. 1427, line 15

ਪਤਿਤ ਉਧਾਰਨ ਭੈ ਹਰਨ ਹਰਿ ਅਨਾਥ ਕੇ ਨਾਥ ॥ਕਹੁ ਨਾਨਕ ਤਿਹ ਜਾਨੀਐ ਸਦਾ ਬਸਤੁ ਤੁਮ ਸਾਥਿ ॥੬॥

God can transform the sinners and erase their sins; He is the one who can rid you of fear; He is the support of those who have no support. Says Nanak, realize and know the One who is always with you.

Fifth Guru GGS p. 961, line 15

ਜਿਸ ਨੋ ਤੇਰੀ ਨਦਰਿ ਨ ਲੇਖਾ ਪੁਛੀਐ ॥

One who is blessed with Your Grace is not called to account.

Third Guru GGS p. 1089, line 11

ਤਿਸੁ ਸਰਣਾਈ ਛੂਟੀਐ ਲੇਖਾ ਮੰਗੈ ਨ ਕੋਇ ॥

In His Sanctuary, one is exonerated, and not called to account.

Fifth Guru GGS p. 1096, line 17

ਲੇਖਾ ਕੋਇ ਨ ਪੁਛਈ ਜਾ ਹਰਿ ਬਖਸੰਦਾ ॥

No one is called to account after being pardoned by God.

First Guru GGS p. 56, line 10

ਬਿਨੁ ਗੁਰ ਕਰਮ ਨ ਛੁਟਸੀ ਕਹਿ ਸੁਣਿ ਆਖਿ ਵਖਾਣੁ ॥੭॥

One cannot break free (of the Karma record which leads one to the cycle of birth and death) without the Mercy/Grace of the Guru (the Divine), although much is said and heard in sermons.

First Guru GGS p. 156, line 4

ਜਨਮ ਜਨਮ ਕੇ ਪਾਪ ਕਰਮ ਕੇ ਕਾਟਨਹਾਰਾ ਲੀਜੈ ਰੇ ॥੧॥

Take to the Divine, the Destroyer of the sins and Karma of past incarnations.

Fifth Guru GGS p. 183, line 12

ਆਵਣ ਜਾਣ ਰਖੇ ਕਰਿ ਕਰਮ ॥੨॥

He saves one from the cycle of birth and death with His mercy.

Saint Kabir GGS p. 344, line 18

ਬਾਹਰਿ ਭੀਤਰਿ ਭਇਆ ਪ੍ਰਗਾਸੁ ॥ ਤਬ ਹੂਆ ਸਗਲ ਕਰਮ ਕਾ ਨਾਸੁ ॥੭॥

When illuminated (enlightened) inside and out, all your Karma will be erased.

Saint Rama Nand Ji GGS p. 1195, line 15

ਗੁਰ ਕਾ ਸਬਦੁ ਕਾਟੈ ਕੋਟਿ ਕਰਮ ॥੩॥੧॥

(Immersing in the) Divine Sound eradicates the Karma of millions of past actions.

Fourth Guru GGS p. 1115, line 4

ਜਿਨ ਕਉ ਤੂ ਹਰਿ ਮੇਲਹਿ ਸੁਆਮੀ ਸਭੁ ਤਿਨ ਕਾ ਲੇਖਾ ਛੁਟਕਿ ਗਇਆ ॥

Those whom You unite with Yourself, O' my Master, they are no longer held to account.

Fourth Guru GGS p. 1118, line 6

ਜਿਸ ਨੋ ਨਾਮੁ ਦੇਇ ਮੇਰਾ ਸੁਆਮੀ ਤਿਸੁ ਲੇਖਾ ਸਭੁ ਛਡਾਵੀਐ ਰੇ ॥੨॥

Those whom my Master blesses with His awareness (Name), their entire account is forgiven.

Third Guru GGS p. 1346, line 9

ਜਿਥੈ ਲੇਖਾ ਮੰਗੀਐ ਤਿਥੈ ਦੇਹ ਜਾਤਿ ਨ ਜਾਇ ॥

One's body and social status do not accompany to the place where one is called to account.

Fourth Guru GGS p. 1422, line 19

ਦਰਗਹਿ ਲੇਖਾ ਮੰਗੀਐ ਕੋਈ ਅੰਤਿ ਨ ਸਕੀ ਛਡਾਇ ॥

In the Divine Court where you are called to account in the end, no one is able to help.

Chapter 6: Can one see God?

> ➢ *God and the Divine System can be witnessed and experienced.*
> ➢ *The Human Body is priceless and is a rare opportunity to witness God.*
> ➢ *Human body is equipped with the ability to witness God while living.*
> ➢ *Tenth gate in the body to witness the Divine?*
> ➢ *Loving devotional faith is the best way to open the Tenth Gate and to connect with God.*
> ➢ *Remembrance and exploration of the Divine is everybody's birth right.*

God and the Divine System can be witnessed and experienced.

Even though God does not have a form that can be described using our vocabulary or building on our observations and experiences in this world, God and the Divine system can be experienced and seen through one's own eyes and mind.

The Sikh Gurus and saints from other faiths whose statements are recorded in Guru Granth Sahib describe in many verses that they have seen, witnessed, or experienced the Divine and the Divine System with their own eyes and mind. However, they say that the eyes that behold the Divine are different from the eyes that we use to see the world around us. They state that God's image is nothing like you have ever seen before. According to them, when you behold the Divine and the Divine System, you become joyful and ecstatic because you realize that you are not the fragile and vulnerable body you thought was you, but an eternally living soul or manifestation of God that never dies. You understand the true nature of your existence and see that all the sorrow and suffering without this realization was due to ignorance. You see the Grand Divine Drama in play and find it enchanting.

Having experienced the Divine, one sees the same Divine everywhere and in everyone. Only upon beholding the Divine, you can comprehend the Divine Reality. Having seen the Divine experientially, the mind of the beholder is forever ecstatic and absorbed in the Divine. One sees that the Divine, which looks like nothing you have ever seen before, is always there within us and around us and everything animate and inanimate is a manifestation of Him.

Beholding the Divine, one becomes free of desire and no longer has the fear of the pain of birth and death. After experiencing the Immaculate Divine everywhere, skepticism vanishes, and one is filled with cool tranquility and peace. At that time, all suffering disappears, and the mind gets ecstatic. Only a few are lucky enough to witness the incredibly beautiful Divine while alive.

In their own words:

First Guru GGS p. 764, line 19

ਦਰਸਨੁ ਦੇਖਿ ਭਈ ਨਿਹਕੇਵਲ ਜਨਮ ਮਰਣ ਦੁਖੁ ਨਾਸਾ ॥

Beholding the Divine, I have become free of desire; I no longer have the fear of the pain of birth and death.

First Guru GGS p. 224, line 5

ਦਰਸਨੁ ਦੇਖਿ ਭਈ ਮਤਿ ਪੂਰੀ ॥

Beholding the Divine, my understanding has been perfected.

First Guru GGS p. 1256, line 8

ਅਣਡੀਠਾ ਕਿਛੁ ਕਹਣੁ ਨ ਜਾਇ ॥

Without seeing Him, one cannot say anything about Him.

First Guru GGS p. 909, line 24 and 25

ਲੋਇਣ ਦੇਖਿ ਰਹੇ ਬਿਸਮਾਦੀ ਚਿਤੁ ਅਦਿਸਟਿ ਲਗਾਈ ॥੨੪॥

ਅਦਿਸਟੁ ਸਦਾ ਰਹੈ ਨਿਰਾਲਮੁ ਜੋਤੀ ਜੋਤਿ ਮਿਲਾਈ ॥੨੫॥

The eyes gaze ecstatically at the Divine with the mind absorbed in the Divine which looks nothing like seen before. The Invisible which looks like nothing-you-have-ever-seen before is always immaculate and your light merges into the Divine Light.

Fourth Guru, GGS, p. 87, line 19

ਅਦਿਸਟੁ ਅਗੋਚਰੁ ਅਲਖੁ ਨਿਰੰਜਨੁ ਸੋ ਦੇਖਿਆ ਗੁਰਮੁਖਿ ਆਖੀ ॥੧੨॥

True seekers of the Divine have seen the Invisible, Imperceptible, Unknowable, Immaculate Divine with their own eyes.

Fifth Guru GGS p. 894, line 8
ਸੋ ਬੋਲਹਿ ਜੋ ਪੇਖਹਿ ਆਖੀ ॥

The enlightened ones speak only of what they have seen with their own eyes.

Fifth Guru GGS p. 577, line 13
ਨਾਨਕ ਸੇ ਅਖੜੀਆਂ ਬਿਅੰਨਿ ਜਿਨੀ ਡਿਸੰਦੋ ਮਾ ਪਿਰੀ ॥੧॥

Says Nanak, the eyes which behold my Beloved Divine are not the eyes (we generally refer to).

First Guru, GGS, p. 1041, line 13
ਗੁਰਮਤਿ ਆਖੀ ਦੇਖਹੁ ਊਚਾ ॥

Following the path to the Divine, you can behold the lofty Divine with your own eyes.

Fifth Guru, GGS, p. 452, line 13
ਕਹੁ ਨਾਨਕ ਹਰਿ ਸਿਉ ਮਨੁ ਮਾਨਿਆ ਸੋ ਪ੍ਰਭੁ ਨੈਣੀ ਡੀਠਾ ॥੧॥

Says Nanak, having seen the Divine with my own eyes, my mind is engrossed in the Divine.

Fifth Guru GGS p. 530, line 2
ਸੋ ਪ੍ਰਭੁ ਜਤ ਕਤ ਪੇਖਿਓ ਨੈਣੀ ॥

I see the Divine everywhere with my own eyes.

Fifth Guru, GGS, p. 1077, line 4
ਨੈਣੀ ਪੇਖਾ ਅਗਮ ਅਥਾਹਾ ॥

With my eyes, I behold the inaccessible and unfathomable God.

Fifth Guru GGS p. 197, line 17

ਨਾਨਕ ਕਉ ਮਿਲਿਆ ਅੰਤਰਜਾਮੀ ॥੪॥੮੯॥੧੫੮॥

Nanak has met the all-knowing, omniscient Divine.

Fifth Guru GGS p. 261, line 16

ਮੋਹੀ ਦੇਖਿ ਦਰਸੁ ਨਾਨਕ ਬਲਿਹਾਰੀਆ ॥੧॥

Says Nanak, beholding the Divine, I am so ecstatic; I can sacrifice my life for Him.

Fifth Guru GGS p. 804, line 6

ਨੈਨ ਸੰਤੋਖੇ ਪ੍ਰਭ ਦਰਸਨੁ ਪਾਇਆ ॥

Beholding the Divine, my eyes are gratified.

Fifth Guru GGS p. 1211. Line 17

ਨੈਨਹੁ ਦੇਖਿਓ ਚਲਤੁ ਤਮਾਸਾ ॥

With my own eyes, I have seen the wondrous Play of the Divine.

Fifth Guru GGS p. 890, line 15

ਸਰਬ ਅਨੰਦ ਜਬ ਦਰਸਨੁ ਪਾਈਐ ॥

Beholding the Divine, you are in a total blissful state.

Saint Naam Dev GGS p 1164, line 1

ਨਾਮੇ ਹਰਿ ਕਾ ਦਰਸਨੁ ਭਇਆ ॥੪॥੩॥

Says Nama, I had the Blessed Vision of the Divine.

Saint Kabir GGS p. 1350, line 4

ਕਹਿ ਕਬੀਰ ਮੇਰੀ ਸੰਕਾ ਨਾਸੀ ਸਰਬ ਨਿਰੰਜਨੁ ਡੀਠਾ ॥੪॥੩॥

Says Kabir, beholding the Immaculate Divine everywhere, I have no skepticism left.

Saint Kabir GGS p. 1370, line 15

ਕਬੀਰ ਨੈਨ ਨਿਹਾਰਉ ਤੁਝ ਕਉ ਸ੍ਰਵਨ ਸੁਨਉ ਤੁਅ ਨਾਉ ॥

Says Kabir, I behold You with my eyes; I hear Your Name with my ears.

Fifth Guru GGS p. 805, Line 7
ਪਾਰਬ੍ਰਹਮੁ ਸੋ ਨੈਨਹੁ ਪੇਖਿਆ ॥੩॥
I have seen the Divine with my own eyes.

Fifth Guru GGS p. 254, line 16
ਭਈ ਕ੍ਰਿਪਾ ਤਬ ਦਰਸਨੁ ਪਾਇਓ ॥
One is able to behold the Divine only with the Divine Grace.

Fifth Guru GGS p. 1150, line 13
ਜੋਤਿ ਸਰੂਪ ਜਾ ਕੀ ਸਭ ਵਥੁ ॥
He is the embodiment of Light; all beings belong to Him.

Fifth Guru GGS p. 108, line 16
ਉਧ ਕਵਲੁ ਜਿਸੁ ਹੋਇ ਪ੍ਰਗਾਸਾ ਤਿਨਿ ਸਰਬ ਨਿਰੰਜਨੁ ਡੀਠਾ ਜੀਉ ॥੨॥
The person whose inverted lotus inside becomes illuminated, sees the Immaculate Divine everywhere.

Fifth Guru, GGS p. 200, line 5
ਨਾਨਕ ਦਰਸਨੁ ਦੇਖਿ ਨਿਹਾਲੁ ॥੨॥੧੦੧॥੧੭੦॥
Says Nanak, Beholding the Divine, one is so enraptured.

Fifth Guru GGS, p. 202, line 11
ਦਰਸਨ ਦੇਖਿ ਸੀਤਲ ਮਨ ਭਏ ॥
Beholding the Divine, mind is showered with cool tranquility and peace.

Fifth Guru, GGS p. 217, line 8
ਦਰਸਨ ਪੇਖਤ ਸਭ ਦੁਖ ਪਰਹਰਿਆ ਜੀਉ ॥
Beholding the Divine, all suffering disappears.

Fifth Guru, GGS p. 282, line 18

ਗੁਰ ਦਰਸਨੁ ਦੇਖਿ ਮਨਿ ਹੋਇ ਬਿਗਾਸੁ ॥

Beholding the Divine, the mind gets ecstatic.

Fifth Guru GGS p. 101, line 8
ਵਡਭਾਗੀ ਦਰਸਨੁ ਕੋ ਵਿਰਲਾ ਪਾਏ ॥

Only a few are fortunate enough to be able to behold the Divine.

Second Guru GGS p. 146, line 4
ਦਰਸਨਿ ਰੂਪਿ ਅਥਾਹ ਵਿਰਲੇ ਪਾਈਅਹਿ ॥

Only a few are able to behold the unimaginably Beauteous Divine.

Third Guru GGS p. 160, line 11
ਏਕੁ ਅਚਰਜੁ ਏਕੋ ਹੈ ਸੋਈ ॥

The One Divine is wondrous and amazing! He is the One, the One and Only.

Fifth Guru GGS p. 887, line 12
ਤਾ ਇਹੁ ਅਚਰਜੁ ਨੈਨਹੁ ਡੀਠਾ ॥੧॥

And then, I saw this Wonder with my own eyes.

The Human Body is priceless and is a rare opportunity to witness God.

The human body is a rare opportunity for self-realization and getting out of the Karma-driven cycle of birth and death. It is a blessing. One must not waste this rare opportunity to witness the divine. The Divine has placed all that is needed to see the Divine within this body. Even the deities, gods and goddesses crave this human body. In this world, we humans have the upper hand. All other forms of life are subordinate to humans. We have wandered through countless incarnations until finally attaining this priceless human life.

In their own words:

Third Guru GGS p. 1064, line 17
ਇਸੁ ਦੇਹੀ ਵਿਚਿ ਸਭ ਵਥੁ ਪਾਈ ॥
The Divine has placed all that is needed (to see the Divine) within this body.

First Guru GGS p. 1026, line 9
ਦੇਹੀ ਅੰਦਰਿ ਨਾਮੁ ਨਿਵਾਸੀ ॥
The Naam (the Divine) resides (is found) within the body.

Saint Kabir GGS p. 1159, line 7
ਇਸ ਦੇਹੀ ਕਉ ਸਿਮਰਹਿ ਦੇਵ ॥
Even the gods crave for this human body.

Fifth Guru GGS p. 374, line 5
ਅਵਰ ਜੋਨਿ ਤੇਰੀ ਪਨਿਹਾਰੀ ॥ ਇਸੁ ਧਰਤੀ ਮਹਿ ਤੇਰੀ ਸਿਕਦਾਰੀ ॥
All other forms of life are subordinate to you. In this world, you (human) have the upper hand.

Fifth Guru GGS p. 188, line 5
ਨਾਮੁ ਨ ਜਪਹਿ ਤੇ ਆਤਮ ਘਾਤੀ ॥੧॥
Not meditating on the Divine Naam is like committing suicide.

Ninth Guru GGS p. 219, line 15
ਮਾਨਸ ਜਨਮੁ ਅਮੋਲਕੁ ਪਾਇਓ ਬਿਰਥਾ ਕਾਹਿ ਗਵਾਵਉ ॥੧॥ ਰਹਾਉ ॥
You have been blessed with the priceless jewel of this human life; why are you squandering it?

Ninth Guru GGS p. 631, line 16
ਫਿਰਤ ਫਿਰਤ ਬਹੁਤੇ ਜੁਗ ਹਾਰਿਓ ਮਾਨਸ ਦੇਹ ਲਹੀ ॥
After wandering around for ages and growing weary, finally, you obtained this human body.

103

Fifth Guru GGS p. 1207, line 7

ਅਨਿਕ ਜਨਮ ਭ੍ਰਮਤੇ ਹੀ ਆਇਓ ਮਾਨਸ ਜਨਮੁ ਦੁਲਭਾਹੀ ॥

You wandered through countless incarnations, until finally you attained this priceless human life.

Saint Kabi GGS p. 1366, line 1

ਕਬੀਰ ਮਾਨਸ ਜਨਮੁ ਦੁਲੰਭੁ ਹੈ ਹੋਇ ਨ ਬਾਰੈ ਬਾਰ ॥

Says Kabir, the human body is a rare (gift); you do not get this opportunity over and over again.

Third Guru GGS p. 789, line 18

ਇਹੁ ਮਾਨਸ ਜਨਮੁ ਦੁਲੰਭੁ ਸਾ ਮਨਮੁਖ ਸੰਤਾਪੇ ॥

This human body is a rare opportunity. Following the wayward mind, people suffer in pain.

Ninth Guru GGS p, 902, line 10

ਮਾਨਸ ਜਨਮੁ ਦੀਓ ਜਿਹ ਠਾਕੁਰਿ ਸੋ ਤੈ ਕਿਉ ਬਿਸਰਾਇਓ ॥

Why have you forgotten the Divine Master who blessed you with this human life?

Saint Kabir GGS p. 1159, line 8

ਮਾਨਸ ਜਨਮ ਕਾ ਏਹੀ ਲਾਹੁ ॥੧॥ ਰਹਾਉ ॥

Attaining awareness of the Divine is the best remuneration of human life.

Ninth Guru GGS p.411 line 7

ਮਾਨਸ ਜਨਮ ਅਕਾਰਥ ਖੋਵਤ ਲਾਜ ਨ ਲੋਕ ਹਸਨ ਕੀ ॥

You are living this human life in vain; you are not ashamed that you may be mocked at for squandering this opportunity.

Third Guru GGS p. 1334, line 10

ਮਾਨਸ ਜਨਮਿ ਸਤਿਗੁਰੂ ਨ ਸੇਵਿਆ ਬਿਰਥਾ ਜਨਮੁ ਗਵਾਇਆ ॥

Not having served the Divine as a human, you have squandered the human life.

Saint Kabir GGS p. 1366, line 1
ਕਬੀਰ ਮਾਨਸ ਜਨਮੁ ਦੁਲੰਭੁ ਹੈ ਹੋਇ ਨ ਬਾਰੈ ਬਾਰ ॥
Says Kabir, human life is a rare opportunity; you do not get it over and over again.

Human body is equipped with the ability to witness God while living.

Human body is equipped with the capability to see and experience the Divine while living this life. The Human Body is priceless and a rare opportunity to see and experience God, and one must not squander away this rare opportunity to witness the Divine. To experience the Divine while living, one should start with contemplation and remembrance of the existence of God using any expression or Naam (Name), which reminds you of His attributes. Because the Naam you contemplate on is a name for God, those who experienced God have also used the word Naam at times as a synonym for God. As you cultivate remembrance of God focusing on various attributes of God, the mind starts to quieten other internal chatter and begins to focus on Naam. With a deep, sustained practice of remembrance of God, the mind increasingly focuses and ultimately tunes into the Divine Sound called Shabad. Sustained contemplation and meditation on God transforms the mind and makes one eligible for Divine Grace and witnessing the Divine.

The body is a mansion, a temple, the home of the Divine; He has infused His Infinite Light into it. Everything (that is outside) is also within the human body. Within this body are countless vast vistas- the continents, worlds, and the worlds beyond. Using Naam as a synonym for God, they say the Naam (the Divine) resides (is found) within the body. The true seeker comes to realize that having a human body is like striking gold, as it provides a pathway to the Divine.

In their own words:

First Guru GGS p. 1256, line 3
ਕਾਇਆ ਮਹਲੁ ਮੰਦਰੁ ਘਰੁ ਹਰਿ ਕਾ ਤਿਸੁ ਮਹਿ ਰਾਖੀ ਜੋਤਿ ਅਪਾਰ ॥

The body is a mansion, a temple, the home of the Divine; He has infused His Infinite Light into it.

Third Guru GGS p. 1056, line 16
ਦੇਹੀ ਅੰਦਰਿ ਵਸਤੁ ਅਪਾਰਾ ॥

Within the body, there is the priceless object.

Third Guru GGS p. 754, line 7
ਕਾਇਆ ਅੰਦਰਿ ਸਭੁ ਕਿਛੁ ਵਸੈ ਖੰਡ ਮੰਡਲ ਪਾਤਾਲਾ ॥

Everything (that is outside) is also within the human body – the continents, worlds and nether regions.

Third Guru GGS p. 112, line 12
ਇਸੁ ਕਾਇਆ ਅੰਦਰਿ ਬਹੁਤੁ ਪਸਾਰਾ ॥

Within this body are countless vast vistas.

Third Guru GGS p. 754, line 12
ਇਸੁ ਕਾਇਆ ਅੰਦਰਿ ਨਾਮੁ ਨਉ ਨਿਧਿ ਪਾਈਐ ਗੁਰ ਕੈ ਸਬਦਿ ਵੀਚਾਰਾ ॥

By contemplating on the Divine Shabad, one can attain the Divine Naam, which is more precious than nine treasures (commonly described as the ultimate riches in the world).

Third Guru GGS p. 427, line 18

ਨਾਨਕ ਇਸੁ ਦੇਹੀ ਵਿਚਿ ਨਾਮੁ ਨਿਧਾਨੁ ਹੈ ਪਾਈਐ ਗੁਰ ਕੈ ਹੇਤਿ ਅਪਾਰਿ ॥

Says Nanak, within this body is the treasure of the Naam, the abode of the Divine; it is found through the love of the Divine.

First Guru GGS p. 1026, line 9

ਦੇਹੀ ਅੰਦਰਿ ਨਾਮੁ ਨਿਵਾਸੀ ॥

The Naam (the Divine) resides (is found) within the body.

Third Guru GGS p. 117, line 12

ਕਾਇਆ ਸਰੀਰੈ ਵਿਚਿ ਸਭੁ ਕਿਛੁ ਪਾਇਆ ॥

(The Divine) has equipped the body with all that is needed (to experience the Divine).

First Guru GGS p. 1039, line 19

ਨਾਨਕ ਖੋਜਿ ਲਹਹੁ ਘਰੁ ਅਪਨਾ ਹਰਿ ਆਤਮ ਰਾਮ ਨਾਮੁ ਪਾਇਆ ॥੫॥

Says Nanak, search and look through your own home (inner self), and you shall find the Supreme Soul, the Naam (existence) of the Divine.

First Guru GGS p. 1013, line 13

ਗ੍ਰਿਹੁ ਸਰੀਰੁ ਗੁਰਮਤੀ ਖੋਜੇ ਨਾਮੁ ਪਦਾਰਥੁ ਪਾਏ ॥੮॥

Searching for the home of the Divine through the body, following the Guru's teachings, one obtains the precious Naam.

ਕੰਚਨ ਕਾਇਆ ਗੁਰਮੁਖਿ ਬੂਝੈ ਜਿਸੁ ਅੰਤਰਿ ਨਾਮੁ ਨਿਵਾਸੀ ਹੇ ॥੪॥

The true seeker comes to understand that having the human body is like striking gold; it is where the Naam (Divine) resides.

First Guru GGS p. 567, Line 9

ਕੰਚਨ ਕਾਇਆ ਸੁਇਨੇ ਕੀ ਢਾਲਾ ॥

Your body is so precious, as if cast in gold.

First Guru GGS p. 597, line 7

ਘਟ ਘਟ ਅੰਤਰਿ ਬ੍ਰਹਮੁ ਲੁਕਾਇਆ ਘਟਿ ਘਟਿ ਜੋਤਿ ਸਬਾਈ ॥

*The Divine is hiding deep within each and every heart;
His Light is in each and every heart.*

Third Guru GGS p. 1066, line 12

ਮੇਰੈ ਪ੍ਰਭਿ ਅੰਦਰਿ ਆਪੁ ਲੁਕਾਇਆ ॥

My (beloved) God has hidden Himself deep within all of us.

Third Guru GGS 1066, line 13

ਇਸੁ ਕਾਇਆ ਕੀ ਕੀਮਤਿ ਕਿਨੈ ਨ ਪਾਈ ॥

People do not know about the (real) value of this body.

Saint Kabir GGS p. 1160, line 1

ਕਾਜੀ ਸੋ ਜੁ ਕਾਇਆ ਬੀਚਾਰੈ ॥

He alone is a Qazi, who ponders over (the nature) of the human body.

Fourth Guru GGS p. 442, line 18

ਸਮੁੰਦੁ ਵਿਰੋਲਿ ਸਰੀਰੁ ਹਮ ਦੇਖਿਆ ਇਕ ਵਸਤੁ ਅਨੂਪ ਦਿਖਾਈ ॥

Churning the ocean of the body, I have seen an incomparable thing come into view.

Saint Kabir GGS p. 857, line 6

ਸਰੀਰ ਸਰੋਵਰ ਭੀਤਰੇ ਆਛੈ ਕਮਲ ਅਨੂਪ ॥

Like a beautiful lotus in a water body, there is this thing of incomparable beauty in the human body.

Fourth Guru GGS p. 1191, line 12

ਮੈ ਨਿਰਖਤ ਨਿਰਖਤ ਸਰੀਰੁ ਸਭੁ ਖੋਜਿਆ ਇਕੁ ਗੁਰਮੁਖਿ ਚਲਤੁ ਦਿਖਾਇਆ ॥

I have examined and looked through my entire body in seeking the Divine and I behold a miraculous wonder.

Fifth Guru GGS p. 612, line 13

ਦੇਖਹੁ ਅਚਰਜੁ ਭਇਆ ॥ ਜਿਹ ਠਾਕੁਰ ਕਉ ਸੁਨਤ ਅਗਾਧਿ ਬੋਧਿ ਸੋ ਰਿਦੈ ਗੁਰਿ ਦਇਆ ॥

Behold, a wondrous miracle has happened! That Divine Master, who is said to be unfathomable and Incomprehensible, by His Grace, I see is enshrined within my heart.

Fourth Guru GGS p. 235, line 1

ਮਨ ਕਰਹਲਾ ਮੇਰੇ ਪਿਆਰਿਆ ਵਿਚਿ ਦੇਹੀ ਜੋਤਿ ਸਮਾਲਿ ॥

O' my dear wandering mind (restless like a camel's newborn offspring), focus on the Divine Light within the body.

First Guru GGS p. 1329, line 5

ਆਪਾ ਮਧੇ ਆਪੁ ਪਰਗਾਸਿਆ ਪਾਇਆ ਅੰਮ੍ਰਿਤੁ ਨਾਮੁ ॥੧॥

Within the self, the Divine is revealed, when one is blessed with the Ambrosial Naam of the Divine.

Third Guru GGS p. 120, line 8

ਨਾਨਕ ਏਕੋ ਨਾਮੁ ਵਰਤੈ ਮਨ ਅੰਤਰਿ ਗੁਰ ਪਰਸਾਦੀ ਪਾਵਣਿਆ ॥੮॥

Says Nanak, the One Naam is pervading deep within the mind; it is attained by Divine's Grace.

Second Guru GGS p. 146, line 9

ਤਿਸੁ ਵਿਚਿ ਨਉ ਨਿਧਿ ਨਾਮੁ ਏਕੁ ਭਾਲਹਿ ਗੁਣੀ ਗਹੀਰੁ ॥

(Within the body) resides the Divine Naam, the source of all (nine) treasures; The virtuous ones seek it out.

Tenth gate in the body to witness the Divine?

Those who experienced the Divine state that there are 10 external gates or outlets of the body. While the nine gates (two eyes, two nostrils, two ears, mouth, and the two organs of excretion and procreation, the anus and the urethra) are open and operational, the 10th gate, which is at the apex of the brain, is closed. The tenth gate is closed per Divine design.

As mentioned in Guru Granth Sahib, the tenth gate opens into the realm of the Divine and enables you to witness the incredible, invisible, indescribable Divine. The tenth gate, called the Dasam Dwaar, is the gateway to witnessing the Divine[17]. Deep within the body-village is a fortress. The 10th gate leads to where the Divine resides. The hard and heavy doors of the Tenth Gate are closed and closed hard. Through the Divine Shabad, they are flung open.[18] The Tenth Gate is found after getting rid of (preconceptions that cause) egotistical pride.

<u>In their own words:</u>

First Guru GGS p. 1031, line 10

---

[17] An article published in the MIT's Journal of Cognitive Neuroscience "Ecstatic or Mystical Experience through Epilepsy" by Fabienne Picard (September 1, 2023) states that based on a number of case studies, they have identified the *dorsal anterior insula* in the brain as a key structure in the generation of the blissful or revelatory state of mind. They postulate that this is the first significant breakthrough in understanding the neural correlates of ecstatic mystical experiences.

[18] In Buddhism, the tenth gate is referred to as the brilliant or supreme gate.

ਦੇਹੀ ਨਗਰੀ ਨਉ ਦਰਵਾਜੇ ਸੋ ਦਸਵਾ ਗੁਪਤੁ ਰਹਾਤਾ ਹੇ ॥੪॥

The body is like a village with nine gates (open); the Tenth Gate remains hidden.

First Guru GGS p. 1039, line 17

ਦੇਹੀ ਨਗਰੀ ਨਉ ਦਰਵਾਜੇ ॥ ਸਿਰਿ ਸਿਰਿ ਕਰਣੈਹਾਰੈ ਸਾਜੇ ॥ ਦਸਵੈ ਪੁਰਖੁ ਅਤੀਤੁ ਨਿਰਾਲਾ ਆਪੇ ਅਲਖੁ ਲਖਾਇਆ ॥

The body is like a village with 9 gates (open). The Creator fashioned it this way for everyone. The Tenth Gate goes to the Primal Being, the Immaculate and Incomparable Divine. The Indescribable Himself has revealed this.

First Guru GGS p. 152, line 3

ਨਉ ਦਰਵਾਜੇ ਦਸਵਾ ਦੁਆਰੁ ॥

It has nine doors, and then there is the Tenth Gate.

Third Guru GGS p. 922, line 11

ਵਜਾਇਆ ਵਾਜਾ ਪਉਣ ਨਉ ਦੁਆਰੇ ਪਰਗਟੁ ਕੀਏ ਦਸਵਾ ਗੁਪਤੁ ਰਖਾਇਆ ॥ ਗੁਰਦੁਆਰੈ ਲਾਇ ਭਾਵਨੀ ਇਕਨਾ ਦਸਵਾ ਦੁਆਰੁ ਦਿਖਾਇਆ ॥

Blowing the breath of life into the body as if it is a musical instrument, He kept the nine doors in the body open but kept the Tenth Gate hidden. The Tenth Gate is revealed to those who are blessed with a longing to see the Divine.

Saint Baini JI GGS p. 974, line 11

ਦਸਮ ਦੁਆਰਾ ਅਗਮ ਅਪਾਰਾ ਪਰਮ ਪੁਰਖ ਕੀ ਘਾਟੀ ॥

The Tenth Gate leads to the home of the inaccessible, infinite Supreme Being.

First Guru GGS p. 1033, line 9

ਕਾਇਆ ਨਗਰੁ ਨਗਰ ਗੜ ਅੰਦਰਿ ॥ ਸਾਚਾ ਵਾਸਾ ਪੁਰਿ ਗਗਨੰਦਰਿ ॥ ਬਜਰ ਕਪਾਟ ਜੜੇ ਜੜਿ ਜਾਣੈ ਗੁਰ ਸਬਦੀ ਖੋਲਾਇਦਾ ॥

111

Deep within the body-village is a fortress. The 10ᵗʰ gate goes to where the Divine resides. The hard and heavy doors of the Tenth Gate are closed and closed hard. Through the Divine Shabad, they are flung open.

First Guru GGS p. 1033, line 11

ਭੀਤਰਿ ਕੋਟ ਗੁਫਾ ਘਰ ਜਾਈ ॥ ਨਉ ਘਰ ਥਾਪੇ ਹੁਕਮਿ ਰਜਾਈ ॥ ਦਸਵੈ ਪੁਰਖੁ ਅਲੇਖੁ ਅਪਾਰੀ ਆਪੇ ਅਲਖੁ ਲਖਾਇਦਾ ॥

Within the body fortress is the cave, the home of the Divine. He established the nine gates of this house, by His Command and Will. The Tenth Gate is the one that goes to the Primal Divine, the Indescribable and Infinite. Only He Himself reveals His Unseen self.

Third Guru GGS p. 954, line 12

ਨਉ ਦਰਵਾਜੇ ਕਾਇਆ ਕੋਟੁ ਹੈ ਦਸਵੈ ਗੁਪਤੁ ਰਖੀਜੈ ॥

The fortress of the body has nine gates; the tenth gate has been kept hidden.

Loving devotional faith is the best way to open the Tenth Gate and to connect with God.

According to Guru Granth Sahib, everybody gets to see glimpses of the Divine System after death when the veil of ignorance is lifted. However, some people may also desire to experience and witness the divine while they are alive. For these seekers of the Divine, Guru Granth Sahib outlines the path and guides on how to cultivate the practice of remembering God by contemplating on various Divine attributes. Such contemplation helps one in quietening the mind of constant internal chatter and perfecting the practice of tuning into the Divine Sound which ultimately takes one to the Divine, the source of that sound. The optimal approach to unlock the Tenth Gate is by maintaining constant remembrance of God and nurturing devotional faith.

India had a rich tradition of pursuit of the Divine, and at the time when Sikhism came into being, it was common for people who wanted to see the Divine to go to the forests and mountains away from the world to concentrate and meditate. There were many sects of ascetics guiding people in their pursuit. Many of the sects at the time were engaged in torturous physical practices (called Hatha Yoga) to control their breathing and forcibly energizing the kundalini to eventually open the Tenth Gate. Many sects were promoting the use of psychedelic substances and liquor to jump-start their efforts to see God. Guru Granth Sahib admonishes against that approach because it does not make someone a better person and does not help them gain better control over anger, lust, greed, attachment, and ego, even though it might open up some energy channels and give them a glimpse of the super-natural phenomena more quickly.

Sikh Gurus and non-Sikh saints whose descriptions of the Divine are included in Guru Granth Sahib were aware of a number of stories of how some ascetics, who had meditated a lot and acquired certain occult powers, ended up using them to put curses on people and harm them. Some ascetics actually enjoyed having those powers and used them to control people. Guru Nanak explained that the reason for that problem was that Hatha Yoga meditation did not actually transform a person's mind and did not make them kinder, gentler human beings.

Guru Nanak actually traveled to the mountains and had discourses with various sects of ascetics who had renounced normal worldly life in pursuit of God. He explained that while

Hatha Yoga could enable a person to attain some supernatural abilities, it does not help them control their anger, ego, and other base instincts. Guru Nanak tried to show them the power of devotional faith and constant remembrance of God. Guru Nanak argued that compassion, kindness, contentment, and control over anger are more important than the garb they wore and the rituals they practiced.

Guru Nanak's approach to opening the Tenth Gate and witnessing the Divine, which subsequent Gurus propagated in their writings, emphasizes deep faith and constant remembrance of God. The devotional faith-based transformational meditation approach gradually clears the mind of distracting internal chatter. Because it is based on remembrance of God's various attributes, it creates an intense longing to see the Divine. As the mind quietens, the concentration gets better and better. This approach is considered superior to Hatha Yoga because it transforms the mind simultaneously, fostering kindness, contentment, and conscientiousness.

The intensity of the longing to connect with the Creator and devotional meditation is the most efficient way to quieten the mind and to focus single-mindedly to witness the Divine. This approach outlined in the Guru Granth Sahib is commonly referred to as Sehaj Yog, a slow and steady way to connect with God, as opposed to forcibly energizing the Kundalini power. It is also referred to as Prema-Bhagti or meditation based on love and a longing to see the Divine. In contrast to Hatha Yoga, Sehaj Yog tempers various human afflictions like anger, greed, lust, ego and excessive attachment to this world and makes them better people. Sehaj Yog results in opening up the energy channels and accessing the Tenth Gate in a slow, steady, and spontaneous way instead of the efforts to forcibly open it through physical maneuvers and postures.

In addition to the Sikh Gurus' writings about the devotional faith-based approach to the Divine, Guru Granth Sahib includes writings of saints of other faiths who achieved enlightenment using devotional faith or the Sehaj Yog method. Saint Kabir, in particular, detailed how instead of the psychedelic and intoxication-based Hatha Yoga being practiced by many at the time, contemplation, remembrance and longing to see God can be a faster and more effective method to witness God.

In their own words:

Fifth Guru GGS p. 1302, line 18

ਆਗੈ ਦ੍ਰਿਸਟਿ ਆਵਤ ਸਭ ਪਰਗਟ ਈਹਾ ਮੋਹਿਓ ਭਰਮ ਅੰਧੇਰੋ ॥੧॥

Hereafter (when you leave the body), everything is revealed for you to see, but the darkness of ignorance keeps all enticed here in this world.

First Guru GGS p. 905, line 4

ਹਠੁ ਨਿਗ੍ਰਹੁ ਕਰਿ ਕਾਇਆ ਛੀਜੈ ॥

Practicing torturous methods of Hatha Yoga, the body wears away.

First Guru GGS p. 905, line 19

ਹਠੁ ਅਹੰਕਾਰੁ ਕਰੈ ਨਹੀ ਪਾਵੈ ॥

One cannot witness the Divine egotistically and through Hatha (forcibly opening up the energy channels).

First Guru GGS p. 844, line 1

ਭੇਖੁ ਭਵਨੀ ਹਠੁ ਨ ਜਾਨਾ ਨਾਨਕਾ ਸਚੁ ਗਹਿ ਰਹੇ ॥੧॥

Holding tight to the (Divine) Reality, says Nanak, I think nothing of religious garb, pilgrimages, or Hatha (forcible ways of opening up the 10th gate).

First Guru GGS p. 55, line 6
ਜੋਤਿ ਨਿਰੰਤਰਿ ਜਾਣੀਐ ਨਾਨਕ ਸਹਜਿ ਸੁਭਾਇ ॥੮॥੩॥
(Following the devotional Sehaj Yog approach) Says Nanak, the Divine Light that pervades within is revealed naturally and spontaneously.

First Guru GGS p. 685, line 15
ਪ੍ਰੇਮ ਭਗਤਿ ਕਰਿ ਸਹਜਿ ਸਮਾਇ ॥
Through loving devotional worship, one merges in the Divine spontaneously without torturing the body.

First Guru GGS p. 1023, line 10
ਗੁਰਮੁਖਿ ਜਾਤਾ ਤੁਧੁ ਸਾਲਾਹੀ ॥
The seekers of the Divine come to know of the Divine through remembrance of God's attributes.

Fifth Guru GGS p. 901, line 3
ਗੁਣ ਗਾਵਤ ਹੋਵਤ ਪਰਗਾਸੁ ॥
Singing the glorious attributes of the Divine leads to enlightenment.

First Guru GGS p. 685, line 18
ਗੁਰਮੁਖਿ ਭਗਤਿ ਸਹਜਿ ਬੀਚਾਰੀ ॥
The Divine seeker engages in effortless contemplation of the Divine.

First Guru GGS p. 686, line 4
ਸਹਜਿ ਮਿਲੈ ਮਿਲਿਆ ਪਰਵਾਣੁ ॥
Witnessing the Divine through steady devotional contemplation is a Divinely approved way (as opposed to

opening the tenth gate through torturous physical methods).

First Guru GGS p. 942, line 4
ਗੁਰਮੁਖਿ ਲਾਗੈ ਸਹਜਿ ਧਿਆਨੁ ॥

(Through the slow and steady devotional method), the Divine seeker's mind gets focused on the Divine.

Fifth Guru GGS p. 288, line 11
ਭਗਤਿ ਭਾਇ ਆਤਮ ਪਰਗਾਸ ॥

Through devotional meditation, the soul is enlightened.

First Guru GGS p. 661, line 12
ਸਚਿ ਸਿਮਰਿਐ ਹੋਵੈ ਪਰਗਾਸੁ ॥

Remembering the Eternal Divine, one is enlightened.

Third Guru GGS p. 429, line 1
ਸਹਜੇ ਨਾਮੁ ਧਿਆਈਐ ਗਿਆਨੁ ਪਰਗਟੁ ਹੋਇ ॥੧॥

Meditating on the Divine Naam in a natural and steady way (without exacting practices), Reality is revealed. ||1||

Fourth Guru GGS p. 1069, line 6
ਗੁਰ ਪਰਸਾਦੀ ਸਹਜਿ ਸਮਾਹੀ ॥

(Using the devotional meditation method) By Guru's Grace, the seeker merges into the Divine.

First Guru GGS p. 1109, line 1
ਦਹ ਦਿਸਿ ਸਾਖ ਹਰੀ ਹਰੀਆਵਲ ਸਹਜਿ ਪਕੈ ਸੋ ਮੀਠਾ ॥

(Using a fruit tree's example) with all the branches green and alive, the fruit which ripens naturally and slowly is sweet.

First Guru GGS p. 1109, line 3
ਦੀਪਕੁ ਸਹਜਿ ਬਲੈ ਤਤਿ ਜਲਾਇਆ ॥

Properly lit lamp (with only the oiled part or the essence of the wick burning) keeps lighting in a steady way.

First Guru GGS p. 1112, line 5
ਜਗਜੀਵਨੁ ਦਾਤਾ ਪੁਰਖੁ ਬਿਧਾਤਾ ਸਹਜਿ ਮਿਲੇ ਬਨਵਾਰੀ ॥

The Giver of Life to the World, the Primal Divine Being, the architect of the whole Divine System is met spontaneously.

First Guru GGS p. 1113, line 4
ਏ ਮਨ ਮੇਰਿਆ ਗੁਣ ਗਾਵਹਿ ਸਹਜਿ ਸਮਾਵਹੀ ਰਾਮ ॥

O' my mind, singing the glorious praises of the Divine, you shall merge unto Him spontaneously.

First Guru GGS p. 1273, line 13
ਸਭ ਮਹਿ ਜੀਉ ਜੀਉ ਹੈ ਸੋਈ ਘਟਿ ਘਟਿ ਰਹਿਆ ਸਮਾਈ ॥ ਗੁਰ ਪਰਸਾਦਿ ਘਰ ਹੀ ਪਰਗਾਸਿਆ ਸਹਜੇ ਸਹਜਿ ਸਮਾਈ ॥੭॥

He is the life within all beings and permeates and pervades each and every heart. By Divine Grace, He is revealed within (this body) naturally thus merging one effortlessly onto Him.

Fourth Guru GGS p. 1317, line 7
ਮੈ ਪ੍ਰਭੁ ਸਜਣੁ ਪਾਇਆ ਜਨ ਨਾਨਕ ਸਹਜਿ ਮਿਲੇਇ ॥੧॥

I have found God, my Best Friend; says humble Nanak, having spontaneously met the Divine.

Fifth Guru GGS p. 1349, line 3
ਹਰਿ ਜਨ ਲਾਵਹਿ ਸਹਜਿ ਧਿਆਨੁ ॥

God's humble seekers focus their attention slowly and steadily on Him.

First Guru GGS p.766, line 10
ਆਪਨੜਾ ਪ੍ਰਭੁ ਸਹਜਿ ਪਛਾਤਾ ਜਾ ਮਨੁ ਸਾਚੈ ਲਾਇਆ ॥

Focusing the mind on the Eternal Divine (slowly and steadily), one spontaneously realizes the Divine.

Third Guru GGS p. 232, line 8
ਨਾਮੇ ਸੇਵੇ ਨਾਮਿ ਸਹਜਿ ਸਮਾਵੈ ॥

Those who contemplate on Naam (the Divine), immerse in the Divine spontaneously (without exacting practices).

Fifth Guru GGS p. 781, line 3
ਹਰਿ ਹਰਿ ਜਪੁ ਜਪੀਐ ਦਿਨੁ ਰਾਤੀ ਲਾਗੈ ਸਹਜਿ ਧਿਆਨਾ ॥

We should chant God's Name and contemplate day and night to help focus on the Divine spontaneously.

Saint Kabir GGS p. 478, line 7
ਸਹਜਿ ਬਿਲੋਵਹੁ ਜੈਸੇ ਤਤੁ ਨ ਜਾਈ ॥੧॥

(Referring to reciting Naam and comparing it to how butter is extracted best by churning it slowly), Churn it slowly and steadily, so that the essence, (which is to witness the Divine) may not be lost.

Saint Kabir GGS p. 481, line 2
ਗੁਰ ਪ੍ਰਸਾਦਿ ਸਹਜਿ ਤਰੇ ਕਬੀਰਾ ॥੫॥੬॥੧੯॥

By Divine Grace, Says Kabir, I have crossed over, using the slow and steady method.

First Guru GGS p. 489, line 14
ਨਾਨਕ ਸਹਜਿ ਮਿਲੇ ਜਗਜੀਵਨ ਨਦਰਿ ਕਰਹੁ ਨਿਸਤਾਰਾ ॥੪॥੨॥

Says Nanak, you meet the Divine, the life of the world using the Sehaj method with Divine Grace emancipating you.

Fifth Guru GGS p. 531, line 17
ਨਾਮੁ ਨਿਧਾਨੁ ਗਾਵਤ ਗੁਣ ਗੋਬਿੰਦ ਲਾਗੋ ਸਹਜਿ ਧਿਆਨਾ ॥੧॥

Reciting precious Naam and singing the glorious praises of God, mind focuses on the Divine spontaneously.

Fourth Guru GGS P. 572, line 8
ਹਉਮੈ ਰੋਗੁ ਗਇਆ ਦੁਖੁ ਲਾਥਾ ਹਰਿ ਸਹਜਿ ਸਮਾਧਿ ਲਗਾਈ ॥
The disease of egotism has been eradicated and suffering has been eliminated resulting in a state of deep spontaneous meditation of the Divine.

Third Guru GGS p. 591, line 9
ਨਾਨਕ ਗੁਰਮੁਖਿ ਸਹਜਿ ਮਿਲੈ ਸਚੇ ਸਿਉ ਲਿਵ ਲਾਉ ॥
Says Nanak, the seeker witnesses the Divine in a slow and steady way by focusing on the Divine.

Third Guru GGS p. 650, line 13
ਗੁਣ ਨਿਧਾਨੁ ਹਰਿ ਪਾਇਆ ਸਹਜਿ ਕਰੇ ਵੀਚਾਰੁ ॥
One finds the Divine, the treasure of all virtue, contemplating on Him in a slow and steady way.

First Guru GGS p. 416, line 11
ਬੰਧਨ ਤੋਰੇ ਸਹਜਿ ਧਿਆਨੁ ॥
Meditating in a slow and steady way, one is able to break free (of the Karma driven cycle of birth and death.)

Third Guru GGS p. 26, line 8
ਹਿਰਦੈ ਕਮਲੁ ਪ੍ਰਗਾਸਿਆ ਲਾਗਾ ਸਹਜਿ ਧਿਆਨੁ ॥
When one is absorbed in sustained effortless meditation, the heart blossoms forth like a lotus flower.

Fifth Guru GGS p. 97, line 10
ਅਨਹਦੁ ਵਾਜੈ ਸਹਜਿ ਸੁਹੇਲਾ ॥
The Unstruck Divine Melody resounds and resonates spontaneously.

Third Guru GGS p. 119, line 5

ਅੰਮ੍ਰਿਤੁ ਵਰਸੈ ਸਹਜਿ ਸੁਭਾਏ ॥

Spontaneously the Ambrosial Nectar rains down, softly and gently.

Fifth Guru GGS p. 185, line 19

ਹਰਿ ਗੁਣ ਗਾਵਹ ਸਹਜਿ ਸੁਭਾਇ ॥੧॥

Sing the Glorious Praises of the Divine naturally as a matter of habit.

First Guru GGS p. 222, line 13

ਗੁਰਮੁਖਿ ਦੀਸੈ ਸਹਜਿ ਸੁਭਾਇ ॥

The seeker sees the Divine with effortless meditation.

Fifth Guru GGS p. 263, line 13

ਪ੍ਰਭ ਕੈ ਸਿਮਰਨਿ ਸਹਜਿ ਸਮਾਨੀ ॥

Remembering God, one effortlessly immerses into Him.

Saint Kabir GGS p. 328, line 15

ਸਹਜਿ ਸਹਜਿ ਗੁਣ ਰਮੈ ਕਬੀਰੁ ॥੩॥੨੬॥

I, Kabir, keep contemplating on the attributes of God in a slow and steady way.

Third Guru GGS p. 361, line 19

ਸਬਦਿ ਤਰੇ ਜਨ ਸਹਜਿ ਸੁਭਾਇ ॥

Through the Divine Sound or Shabad, the humble seekers swim across effortlessly.

Third Guru GGS p. 364, line 18

ਗੁਰ ਕਾ ਸਬਦੁ ਸਹਜਿ ਵੀਚਾਰੁ ॥

Contemplate on the Divine Sound in a slow and steady way.

Remembrance and exploration of the Divine is everybody's birth right.

At the time of the Sikh Gurus (1469-1708), and the other saints whose descriptions of the Divine are recorded in the Sikh scripture, Hinduism was the dominant religion in India. It had instituted a birth-based caste system which divided the society into four classes. The Hindu scriptures maintained that the caste system was ordained by God, where only the priestly Brahmin class had the right to education and spiritual development, while the lowest class, handling the filthiest clean-up work in the society, was declared untouchable. It was a division of society based on birth in a class with no upward mobility. Per the caste system, education and exploration of the Divine were reserved for the highest Brahmin caste, while the untouchables were prohibited from reciting God's name or hearing God's name.

Sikh Gurus and other non-Sikh saints, whose descriptions of the Divine are recorded in the Guru Granth Sahib, were vocal critics of the birth-based caste system. The Sikh scripture proclaims that exploration of the Divine and meditating on the Name of God is every human's birth right. It emphatically declares that we are all made of the same clay and the same Divine Energy runs through us all, and it is wrong to characterize some as inherently high or inherently low based on birth, color, or race. As a testament to the Sikh Gurus' declarations of equality, human dignity, and honor, Guru Granth Sahib includes hymns of non-Sikh saints from untouchable classes who experienced the Divine.

The Sikh Gurus stressed that neither the body nor the high caste goes with one after death and that in the Divine Court, everybody is judged based on their deeds. Instead of designating someone as a Brahmin based on caste of birth, the scripture states that only those who know about the Creator (referred to as Brahma in Hinduism) deserve to be called Brahmins. The Sikh Gurus spread the Divine message that anybody who remembers God is emancipated regardless of their caste or class.

In their own words:

Third Guru GGS p.112, line 1

ਦੇਹੀ ਜਾਤਿ ਨ ਆਗੈ ਜਾਏ ॥ ਜਿਥੈ ਲੇਖਾ ਮੰਗੀਐ ਤਿਥੈ ਛੁਟੈ ਸਚੁ ਕਮਾਏ ॥

Your body or high caste will not go with you to the world hereafter. When called to account (in the Divin court), you will be emancipated only by how much you labored for the Divine.

First Guru GGS p. 349, line 13

ਜਾਣਹੁ ਜੋਤਿ ਨ ਪੂਛਹੁ ਜਾਤੀ ਆਗੈ ਜਾਤਿ ਨ ਹੇ ॥੧॥ ਰਹਾਉ ॥

Recognize the Divine light within each and do not ask what caste someone belongs to; there are no classes or castes in the world hereafter.

Third Guru GGS p. 363, line 11

ਆਗੈ ਜਾਤਿ ਰੂਪੁ ਨ ਜਾਇ ॥

Social status and how one looks will not go with you hereafter.

Fifth Guru GGS p. 1001, line 12

ਖਤ੍ਰੀ ਬ੍ਰਾਹਮਣ ਸੂਦ ਵੈਸ ਸਭ ਏਕੈ ਨਾਮਿ ਤਰਾਨਥ ॥

(Referring to each of the four castes in the caste hierarchy in India), the Kshatriyas, Brahmins, Soodras and Vaisyas can all cross over, through the Name of the One Divine.

Third Guru, GGS p. 514, line 17

ਆਗੈ ਨਾਉ ਜਾਤਿ ਨ ਜਾਇਸੀ ਮਨਮੁਖਿ ਦੁਖੁ ਖਾਤਾ ॥

Your name and caste will not go with you hereafter; those who foolishly follow their mind and believe otherwise end up in misery.

Fifth Guru GGS p. 274, line 16
ਚਹੁ ਵਰਨਾ ਕਉ ਦੇ ਉਪਦੇਸੁ ॥ ਨਾਨਕ ਉਸੁ ਪੰਡਿਤ ਕਉ ਸਦਾ ਅਦੇਸੁ॥੪॥

(Referring to the edict in Hindu scriptures in India banning untouchable low caste people from reciting God's name), Says Nanak, I bow in salute to a Pandit who gives sermons to all four castes.

Third Guru GGS p. 1127, line 19
ਜਾਤਿ ਕਾ ਗਰਬੁ ਨ ਕਰੀਅਹੁ ਕੋਈ ॥ ਬ੍ਰਹਮੁ ਬਿੰਦੇ ਸੋ ਬ੍ਰਾਹਮਣੁ ਹੋਈ ॥੧॥

No one should take pride just in being born to a (high) caste. He alone is a Brahmin who know Brahm (God).

Fifth Guru GGS p. 274, line 16
ਚਹੁ ਵਰਨਾ ਮਹਿ ਜਪੈ ਕੋਊ ਨਾਮੁ ॥

(Speaking in the context of Hindu scriptures forbidding the untouchable castes from reciting God's name) Anyone, from any of the four castes may chant the Naam.

Third Guru GGS Page 1128, line 1
ਚਾਰੇ ਵਰਨ ਆਖੈ ਸਭੁ ਕੋਈ ॥ ਬ੍ਰਹਮੁ ਬਿੰਦ ਤੇ ਸਭ ਓਪਤਿ ਹੋਈ ॥੨॥

Everyone says that there are four castes (four social classes). (Referring to the Brahmin' claim that only Brahmins emanated from Brahma), all emanated from the same God.

Third Guru GGS p. 1128, line 2
ਮਾਟੀ ਏਕ ਸਗਲ ਸੰਸਾਰਾ ॥ ਬਹੁ ਬਿਧਿ ਭਾਂਡੇ ਘੜੈ ਕੁਮ੍ਹਾਰਾ ॥੩॥

The entire world is made of the same clay. The Potter has shaped it into various sorts of vessels.

Fourth Guru GGS p. 96, line 9

ਏਕੋ ਪਵਣੁ ਮਾਟੀ ਸਭ ਏਕਾ ਸਭ ਏਕਾ ਜੋਤਿ ਸਬਾਈਆ ॥

All are made of the same clay and breathe the same air and have the same one Light running through all of them.

Fifth Guru GGS p. 188, line 10

ਏਕਾ ਮਾਟੀ ਏਕਾ ਜੋਤਿ ॥

Made of same clay and same Light running through all.

Saint Kabir GGS p. 479, line 18

ਕੁਮ੍ਹਾਰੈ ਏਕ ਜੁ ਮਾਟੀ ਗੂੰਧੀ ਬਹੁ ਬਿਧਿ ਬਾਨੀ ਲਾਈ ॥

The (Divine) potter working the same clay, has shaped it in various ways.

Saint Kabir, GGS p. 1350, line 2

ਮਾਟੀ ਏਕ ਅਨੇਕ ਭਾਂਤਿ ਕਰਿ ਸਾਜੀ ਸਾਜਨਹਾਰੈ ॥

The clay is the same, but the (Divine) fashioner has fashioned it in various ways.

Fourth Guru, GGS p. 733, line 9

ਪਤਿਤ ਜਾਤਿ ਉਤਮੁ ਭਇਆ ਚਾਰਿ ਵਰਨ ਪਏ ਪਗਿ ਆਇ ॥੨॥

(Speaking of Saint Ravidas who belonged to the untouchable class processing raw hides) Although he was of low social status, he was elevated to a high status (by his remembrance of God) and people from all four castes came and bowed at his feet.

Fifth Guru GGS p. 747, line 19

ਖਤ੍ਰੀ ਬ੍ਰਾਹਮਣ ਸੂਦ ਵੈਸ ਉਪਦੇਸੁ ਚਹੁ ਵਰਨਾ ਕਉ ਸਾਝਾ ॥ਗੁਰਮੁਖਿ
ਨਾਮੁ ਜਪੈ ਉਧਰੈ ਸੋ ਕਲਿ ਮਹਿ ਘਟਿ ਘਟਿ ਨਾਨਕ ਮਾਝਾ ॥

Says Nanak my message to all the four castes- the Kshatriyas, Brahmins, Soodras and Vaisyas – is the same and that is that in the age of Kal Yug, whoever remembers God pervading in everyone, will be emancipated.

Fourth Guru GGS p. 861, line 7

ਬ੍ਰਹਮਣੁ ਖਤ੍ਰੀ ਸੂਦ ਵੈਸ ਚਾਰਿ ਵਰਨ ਚਾਰਿ ਆਸ੍ਰਮ ਹਹਿ ਜੋ ਹਰਿ ਧਿਆਵੈ ਸੋ ਪਰਧਾਨੁ ॥

(Speaking of four castes in Hindu scriptures), there are four castes: Brahmin, Kshatriya, Soodra and Vaisya, and there are four stages of life. One who meditates on the Divine, is the most distinguished and renowned.

Fifth Guru GGS p. 1150, line 11

ਜਾਤਿ ਅਜਾਤਿ ਜਪੈ ਜਨੁ ਕੋਇ ॥

(Speaking in the context of Hindu scriptures forbidding low caste people from reciting God's name) High caste or low caste, anyone may engage in remembrance of God.

First Guru GGS p. 1330, line 8

ਸਾ ਜਾਤਿ ਸਾ ਪਤਿ ਹੈ ਜੇਹੇ ਕਰਮ ਕਮਾਇ ॥

Your caste or status is what your actions reveal.

Chapter 7: Witnessing the Divine-Contemplation

➢ *Contemplation or the Naam method to witness the Divine.*

➢ *God can be remembered by various attributes or names.*

➢ *Focus on One Divine who is pervading everywhere.*

➢ *With practice, meditation becomes an enjoyable experience and is no longer an arduous task.*

➢ *Contemplation on Divine Naam prepares the mind for the ultimate experience of the Divine.*

➢ *Naam method provides a roadmap for ordinary people to explore the Divine*

➢ *Meditation on Divine Naam helps one get rid of the Karma record.*

Contemplation or the Naam method to witness the Divine

Contemplation (also known as the Naam method) is based on training the mind to overcome various distractions and focus on the exploration of inner depths in pursuit of the Divine. It is a devotional faith-based approach and is also called Sehaj Yog or the slow and steady approach which transforms a person's inner self.

Naam in the Punjabi language (which is the language in which Guru Granth Sahib is written) literally means name, but in Guru Granth Sahib, it refers to a name that denotes the very existence or identity of the Divine. So, in the context of the pursuit of the Divine, Naam refers to contemplating on the existence of the Divine using various attributes of the Divine that enlightened people have described over time. In many verses, Naam refers to the Divine Himself or the Divine Energy, which has created everything, provides sustenance to everything, and ultimately leads to the dissolution of every life form.

Using the approach of Sehaj Yog, the first step in the journey is to develop a longing to connect with God through contemplation and remembrance of various attributes or names of the Divine which are indicative of the Divine power and nature. Various religions describe various attributes of God such as God is omnipotent, omniscient, eternal, kind and compassionate among other things. Followers of Sikh religion are generally advised to start with contemplation of the awesome Energy that God radiates all around us, through observation, thinking or uttering the words "Wahguru" which literally means *"God, I am in awe thinking of You"*. One should focus on any attributes of God that strengthen the longing to connect with Him. The attribute (s) you use to contemplate on God is referred to as Naam. Naam is the primary vehicle to begin the journey to explore the mysteries of our life and to try to connect with the Divine. With practice, meditation using the Naam method becomes an enjoyable experience and is not an arduous task.

Growing up, I used to wonder why God wanted us to chant His name or think of Him and wished that God would just do his job of taking care of us. It took me a long time to make sense of it. Chanting or reciting God's Name or contemplating on the Divine attributes is not a form of flattery of God. It is not that God likes to be flattered by us as we like others to flatter us by saying nice things about us. God wants us to stay connected to Him for our own sake so we do not go astray and can find our way back home to the Divine after the end of this life. Remembrance of God is akin to plugging into God's abounding creative energy and support. Connecting with God helps us stay on the right track and refrain from bad Karma. It is energizing and inspirational and helps us navigate rough waters in this world.

People with a scientific bent of mind trying to explore and verify the existence of God might find it unacceptable to have devotional faith without having proven the hypothesis that God exists because it sounds so unscientific. However, since the pathway to God goes through the mind, one cannot embark on this journey unless the mind is engaged and the internal chatter subsides. It really does require a leap of faith.

God can be remembered by various attributes or names.

Naam is the primary vehicle to begin our journey to explore the mysteries of our life and to try to connect with the Divine. Written in beautiful, melodious mystic poetry, most of the verses in Guru Granth Sahib implore us to recognize the higher Divine Energy and to think, contemplate, recite, or chant a Name that best describes the Divine for us and inspires us to connect with the Divine. As described at the outset of this book, the Divine is described in the Sikh scripture as One and Only One, the source from which all forms emanate, eternal energy personified which is self-existent, never was born, and never will die. The Divine is fearless and never has enmity towards anyone. The Divine Image is beyond Time, was there in the beginning, has been there through the ages and will always be there. God is described as kind and compassionate. God is playful and blissful. Contemplating on any or all of these Divine attributes or whatever your mind can hold on to is a good start.

So, pick the one that best inspires you to get on this journey of exploration and connection.

In their own words:

Fifth Guru GGS p. 45, line 1
ਮੇਰੇ ਮਨ ਹਰਿ ਹਰਿ ਨਾਮੁ ਧਿਆਇ ॥

O' my mind, meditate on the Divine Name.

First Guru GGS p. 358, line 14
ਤੇਰੇ ਨਾਮ ਅਨੇਕਾ ਰੂਪ ਅਨੰਤਾ ਕਹਣੁ ਨ ਜਾਹੀ ਤੇਰੇ ਗੁਣ ਕੇਤੇ ॥੧॥ ਰਹਾਉ ॥

Your Names are so many, and Your Forms are endless. No one can describe how many glorious attributes You have.

Fourth Guru GGS p. 1319, line 5
ਹਰਿ ਕੇ ਨਾਮ ਅਸੰਖ ਅਗਮ ਹਹਿ ਅਗਮ ਅਗਮ ਹਰਿ ਰਾਇਆ ॥

The Divine has countless Names and is unfathomable. The Sovereign Divine is just unfathomable.

Fifth Guru GGS p. 986, line 12

ਅਗਮ ਰੂਪੁ ਗੋਬਿੰਦ ਕਾ ਅਨਿਕ ਨਾਮ ਅਪਾਰ ॥

The indescribable image of the Master of the Universe is profound and unfathomable; His Names are innumerable.

Focus on One Divine who is pervading everywhere

Focus on the One who is the beginning and the end of everything animate or inanimate. Think of the One who is the Creator of everything with or without a form, provides for all and the one who finally subsumes everything onto Himself. Be in awe about the One who holds countless planetary bodies in place.

In their own words:

Fifth Guru GGS p. 209, line 14

ਜਿਨਿ ਧਾਰੇ ਬ੍ਰਹਮੰਡ ਖੰਡ ਹਰਿ ਤਾ ਕੋ ਨਾਮੁ ਜਪੀਜੈ ਰੇ ॥

Chant the Naam of the Divine who established the solar systems and the cosmos.

Fifth Guru GGS p. 284, line 11

ਨਾਮ ਕੇ ਧਾਰੇ ਸਗਲੇ ਜੰਤ ॥

The Divine Naam (Energy) is what keeps all creatures alive.

Fifth Guru GGS p. 284, line 11

ਨਾਮ ਕੇ ਧਾਰੇ ਖੰਡ ਬ੍ਰਹਮੰਡ ॥

The Divine Naam (Energy) is what keeps planets and solar systems in place.

Fifth Guru GGS p. 284, line 12
ਨਾਮ ਕੇ ਧਾਰੇ ਆਗਾਸ ਪਾਤਾਲ ॥ ਨਾਮ ਕੇ ਧਾਰੇ ਸਗਲ ਆਕਾਰ ॥
The Divine Naam (Energy) is what keeps the space above and below us in place. The Divine Naam is the source of all forms of life.

Fifth Guru GGS p. 284, line 13
ਨਾਮ ਕੇ ਧਾਰੇ ਪੁਰੀਆ ਸਭ ਭਵਨ ॥
The Divine Naam is the Support of all worlds and realms.

With practice, meditation becomes an enjoyable experience and is not an arduous task.

In their own words:

First Guru GGS p. 155, line 6
ਕੂਜਾ ਮੇਵਾ ਮੈ ਸਭ ਕਿਛੁ ਚਾਖਿਆ ਇਕੁ ਅੰਮ੍ਰਿਤੁ ਨਾਮੁ ਤੁਮਾਰਾ ॥੪॥
Having tasted sweet treats and nuts and all, I say Your Naam alone is the Ambrosial Nectar (the tastiest of all).

Fifth Guru GGS p. 1229, line 16
ਨਹੀ ਤੁਲਿ ਗੋਬਿਦ ਨਾਮ ਧੁਨੇ ॥
There is nothing like the celestial melody of the Divine Naam.

Third Guru GGS p. 361, line 17
ਹਰਿ ਕਾ ਨਾਮੁ ਮੀਠਾ ਅਤਿ ਰਸੁ ਹੋਇ ॥
The Divine Naam is so succulent and sweet.

First Guru GGS p. 349, line 18

ਨਾਨਕ ਨਾਮ ਵਿਟਹੁ ਕੁਰਬਾਣੁ ॥

Says Nanak, I can give my life for Divine Naam.

First Guru GGS p. 58, line 1

ਮੈ ਧਨੁ ਨਾਮੁ ਨਿਧਾਨੁ ਹੈ ਗੁਰਿ ਦੀਆ ਬਲਿ ਜਾਉ ॥੧॥ ਰਹਾਉ ॥

Having the Treasure of the Wealth of the Naam; I can give my life for the (Divine) Guru.

First Guru GGS p. 62, line 10

ਰਾਮ ਨਾਮਿ ਮਨੁ ਬੇਧਿਆ ਗੁਰਿ ਦੀਆ ਸਚੁ ਦਾਨੁ ॥੪॥

The Naam of the all-pervading Divine has pierced my mind; this true gift is from the Divine.

Fourth Guru GGS p. 367, line 2

ਜਪਿ ਜਪਿ ਨਾਮੁ ਮਨਿ ਭਇਆ ਅਨੰਦਾ ॥

Mind becomes ecstatic and blissful chanting the Divine Naam over and over.

Fifth Guru p. 382, line 14

ਅੰਮ੍ਰਿਤ ਨਾਮੁ ਅੰਮ੍ਰਿਤ ਨਾਮੁ ਤੁਮਾਰਾ ਠਾਕੁਰ ਏਹੁ ਮਹਾ ਰਸੁ ਜਨਹਿ ਪੀਓ ॥

O' my Master, your Naam is the Ambrosial Nectar; your humble servant has tasted this supreme elixir.

Third Guru GGS p. 666, line 3

ਹਰਿ ਨਾਮੁ ਅਚਰਜੁ ਪ੍ਰਭੁ ਆਪਿ ਸੁਣਾਏ ॥

The Divine Himself imparts wonderfully unique Naam.

First Guru GGS p. 352, line 18

ਅੰਮ੍ਰਿਤ ਨਾਮੁ ਸਤਿਗੁਰਿ ਦੀਆ ॥

The ambrosial Naam is a gift from the Divine.

Third Guru GGS p. 112, line 12

ਨਾਮੁ ਨਿਰੰਜਨੁ ਅਤਿ ਅਗਮ ਅਪਾਰਾ ॥

The Divine (whose Naam we contemplate on) is not subject to the darkness (the veil of ignorance) and is extremely unfathomable and infinite.

Contemplation on Divine Naam prepares the mind for the ultimate experience of the Divine.

In starting our pursuit to connect with the Divine, the Sikh scripture tells us to start by chanting or reciting the Naam. Starting with reciting the Divine Naam with the tongue, one progresses to contemplating the various attributes of the Divine with the mind, which puts aside the constant internal chatter. The goal is to focus on the Divine with single-mindedness, getting clutter of thoughts out of our minds, which can take varying amounts of time for various people.

In their own words:

First Guru GGS p. 946, line 13

ਨਾਮੇ ਹੀ ਤੇ ਸਭੁ ਪਰਗਟੁ ਹੋਵੈ ਨਾਮੇ ਸੋਝੀ ਪਾਈ ॥

Through the Divine Naam, everything is revealed; through the Naam, enlightenment is obtained.

Fifth Guru GGS p. 300, line 2

ਦੁਰਮਤਿ ਮਿਟੀ ਹਉਮੈ ਛੁਟੀ ਸਿਮਰਤ ਹਰਿ ਕੋ ਨਾਮ ॥

Evil-mindedness disappears, and the ego goes away, when one remains in remembrance of Divine Naam.

Fourth Guru GGS p. 309, line 17

ਅੰਤਰ ਜੋਤਿ ਪ੍ਰਗਾਸੀਆ ਨਾਨਕ ਨਾਮਿ ਸਮਾਇ ॥੨॥

Says Nanak, immersed in Naam (Divine), one's inner self is illuminated with the Divine Light.

Saint Kabir GGS p. 333, line 2

ਕਹੁ ਕਬੀਰ ਅਨਭਉ ਇਕੁ ਦੇਖਿਆ ਰਾਮ ਨਾਮਿ ਲਿਵ ਲਾਗੀ ॥

Says Kabir, having experienced and witnessed the One Divine, my mind is attuned to the all-pervading Divine.

First Guru GGS p. 412, line 4

ਅੰਤਰਿ ਨਾਮੁ ਕਮਲੁ ਪਰਗਾਸਾ ॥

With Divine Naam within, your inner self blossoms and opens up like a lotus flower.

Fifth Guru GGS p. 497, line 6

ਸਿਮਰਤ ਨਾਮੁ ਕੋਟਿ ਉਜੀਆਰਾ ਬਸਤੁ ਅਗੋਚਰ ਸੂਝੀ ॥੩॥

Remembering the Divine Naam, a state is achieved where with millions of lights illuminating, you witness the incomprehensible.

Third Guru GGS p. 514, line 11

ਗੁਰ ਸਬਦੀ ਖੋਲਾਈਅਨਿ ਹਰਿ ਨਾਮੁ ਜਪਾਨੀ ॥

Chanting the Divine Naam, the Divine Sound or Shabad opens the doors.

Fifth Guru GGS p. 1144, line 7

ਨਾਮੁ ਲੈਤ ਅਨਹਦ ਪੂਰੇ ਨਾਦ ॥੩॥

Repeating the Divine Naam, the Celestial Musical Sound resounds.

Third Guru GGS p. 427, line 8

ਨਾਨਕ ਨਾਮੇ ਲਾਇ ਸਵਾਰਿਅਨੁ ਸਬਦੇ ਲਏ ਮਿਲਾਇ ॥੮॥੯॥੩੧॥

Says Nanak, the Naam readies (the mind) for the Divine Sound or Shabad which then unites with the Divine.

Third Guru GGS p. 31, line 15

ਨਾਨਕ ਗੁਰਮੁਖਿ ਨਾਮੁ ਧਿਆਈਐ ਸਚਿ ਮਿਲਾਵਾ ਹੋਇ ॥੪॥੧੩॥੪੬॥

Says Nanak, meditating on the Naam, the Divine seeker gets united with the Divine.

First Guru GGS p. 54, line 8
ਦੀਪਕੁ ਸਬਦਿ ਵਿਗਾਸਿਆ ਰਾਮ ਨਾਮੁ ਉਰ ਹਾਰੁ ॥੫॥

With Divine Naam in your mind like a necklace (constantly around your neck), the light of the Shabad is lit inside.

Third Guru GGS p. 33 line 8
ਗੁਰ ਕੈ ਸਬਦਿ ਜੀਵਤੁ ਮਰੈ ਹਰਿ ਨਾਮੁ ਵਸੈ ਮਨਿ ਆਇ ॥੧॥

When the Divine Naam resides in your mind, the Divine Shabad leads you to lose your individual self or ego while still being alive.

Fourth Guru GGS p. 697, line 18
ਹਉ ਬਲਿਹਾਰੀ ਸਤਿਗੁਰ ਅਪੁਨੇ ਜਿਨਿ ਗੁਪਤੁ ਨਾਮੁ ਪਰਗਾਝਾ ॥੨॥

I can sacrifice my life for my Eternal Guru, who has revealed Divine's hidden Naam (existence) to me.

First Guru GGS p. 437, line 9
ਨਾਨਕ ਗੁਰਮੁਖਿ ਸਬਦਿ ਪਛਾਣੈ ਅਹਿਨਿਸਿ ਨਾਮੁ ਧਿਆਈਐ ॥੧॥

Says Nanak, the Divine seeker realizes the Divine Sound or Shabad, meditating every day on the Divine Naam.

Third Guru GGS p. 798, line 16
ਅੰਤਰਿ ਨਾਮੁ ਨਿਧਾਨੁ ਦਿਖਾਇਆ ॥

He has revealed to me the treasure of the Divine Naam inside me.

First Guru GGS p. 843, line 13
ਇਕ ਭਾਇ ਇਕ ਮਨਿ ਨਾਮੁ ਵਸਿਆ ਸਤਿਗੁਰੂ ਹਮ ਮੇਲੀਆ ॥

With single-minded loving devotion, the Naam dwells within and we are united with the Divine, the eternal Guru.

Fifth Guru GGS p. 863, line 6
ਜਲਿ ਥਲਿ ਸਭ ਮਹਿ ਨਾਮੋ ਡੀਠਾ ॥੨॥

Wherever I look, I see the Divine Naam (Energy) in the water, on the land, and everywhere.

Fifth Guru GGS p. 1340, line 19
ਨਾਮੁ ਜਪਤ ਹੋਆ ਪਰਗਾਸੁ ॥

Divine Naam illuminates and dispels darkness.

First Guru GGS p. 941, line 15
ਨਾਮਿ ਰਤੇ ਪਾਵਹਿ ਮੋਖ ਦੁਆਰੁ ॥

Those imbued with the Divine Naam, find the door of liberation (from the Karma-driven cycle of birth and death).

First Guru GGS p. 941, line 15
ਨਾਮਿ ਰਤੇ ਤ੍ਰਿਭਵਣ ਸੋਝੀ ਹੋਇ ॥

Those imbued with the Divine Naam, come to understand all the worlds including those above and below us.

First Guru GGS p. 1012, line 17
ਗੁਰ ਕੈ ਸਬਦਿ ਏਕ ਲਿਵ ਲਾਗੀ ਤੇਰੈ ਨਾਮਿ ਰਤੇ ਤ੍ਰਿਪਤਾਸੀ ॥੧॥

Through the Divine Shabad, they (seekers of the Divine) have single-minded focus on the One Divine; imbued in the Divine Naam, they are fully satiated.

First Guru GGS p. 63, line 6
ਨਾਮ ਵਿਹੂਣੈ ਕਿਆ ਗਈ ਜਿਸੁ ਹਰਿ ਗੁਰ ਦਰਸੁ ਨ ਹੋਇ ॥੬॥

Those who are devoid of Naam and are not able to behold the Divine are not worth noticing.

Naam method provides a roadmap for ordinary people to explore the Divine

The Sikh scripture is very focused on providing a roadmap to the Divine for ordinary people (householders) who must spend a good deal of time providing for their families and living in society. Chanting, reciting and remembering the Naam through the day while working, is described as a way that is practical for most people. In contrast, the Divine pursuit at the time was reserved for people who could renounce the world and be in isolation in the mountains and caves.

In their own words:

First Guru GGS p. 72, line 2

ਏਕੋ ਨਾਮੁ ਹੁਕਮੁ ਹੈ ਨਾਨਕ ਸਤਿਗੁਰਿ ਦੀਆ ਬੁਝਾਇ ਜੀਉ ॥

We are ordained to contemplate on the Naam of the one Divine; says Nanak; the eternal Guru has given me this understanding.

Fifth Guru GGS p. 322, line 9

ਨੇਤ੍ਰੈ ਦੇਖਉ ਪਾਰਬ੍ਰਹਮੁ ਇਕੁ ਨਾਮੁ ਧਿਆਵਉ ॥

Understand that God is close by (and watching) and meditate on Naam, the Name of the One Divine.

First Guru GGS p. 229, line 2

ਘਰਿ ਘਰਿ ਨਾਮੁ ਨਿਰੰਜਨਾ ਸੋ ਠਾਕੁਰੁ ਮੇਰਾ ॥

The One Immaculate Divine pervading in every heart is my Master.

First Guru GGS p. 64, line 2

ਨਾਨਕ ਤਰੀਐ ਸਚਿ ਨਾਮਿ ਸਿਰਿ ਸਾਹਾ ਪਾਤਿਸਾਹੁ ॥

Says Nanak, calling out the Naam of the Divine, the King of kings, one swims across (to the Divine).

Fourth Guru GGS p. 89, line 4

ਸੋ ਐਸਾ ਹਰਿ ਨਾਮੁ ਧਿਆਈਐ ਮਨ ਮੇਰੇ ਜੋ ਸਭਨਾ ਉਪਰਿ ਹੁਕਮੁ ਚਲਾਏ॥

O' my mind, meditate on the Divine Naam whose command rules over all.

Saint Naam, GGS p. 1375, line 19

ਨਾਮਾ ਕਹੈ ਤਿਲੋਚਨਾ ਮੁਖ ਤੇ ਰਾਮੁ ਸੰਮ੍ਹਾਲਿ॥ ਹਾਥ ਪਾਉ ਕਰਿ ਕਾਮੁ ਸਭੁ ਚੀਤੁ ਨਿਰੰਜਨ ਨਾਲਿ ॥੨੧੩॥

(Saint Naam Dev talking to saint Trilochan says), O' Trilochan, recite God's name. While using your hands and feet doing your work, let your mind be focused on the all-knowing Divine.

First Guru GGS p. 152, line 16

ਨਾਮੁ ਰਿਦੈ ਅੰਮ੍ਰਿਤੁ ਮੁਖਿ ਨਾਮੁ ॥

Naam in the heart and the Ambrosial Naam on our lips.

Fifth Guru GGS p. 283, line 3

ਰਾਮ ਨਾਮ ਜਪਿ ਹਿਰਦੇ ਮਾਹਿ ॥

Chant the Naam within your heart.

Third Guru GGS p. 423, line 17

ਹਰਿ ਕਾ ਨਾਮੁ ਰਖਹੁ ਉਰਿ ਧਾਰਿ ॥

Keep the Divine Naam enshrined within your heart.

Fifth Guru GGS p. 916, line 13

ਮਨ ਬਚ ਕ੍ਰਮਿ ਰਾਮ ਨਾਮੁ ਚਿਤਾਰੀ ॥

Contemplating on the all-pervading Divine in thought, word and deed.

Third Guru GGS p. 424, line 12
ਏਕੋ ਨਾਮੁ ਚੇਤਿ ਮੇਰੇ ਭਾਈ ॥

O' my brethren, keep the Naam of the One in your consciousness.

Third Guru GGS p. 426, line 4
ਅੰਤਰਿ ਨਾਮੁ ਮੁਖਿ ਨਾਮੁ ਹੈ ਨਾਮੇ ਸਬਦਿ ਵੀਚਾਰਾ ॥੩॥

With Naam within their hearts and Naam on their lips, they contemplate on the Divine Sound or Shabad.

Fourth Guru GGS p. 690, line 16
ਅਨਦਿਨੁ ਜਪਤ ਰਹੈ ਦਿਨੁ ਰਾਤੀ ਸਹਜੇ ਨਾਮੁ ਧਿਆਇਆ ॥

Contemplating on the Divine Naam continually day and night and effortlessly meditating on the Naam is the way.

First Guru GGS p. 356, line 6
ਸਾਚੁ ਨਾਮੁ ਰਿਦੇ ਰਵੈ ਸਰੀਰ ॥

The Divine Naam running through the heart and body.

First Guru GGS p. 840, line 10
ਅਜਪਾ ਜਾਪੁ ਜਪੈ ਮੁਖਿ ਨਾਮ ॥

Chanting the Divine Naam (in your heart) without actually chanting it with your mouth.

Fifth Guru GGS p. 176, line 17
ਕਰਮ ਭੂਮਿ ਮਹਿ ਬੋਅਹੁ ਨਾਮੁ ॥

In the Karma-based soil (world), plant the seed of the Naam.

Fifth Guru GGS p. 176, line 18
ਹਰਿ ਹਰਿ ਨਾਮੁ ਅੰਤਰਿ ਉਰਿ ਧਾਰਿ ॥

Keep the Divine Naam, the life source of all, enshrined in your heart,

Saint Kabir GGS p. 339, line 3

ਨਾਮੁ ਪਦਾਰਥੁ ਮਨਹਿ ਬਸਾਈਐ ॥

Absorb the precious Divine Naam into the mind.

Fifth Guru GGS p. 394, line 2

ਹਰਿ ਕਾ ਨਾਮੁ ਰਿਦੈ ਨਿਤ ਧਿਆਈ ॥

Remember the Divine Naam in your heart every day.

Fifth Guru GGS p. 184, line 4

ਅੰਮ੍ਰਿਤ ਨਾਮੁ ਰਿਦੈ ਹਰਿ ਜਾਪੈ ॥੧॥

Meditating on the Ambrosial Divine Naam within the heart.

Fifth Guru GGS p. 188, line 5

ਨਾਮੁ ਨ ਜਪਹਿ ਤੇ ਆਤਮ ਘਾਤੀ ॥੧॥

Not contemplating on the Divine Naam is like committing suicide.

Fifth Guru GGS p. 211, line 1

ਜੀਅਰੇ ਓਲ੍ਹਾ ਨਾਮ ਕਾ ॥

O' my soul, your only Support is the Divine Naam.

First Guru GGS p. 877, line 17

ਸਚਿ ਨਾਮਿ ਤਾੜੀ ਚਿਤੁ ਲਾਵੈ ॥੨॥

Focusing one's consciousness deeply on the Divine Naam.

Fifth Guru GGS p. 577, line 16

ਦੇਹ ਅੰਧਾਰੀ ਅੰਧ ਸੁੰਞੀ ਨਾਮ ਵਿਹੂਣੀਆ ॥

The body is pitch dark, blind and desolate without the Naam.

First Guru GGS p. 1039, line 19

ਨਾਨਕ ਖੋਜਿ ਲਹਹੁ ਘਰੁ ਅਪਨਾ ਹਰਿ ਆਤਮ ਰਾਮ ਨਾਮੁ ਪਾਇਆ ॥੫॥

Says Nanak, search and look through your own home (inner self), and you shall find the Supreme Soul, the Naam (existence) of the Divine.

Third Guru GGS p. 1048, line 7
ਕੰਚਨ ਕਾਇਆ ਗੁਰਮੁਖਿ ਬੂਝੈ ਜਿਸੁ ਅੰਤਰਿ ਨਾਮੁ ਨਿਵਾਸੀ ਹੇ ॥੪॥

The true seeker comes to understand that having the human body is like striking gold; it is where the Naam (Divine) resides.

Fourth Guru GGS p. 587, line 9
ਸਹਜੇ ਹੀ ਹਰਿ ਨਾਮੁ ਲੇਹੁ ਹਰਿ ਤਤੁ ਨ ਖੋਈਐ ॥

Contemplate on the Divine Name effortlessly (without torturing your body) so you don't lose the essence of the Divine.

Saint Bheekhan GGS p. 659, line 14
ਹਰਿ ਕਾ ਨਾਮੁ ਅੰਮ੍ਰਿਤ ਜਲੁ ਨਿਰਮਲੁ ਇਹੁ ਅਉਖਧੁ ਜਗਿ ਸਾਰਾ ॥

The Naam of the Divine is like the ambrosial, pristine water which can cure all ills in the world.

Saint Bheekhan GGS p. 659, line 16
ਐਸਾ ਨਾਮੁ ਰਤਨੁ ਨਿਰਮੋਲਕੁ ਪੁੰਨਿ ਪਦਾਰਥੁ ਪਾਇਆ ॥

The Divine Naam is like an invaluable jewel; one begets this most sublime wealth with a virtuous record.

Saint Ravidas GGS p. 694, line 10
ਮਨੁ ਸੁ ਮਧੁਕਰੁ ਕਰਉ ਚਰਨ ਹਿਰਦੇ ਧਰਉ ਰਸਨ ਅੰਮ੍ਰਿਤ ਰਾਮ ਨਾਮ ਭਾਖਉ ॥੧॥

Make your mind like a bumble bee seeking the honey, enshrine Divine image in your heart as if bowing to the Divine's feet and with the tongue, chant the ambrosial Naam of the Divine.

Meditation on Divine Naam helps one get rid of the Karma record

Good Karma leads to a good after-life but does not free one from the Karma-driven cycle of birth and death and does not result in eternal life. It is awareness of the Divine and contemplation and meditation on the Divine Naam which helps one get rid of the Karma record and get out of the Karma-driven cycle of birth and death. Aside from remembering God, there is no other way to erase the Karmic record and break free from the cycle of birth and death.

In their own words:

Ninth Guru GGS p. 220, line 15

ਪਾਵਨ ਨਾਮੁ ਜਗਤਿ ਮੈ ਹਰਿ ਕੋ ਸਿਮਰਿ ਸਿਮਰਿ ਕਸਮਲ ਸਭ ਹਰੁ
ਰੇ॥੧॥

Pure and sublime is the Naam of the Divine in the world. Remembering it over and over, all sins are washed away.

First Guru GGS p. 437, line 6

ਰਾਮ ਨਾਮ ਬਿਨੁ ਮੁਕਤਿ ਨ ਹੋਈ ਨਾਨਕੁ ਕਹੈ ਵੀਚਾਰਾ ॥੪॥੨॥

Without the Divine Naam, there is no liberation (from the Karma-driven cycle of birth and death), so says humble Nanak.

First Guru GGS p. 222, line 16

ਨਾਮ ਬਿਨਾ ਨਾਹੀ ਨਿਜ ਥਾਉ ॥

Without the Naam, none can get (back) to their real home (back with the Divine).

First Guru GGS p. 438, line 15

ਤਿਨੁ ਜਰਾ ਨ ਮਰਣਾ ਨਰਕਿ ਨ ਪਰਣਾ ਜੋ ਹਰਿ ਨਾਮੁ ਧਿਆਵੈ ॥

Those who have God's Naam in their mind, do not wither with time, die and go to hell.

First Guru GGS p. 227, line 5
ਨਾਮਹੁ ਭੁਲੈ ਜਮ ਕਾ ਦੁਖੁ ਸਹਨਾ ॥
Forgetting the Naam (existence of the Divine), people endure the pain of facing the messenger of death.

First Guru GGS p. 57, line 19
ਹਰਿ ਜਪਿ ਨਾਮੁ ਧਿਆਇ ਤੂ ਜਮੁ ਡਰਪੈ ਦੁਖ ਭਾਗੁ ॥
Chant and meditate on the Divine Naam; The messenger of death (who takes you where your actions will be judged) will run away from you, and your suffering will go away.

Third Guru GGS p. 36, line 5
ਰਾਮ ਨਾਮੁ ਸਾਲਾਹਿ ਤੂ ਫਿਰਿ ਆਵਣ ਜਾਣੁ ਨ ਹੋਇ ॥੧॥ ਰਹਾਉ ॥
Praise the Naam, the all-pervading Divine, and you will no longer be subject to the cycle of birth and death.

Fifth Guru GGS p. 104, line 14
ਸਿਮਰਤ ਨਾਮੁ ਕਾਟੇ ਸਭਿ ਫਾਹੇ ॥
Remembrance of Naam (Divine) cuts away all shackles.

First Guru GGS p. 55, line 5
ਪਤਿ ਸਿਉ ਲੇਖਾ ਨਿਬੜੈ ਰਾਮ ਨਾਮੁ ਪਰਗਾਸਿ ॥੨॥
When the radiant light of the Divine Naam illuminates, the account of your actions (Karma) is settled with honor.

First Guru GGS p. 1014, line 3
ਬਿਨੁ ਗੁਰ ਸਬਦ ਨ ਆਪੁ ਪਛਾਣੈ ਬਿਨੁ ਹਰਿ ਨਾਮ ਨ ਕਾਲੁ ਟਰੇ ॥੫॥
Without the Divine Shabad, one does not understand (the essence of) one's own self; without the Divine Naam, one is subject to Time (and death).

First Guru GGS p. 931, line 15

ਨਾਮ ਵਿਹੂਣਾ ਮੁਕਤਿ ਕਿਵ ਹੋਈ ॥੧੫॥

Without the Divine Naam, how can anyone find liberation?

First Guru GGS p. 932, line 9

ਹਰਿ ਨਾਮੁ ਚੇਤਿ ਫਿਰਿ ਪਵਹਿ ਨ ਜੂਨੀ ॥

Remember the Divine Naam to avoid being subjected to the cycle of birth and death.

Fifth Guru GGS p. 45, line 1

ਨਾਮੁ ਸਹਾਈ ਸਦਾ ਸੰਗਿ ਆਗੈ ਲਏ ਛਡਾਇ ॥੧॥ ਰਹਾਉ ॥

The Divine Naam is the companion who will always be with you and will free you in the world hereafter.

Third Guru GGS p. 161, line 1

ਨਾਨਕ ਨਾਮ ਬਿਨਾ ਕੋ ਮੁਕਤਿ ਨ ਹੋਈ ॥੪॥੧੦॥੩੦॥

Says Nanak, without the Divine Naam, no one is liberated from the cycle of birth and death.

Fifth Guru GGS p. 214, line 6

ਹਰਿ ਨਾਮੁ ਲੇਹੁ ਮੀਤਾ ਲੇਹੁ ਆਗੈ ਬਿਖਮ ਪੰਥੁ ਭੈਆਨ ॥

Chant the Divine Naam O' my friend, chant it. Hereafter, the path is terrifying and treacherous.

Third Guru GGS p. 246, line 4

ਰਾਮ ਨਾਮ ਬਿਨੁ ਕੋ ਥਿਰੁ ਨਾਹੀ ਜੀਉ ਬਾਜੀ ਹੈ ਸੰਸਾਰਾ ॥

Nothing has permanent existence other than the Naam of the all-pervading Divine. This world is just a drama.

Fifth Guru GGS p. 264, line 1

ਮਨ ਊਹਾ ਨਾਮੁ ਤੇਰੈ ਸੰਗਿ ਸਹਾਈ ॥

O' my mind, there, only the Divine Naam will accompany you and be your support.

Fifth Guru GGS p, 264, line 2
ਤਹ ਕੇਵਲ ਨਾਮੁ ਸੰਗਿ ਤੇਰੈ ਚਲੈ ॥
Only the Naam shall go along with you over there (not money nor power nor connections).

Fifth Guru GGS p. 264, line 3
ਹਰਿ ਕੋ ਨਾਮੁ ਕੋਟਿ ਪਾਪ ਪਰਹਰੈ ॥
The Divine Naam washes off millions of sins.

Fifth Guru GGS p. 264, line 12
ਹਰਿ ਕਾ ਨਾਮੁ ਸੰਗਿ ਉਜੀਆਰਾ ॥
The Divine Naam shall be the Light with you (after death).

Fifth Guru GGS p. 264, line 12
ਹਰਿ ਕਾ ਨਾਮੁ ਤਹ ਨਾਲਿ ਪਛਾਨੂ ॥
The Divine Naam accompanying you will become your identification.

Fourth Guru GGS p. 310, line 14
ਜਨ ਨਾਨਕ ਨਾਮੁ ਧਿਆਇ ਤੂ ਹਰਿ ਹਲਤਿ ਪਲਤਿ ਛੋਡਾਇਸੀ ॥੧॥
Says humble Nanak, focus on Naam (Divine) which will free you here and hereafter.

Third Guru GGS p. 313, line 11
ਜਨ ਨਾਨਕ ਨਾਮੁ ਸਲਾਹਿ ਤੂ ਜਨਮ ਮਰਣ ਦੁਖੁ ਜਾਇ ॥੧॥
Says humble Nanak, praise the Divine Naam and you will be freed from the pains of birth and death.

First Guru GGS p. 422, line 15
ਜਨਮ ਮਰਣ ਦੁਖ ਮੇਟਿਆ ਜਪਿ ਨਾਮੁ ਮੁਰਾਰੇ ॥
The pain of birth and death is removed, by chanting Divine Naam.

Saint Kabir GGS p. 481, line 10

ਰਾਮ ਨਾਮ ਬਿਨੁ ਮੁਕਤਿ ਨ ਹੋਈ ॥

Without the Divine Naam, no one is liberated.

Saint Kabir GGS p. 332, line 14

ਰਾਮ ਨਾਮ ਕੀ ਗਤਿ ਨਹੀ ਜਾਨੀ ਭੈ ਡੂਬੇ ਸੰਸਾਰੀ ॥

Not fully understanding the value of the all-pervading Divine Naam, people drown in fear in the terrifying world-ocean.

Ninth Guru GGS p. 632, line 7

ਮਹਮਾ ਨਾਮ ਕਹਾ ਲਉ ਬਰਨਉ ਰਾਮ ਕਹਤ ਬੰਧਨ ਤਿਹ ਤੂਟਾ ॥੨॥

How can I fully describe the greatness of the Divine Naam? (But I can tell you that) whoever chants the Divine Naam is freed.

Saint Ravidas GGS p. 659, line 6

ਰਾਮ ਨਾਮ ਬਿਨੁ ਬਾਜੀ ਹਾਰੀ ॥੪॥

Without the Divine Naam, you lose the game (of life) entirely.

Third Guru GGS p. 34, line 5

ਜਨਮ ਮਰਨ ਦੁਖੁ ਪਰਹਰੈ ਸਬਦਿ ਰਹਿਆ ਭਰਪੂਰਿ ॥

The Divine Sound which is permeating everywhere shall liberate you from the pains of death and rebirth.

Saint Naam Dev GGS p. 873, line 12

ਭਜੁ ਨਾਮਾ ਤਰਸਿ ਭਵ ਸਿੰਧੋ ॥੪॥੧॥

Meditate on the Divine Naam to swim across the terrifying world-ocean.

First Guru GGS p. 932, line 9

ਹਰਿ ਨਾਮੁ ਚੇਤਿ ਫਿਰਿ ਪਵਹਿ ਨ ਜੂਨੀ ॥

Remember the Divine Naam to avoid being subjected to the cycle of birth and death.

Third Guru GGS p. 1068, line 8

ਆਵਣ ਜਾਣਾ ਸਬਦਿ ਨਿਵਾਰੇ ॥

It is the Shabad which gets one out of the birth/death cycle.

Saint Ramanand GGS p. 1195, line 15

ਗੁਰ ਕਾ ਸਬਦੁ ਕਾਟੈ ਕੋਟਿ ਕਰਮ ॥੩॥੧॥

(Immersing in the) Divine Sound eradicates the Karma of millions of past actions.

Third Guru GGS p. 1068, line 8

ਆਵਣ ਜਾਣਾ ਸਬਦਿ ਨਿਵਾਰੇ ॥

The coming and going through the cycle of birth and death is ended through the Divine Shabad.

Chapter 8: Witnessing the Divine-the Divine Sound

> *Divine Sound or Shabad is the vehicle to ultimately transport our consciousness to the Divine.*
> *It is the Divine Sound which strikes at the Tenth Gate and opens it for one to behold the Divine.*
> *Shabad, when audible, is very melodious and pleasing.*

What is Shabad?

Shabad literally means an audible word or the sound itself. In the context of unlocking the mysteries of the Divine, who is invisible to us, the word Shabad denotes the Sound Energy which emanates from the Divine and resounds continuously in the universe. It refers to the cosmic sound waves or currents or sound energy permeating everything, animate and inanimate. It is also called Anahad Shabad (which literally means the sound which is not the result of two things striking but it is an unstruck sound which is continuous). This celestial sound emanates from the divine and was the vehicle used by God to create the entire creation. The Shabad is synonymous with the Divine Himself and imbibes the power of the Divine. The energy of the Shabad is what sustains all life. It is this same Energy that maintains the precise orbit of planetary systems.

Divine Shabad is the vehicle to ultimately transport one's consciousness to the Divine.

Contemplation on God's attributes or recitation of Naam cultivates constant remembrance of God. It removes distractions, enables one to quieten the mind effortlessly, and sharpens the focus. When one's practice of remembering or meditating on the Naam gets perfected over time, and the desire to connect with the Divine gets stronger and stronger, it becomes easier to quieten the mind. A quiet and concentrated mind, over time, progresses toward hearing the vibrations of the sound energy of the Divine-the Shabad. As other thoughts are silenced, one starts to hear the sound current of the Divine - the Shabad which is always there, but we are not able to hear.

It is the Divine Sound which strikes at the Tenth Gate and opens it for one to behold the Divine.

As described in the Sikh scripture, the human body has nine gates or openings that are open, but the tenth gate, which is the gateway to witnessing the Divine, is closed and closed hard. The hard and heavy doors of the Tenth Gate are closed and locked. They are flung open through the Divine Shabad.

The meditation on Naam leads one to the Divine Shabad. When one catches hold of the Shabad, at that point, Naam and Shabad become the same- the sound wave of the Divine. Immersing oneself in the Shabad/Naam helps to elevate one's consciousness to the Divine Consciousness. Shabad is the ultimate vehicle to transport our consciousness to the Divine as the Shabad is emanating from the Divine.

When one's consciousness becomes pure of any thoughts and immerses in the Divine Consciousness, that is when the delusion or the veil of ignorance referred to as Maya is dispelled, and one is able to behold the Divine and the Divine System. It is at this point that ignorance and darkness give way to enlightenment of the ultimate Reality. One who successfully labors for the Divine Shabad is liberated while yet alive.

Shabad is described as a melodious harmony of the Divine, which is very pleasing and enticing to the human mind once found. When one is absorbed and immersed in the Shabad, it becomes the vehicle for transporting one's consciousness to Divine Consciousness and the realm of the Divine from where it emanates.

Tuning into the Divine Sound or Shabad (which is always there) requires quietening the mind and focusing one's attention, which takes a lot of practice. Depending on the intensity of the effort and the desire to explore and connect with the higher power, the time required would vary for individuals. Those who have already shed their skepticism about the existence of the Divine, have devotional faith and a longing to see the Divine, will make faster progress because their mind will quieten sooner. As the mind quietens and comes to focus with sustained practice or meditation, they will begin to hear the cosmic sound, which may be faint at first but will become more audible over time. The seeker will kind of ride on the sound frequency, which will, over time, transport the consciousness of the seeker to the source of the Sound, which is the Divine. Various verses in the Sikh scripture expand on the experiences of sound and light as one makes progress.

In their own words:

First Guru GGS p. 1033, line 9

ਕਾਇਆ ਨਗਰੁ ਨਗਰ ਗੜ੍ਹ ਅੰਦਰਿ ॥ ਸਾਚਾ ਵਾਸਾ ਪੁਰਿ ਗਗਨੰਦਰਿ ॥
ਬਜਰ ਕਪਾਟ ਜੜੇ ਜੜਿ ਜਾਣੈ ਗੁਰ ਸਬਦੀ ਖੋਲਾਇਦਾ ॥੨॥

Deep within the body-village is a fortress. The 10th gate goes to where the Divine resides. The hard and heavy doors of the Tenth Gate are closed and closed hard. Through the Divine Shabad, they are flung open.

First Guru GGS p. 1187, line 16

ਗੁਰ ਕੈ ਸਬਦਿ ਪਛਾਨਾ ਤੋਹਿ ॥

One recognizes You (the Divine) through the Divine Shabad.

Third Guru GGS p. 509, line 4

ਸਾਹਿਬੁ ਮੇਰਾ ਸਦਾ ਹੈ ਦਿਸੈ ਸਬਦੁ ਕਮਾਇ ॥

My Divine Master is always there, but is seen only by practicing to get attuned to the Divine Sound.

Third Guru GGS p. 954, line 13

ਬਜਰ ਕਪਾਟ ਨ ਖੁਲਨੀ ਗੁਰ ਸਬਦਿ ਖੁਲੀਜੈ ॥

The rigid door (the tenth gate) cannot be opened except by the Divine Shabad.

Fifth Guru GGS p. 46, line 8

ਸਚੁ ਮਹਲੁ ਘਰੁ ਪਾਇਆ ਗੁਰ ਕਾ ਸਬਦੁ ਪਛਾਨੁ ॥੩॥

Realizing the Divine Shabad, one gets to the True Mansion of His Presence inside.

First Guru GGS p. 1043, line 15

ਗੁਰ ਸਬਦੀ ਸਭੁ ਬ੍ਰਹਮੁ ਪਛਾਨਿਆ ॥

Through the Divine Shabad, I have realized that all is (manifestation of) God.

First Guru GGS p. 56, line 12

ਨਾਨਕ ਸਬਦਿ ਮਿਲਾਵੜਾ ਨਾ ਵੇਛੋੜਾ ਹੋਇ ॥੮॥੫॥

Says Nanak, when one meets the Divine through the Shabad, there is no more separation.

Third Guru GGS p. 1058, line 3

ਜੀਵਨ ਮੁਕਤਿ ਗੁਰ ਸਬਦੁ ਕਮਾਏ ॥

One who successfully labors for the Divine Shabad, is liberated while yet alive.

Third Guru GGS p. 1067, line 18

ਬਿਨੁ ਸਬਦੈ ਹਉਮੈ ਕਿਨੈ ਨ ਮਾਰੀ ॥

Without the Divine Shabad, no one has gotten rid of ego.

Fifth Guru GGS p. 1157, line 5

ਅਚਿੰਤ ਹਮਾਰੈ ਸਬਦਿ ਉਧਾਰ ॥

The Divine Shabad rescues without us even asking.

Third Guru GGS p. 1420, line 12
ਨਾਨਕ ਘਟਿ ਘਟਿ ਏਕੋ ਵਰਤਦਾ ਸਬਦਿ ਕਰੇ ਪਰਗਾਸ ॥੫੮॥

Says Nanak, the One Divine is pervading and permeating each and every being; Shabad illuminates for us to see.

Fourth Guru GGS p. 174, line 18
ਹਰਿ ਅੰਤਰਿ ਨਾਮੁ ਨਿਧਾਨੁ ਹੈ ਮੇਰੇ ਗੋਵਿੰਦਾ ਗੁਰ ਸਬਦੀ ਹਰਿ ਪ੍ਰਭੁ ਗਾਜੈ ਜੀਉ ॥

The treasure of the Naam of the Divine Master is deep within; The Divine Shabad thunderously reveals it.

First Guru GGS p. 19, linme 15
ਬਿਨੁ ਸਬਦੈ ਭਰਮਾਈਐ ਦੁਬਿਧਾ ਡੋਬੇ ਪੂਰੁ ॥੧॥

Without the sound of the Shabad, multitudes of people wander lost and drown in darkness because of the skepticism.

First Guru GGS p. 19, line 15
ਮਨ ਰੇ ਸਬਦਿ ਤਰਹੁ ਚਿਤੁ ਲਾਇ ॥

O' mind, swim across (the ocean of darkness which this world is), by focusing your consciousness on the Shabad.

First Guru GGS p. 60, line 13
ਸੋਹੰ ਆਪੁ ਪਛਾਣੀਐ ਸਬਦਿ ਭੇਦਿ ਪਤੀਆਇ ॥

Pierced through with the Divine Shabad, one realizes how He is residing within everyone.

Third Guru GGS p. 68, line 15
ਭੁਲਿਆ ਸਹਜਿ ਮਿਲਾਇਸੀ ਸਬਦਿ ਮਿਲਾਵਾ ਹੋਇ ॥੭॥

Through the Divine Shabad, the lost ones are united with God effortlessly (spontaneously).

Third Guru GGS p. 68, lime 16
ਸਹਜੇ ਹੀ ਸੋਝੀ ਪਈ ਸਚੈ ਸਬਦਿ ਅਪਾਰਿ ॥

With the Infinite Divine Shabad, one attains understanding (of the Reality) effortlessly.

Third Guru GGS p. 117, line 8
ਉਤਪਤਿ ਪਰਲਉ ਸਬਦੇ ਹੋਵੈ ॥ ਸਬਦੇ ਹੀ ਫਿਰਿ ਓਪਤਿ ਹੋਵੈ ॥

Creation and extinction happens through the Divine Shabad (Sound). It is through the Shabad that Creation happens again.

Third Guru GGS p. 124, line 15
ਬਿਨੁ ਸਬਦੈ ਅੰਤਰਿ ਆਨੇਰਾ ॥

Without the Divine Shabad, there is darkness within.

First Guru GGS p. 152, line 18
ਸਬਦੁ ਬੀਚਾਰਿ ਛੂਟੈ ਹਰਿ ਨਾਇ ॥੨॥

Contemplating the Divine Shabad and the Divine (Naam), we are emancipated (from the Karma-driven cycle of birth and death).

First Guru GGS p. 153, line 6
ਸਬਦਿ ਮਰੈ ਫਿਰਿ ਮਰਣੁ ਨ ਹੋਇ ॥

One who loses oneself (gets rid of ego) through the Divine Shabad, will never again have to die.

Fourth Guru GGS p. 173, line 15
ਸਭੁ ਇਕੋ ਸਬਦੁ ਵਰਤਦਾ ਮੇਰੇ ਗੋਵਿੰਦਾ ਜਨ ਨਾਨਕ ਨਾਮੁ ਧਿਆਇਆ ਜੀਉ ॥

The One and only Divine Shabad of my Divine Master is pervading in everyone, I lowly Nanak meditates on the Divine Naam.

First Guru GGS p. 222, line 14

ਤ੍ਰਿਸਨਾ ਅਗਨਿ ਸਬਦਿ ਬੁਝਾਏ ॥

It is the Divine Shabad which quenches the fire of desire.

First Guru GGS p. 227, line 10
ਬਿਨੁ ਸਬਦੈ ਮੂਠੇ ਦਿਨੁ ਰੈਣੀ ॥੮॥

Without the Shabad, we are robbed of our time day and night.

First Guru GGS p. 228, line 17
ਬਿਨੁ ਸਬਦੈ ਥਿਰੁ ਕੋ ਨਹੀ ਬੁਝੈ ਸੁਖੁ ਹੋਈ ॥੫॥

Knowing that nothing except Divine Shabad shall endure, brings peace.

First Guru GGS p. 351, line 2
ਤਿਸੁ ਰੂਪੁ ਨ ਰੇਖ ਅਨਾਹਦੁ ਵਾਜੈ ਸਬਦੁ ਨਿਰੰਜਨਿ ਕੀਆ ॥੧॥

The Immaculate Divine whose Unstruck Sound resonates constantly has no form or outline.

Third Guru GGS p. 361, line 19
ਸਬਦਿ ਤਰੇ ਜਨ ਸਹਜਿ ਸੁਭਾਇ ॥

The seekers swim across effortlessly through the Divine Shabad.

Third Guru GGS p. 362, line 6
ਬਿਨੁ ਸਬਦੈ ਬਿਰਥਾ ਜਨਮੁ ਗਵਾਇਆ ॥

Without the Divine Shabad, one's life is wasted away in vain.

Third Guru p. 364, line 2
ਮੋਹੁ ਗੁਮਾਨੁ ਗੁਰ ਸਬਦਿ ਜਲਾਏ ॥

The Divine Shabad burns away attachments and pride.

Third Guru GGS p, 364, line 3
ਅੰਤਰਿ ਮਹਲੁ ਗੁਰ ਸਬਦਿ ਪਛਾਣੈ ॥

156

Through the Divine Shabad, one finds the Divine's abode within.

Fifth Guru GGS p. 384, line 14
ਮੰਦਰਿ ਮੇਰੈ ਸਬਦਿ ਉਜਾਰਾ ॥

The Divine Shabad has illuminated the inner mansion within me.

First Guru GGS p. 412, line 7
ਮਾਇਆ ਮੋਹੁ ਗੁਰ ਸਬਦਿ ਜਲਾਏ ॥

The Divine Shabad burns away attachment and the veil of ignorance.

Third Guru GGS p. 1058, line 3
ਜੀਵਨ ਮੁਕਤਿ ਗੁਰ ਸਬਦੁ ਕਮਾਏ ॥

One who successfully labors for the Divine Shabad is liberated while yet alive.

Third Guru GGS p. 1067, line 18
ਬਿਨੁ ਸਬਦੈ ਹਉਮੈ ਕਿਨੈ ਨ ਮਾਰੀ ॥

Without the Divine Shabad, no one has gotten rid of ego.

First Guru GGS p. 412, line 11
ਜੇ ਸਬਦੁ ਬੁਝੈ ਤਾ ਸਚੁ ਨਿਹਾਲਾ ॥

If one catches hold of the Shabad, one can behold the Reality.

First Guru GGS p. 412, line 12
ਸਬਦੁ ਵੀਚਾਰੇ ਏਕ ਲਿਵ ਤਾਰਾ ॥

Contemplate on the Divine Sound single-mindedly.

First Guru GGS p. 414, line 6
ਗੁਰਮੁਖਿ ਸੁਰਤਿ ਸਬਦੁ ਨੀਸਾਨੁ ॥੧॥

The insignia of the Gurmukh (true seeker) is the attunement of own consciousness (surat) into the Divine Shabad.

First Guru GGS p. 414, line 18
ਸਾਚ ਸਬਦ ਬਿਨੁ ਮਹਲੁ ਨ ਪਛਾਣੈ ॥੩॥

Without the eternal Divine Shabad, one cannot recognize the Divine's abode.

First Guru GGS p. 439, line 11
ਸਚੁ ਕਹੈ ਨਾਨਕੁ ਸਬਦਿ ਸਾਚੈ ਮੇਲਿ ਚਿਰੀ ਵਿਛੁੰਨਿਆ ॥੪॥੧॥੫॥

Nanak is proclaiming this truth about the Divine Shabad; it is the Divine Shabad which re-unites those long separated from the Divine, with the Divine.

First Guru GGS p. 597, line 18
ਜਲਿ ਥਲਿ ਮਹੀਅਲਿ ਗੁਪਤੋ ਵਰਤੈ ਗੁਰ ਸਬਦੀ ਦੇਖਿ ਨਿਹਾਰੀ ਜੀਉ ॥

Invisible to us, He is pervading the waters, the lands, and the skies. The Divine Sound reveals that for us to see.

Third Guru GGS p. 604, line 1
ਸਬਦਿ ਮਰਹੁ ਫਿਰਿ ਜੀਵਹੁ ਸਦ ਹੀ ਤਾ ਫਿਰਿ ਮਰਣੁ ਨ ਹੋਈ ॥

Losing your own self (getting rid of the ego) through the Divine Shabad, you shall live forever, and you shall never die again.

First Guru GGS p. 635, line 6
ਸਬਦੁ ਗੁਰ ਪੀਰਾ ਗਹਿਰ ਗੰਭੀਰਾ ਬਿਨੁ ਸਬਦੈ ਜਗੁ ਬਉਰਾਨੰ ॥

The Divine Shabad is the all-knowing profound Guru and the spiritual guide; without the Shabad, the world has no sanity.

Third Guru GGS p. 650, line 12
ਸੋ ਪੜਿਆ ਸੋ ਪੰਡਿਤੁ ਬੀਨਾ ਗੁਰ ਸਬਦਿ ਕਰੇ ਵੀਚਾਰੁ ॥

He alone is educated, and he alone is a wise Pandit, who contemplates on the Divine Shabad.

Fourth Guru GGS p. 776 line 2

ਨਾਨਕ ਪ੍ਰਭੁ ਪਾਇਆ ਸਬਦਿ ਮਿਲਾਇਆ ਜੋਤੀ ਜੋਤਿ ਮਿਲਾਈ ॥੪॥੧॥੪॥

Says Nanak, God is found, by merging in the Shabad which blends one's light into His Light.

First Guru GGS p. 1187, line 16

ਗੁਰ ਕੈ ਸਬਦਿ ਪਛਾਨਾ ਤੋਹਿ ॥

One recognizes You (the Divine) through the Divine Shabad.

First Guru GGS p. 1187, line 19

ਗੁਰ ਸਬਦ ਬੀਚਾਰੇ ਸਹਜ ਭਾਇ ॥੧॥

Contemplates on the Divine Shabad slowly and steadily (without forcibly opening energy channels through Hatha Yoga).

Third Guru GGS p. 797, line 8

ਆਪੇ ਸਤਿਗੁਰੁ ਸਬਦੁ ਹੈ ਆਪੇ ॥

The Divine Himself is the Shabad as well as the Eternal Guru.

First Guru GGS p. 832, line 11

ਕਾਲ ਬਿਕਾਲ ਸਬਦਿ ਭਏ ਨਾਸੁ ॥੭॥

(The cycle of) Birth and death is ended by the Shabad.

First Guru GGS p. 839, line 16

ਗੁਰ ਕੈ ਸਬਦਿ ਪਾਵੈ ਸਭਿ ਪਾਰਿ ॥

All need the Shabad to swim across (from this world to the Divine).

First Guru GGS p. 840, line 15

ਬੁਝਹੁ ਗਿਆਨੀ ਸਬਦੁ ਬੀਚਾਰਿ ॥

O' wise ones, unlock the mystery by contemplating on the Shabad.

First Guru GGS p. 843, line 14
ਸਬਦਿ ਜੋਤਿ ਜਗਾਇ ਦੀਪਕੁ ਨਾਨਕਾ ਭਉ ਭੰਜਨੇ ॥੩॥

Says Nanak, light the lamp (inside) with the spark of the Shabad; it will rid you of all fears.

First Guru GGS p. 844, line 6
ਓਹੁ ਸਬਦਿ ਸਮਾਏ ਆਪੁ ਗਵਾਏ ਤ੍ਰਿਭਵਣ ਸੋਝੀ ਸੂਝਏ ॥

One who loses own self and merges in the Shabad, sees the worlds beyond our world revealed, including those above and below us.

First Guru GGS p. 879, line 16
ਗੁਰ ਕਾ ਸਬਦੁ ਵੀਚਾਰਿ ਜੋਗੀ ॥

O' yogi, contemplate on the Divine Shabad.

Third Guru GGS p. 1250, line 5
ਬਿਨੁ ਸਬਦੈ ਜਗਿ ਆਨੇ੍ਰੁ ਹੈ ਸਬਦੇ ਪਰਗਟੁ ਹੋਇ ॥

Without the Divine Shabad, the world is in darkness/ignorance. The Divine is revealed through the Shabad.

Fourth Guru GGS p. 774, line 17
ਸਹਜੇ ਸਹਜਿ ਮਿਲਿਆ ਜਗਜੀਵਨੁ ਨਾਨਕ ਸੁੰਨਿ ਸਮਾਏ ॥੧॥

Says Nanak when meditation becomes effortless, one gets immersed in the (Divine) void and meets the Divine, the Life of the World.

First Guru GGS p. 931, line 4
ਅੰਤਰਿ ਸਬਦੁ ਸਾਚਿ ਲਿਵ ਲਾਇ ॥੧੦॥

Lovingly centering attention on the Divine Shabad deep inside.

First Guru GGS p. 940, line 7
ਜਿਨਿ ਰਚਿ ਰਚਿਆ ਤਿਸੁ ਸਬਦਿ ਪਛਾਣੈ ਨਾਨਕੁ ਤਾ ਕਾ ਦਾਸੇ ॥੨੧॥
The Shabad is what will help you identify the One who created everything. I, Nanak am sold to Him.

First Guru GGS p. 940, line 16
ਸੋ ਜੋਗੀ ਗੁਰ ਸਬਦੁ ਪਛਾਣੈ ਅੰਤਰਿ ਕਮਲੁ ਪ੍ਰਗਾਸੁ ਥੀਆ ॥
He alone is a Yogi, who has realized the Divine Shabad and whose inner self has been illuminated and blossomed.

First Guru GGS p. 942, line 19
ਭਵਜਲੁ ਸਬਦਿ ਲੰਘਾਵਣਹਾਰੁ ॥੪੩॥
It is the Shabad that can carry us across the terrifying world-ocean.

First Guru GGS p. 943, line 1
ਸਬਦੁ ਗੁਰੂ ਸੁਰਤਿ ਧੁਨਿ ਚੇਲਾ ॥
The Divine Shabad is the Guru; one's consciousness following the Divine sound is the disciple.

First Guru GGS p. 944, line 9
ਸੁ ਸਬਦ ਕਾ ਕਹਾ ਵਾਸੁ ਕਥੀਅਲੇ ਜਿਤੁ ਤਰੀਐ ਭਵਜਲੁ ਸੰਸਾਰੋ ॥
So where is the Divine Shabad that can carry us across the terrifying world ocean said to dwell?

First Guru GGS p. 944, line 12
ਸੁ ਸਬਦ ਕਉ ਨਿਰੰਤਰਿ ਵਾਸੁ ਅਲਖੰ ਜਹ ਦੇਖਾ ਤਹ ਸੋਈ ॥
That Shabad invisibly dwells within everything constantly. Invisible, but wherever I look, I see Him there.

First Guru GGS p. 944, line 15

ਚਿਹਨੁ ਵਰਨੁ ਨਹੀ ਛਾਇਆ ਮਾਇਆ ਨਾਨਕ ਸਬਦੁ ਪਛਾਣੈ ॥੫੯॥

Says Nanak, you find out following the Divine Shabad that the Divine has no form, caste, and is not under the spell of maya or ignorance.

First Guru GGS p. 944, line 11
ਗੁਰਮੁਖਿ ਸਬਦੇ ਸਚਿ ਲਿਵ ਲਾਗੈ ਕਰਿ ਨਦਰੀ ਮੇਲਿ ਮਿਲਾਏ ॥

When the seeker (Gurmukh) gets attuned to the Divine Shabad, the Divine confers His Grace and re-unites with Himself.

First Guru GGS p. 1042, line 6
ਇਹੁ ਭਵਜਲੁ ਜਗਤੁ ਸਬਦਿ ਗੁਰ ਤਰੀਐ ॥

Shabad is the vehicle to cross over this terrifying world-ocean.

First Guru GGS p. 1042, line 7
ਸਬਦ ਸੁਰਤਿ ਬਿਨੁ ਆਈਐ ਜਾਈਐ ॥

Without training one's consciousness to focus on the Divine Shabad, one keeps coming and going (through the cycle of birth and death).

Third Guru GGS p. 1044, line 17
ਸਚੈ ਸਬਦਿ ਤਾੜੀ ਚਿਤੁ ਲਾਏ ॥

Steadily focusing the mind into the Divine Shabad.

Third Guru GGS p. 1052, line 8
ਆਪੇ ਗੁਪਤੁ ਵਰਤੈ ਸਭ ਅੰਤਰਿ ਗੁਰ ਕੈ ਸਬਦਿ ਪਛਾਤਾ ਹੋ ॥੧॥

The Divine Shabad reveals that the Divine Himself invisibly is pervading within all.

First Guru GGS p. 1034, line 18
ਨਿਰਭਉ ਸਬਦੁ ਗੁਰੂ ਸਚੁ ਜਾਤਾ ਜੋਤੀ ਜੋਤਿ ਮਿਲਾਇਦਾ ॥੮॥

When one learns about the Reality through the Divine Shabad and one's light merges with the Divine light, one becomes fearless.

First Guru GGS p. 1034, line 19

ਰੂਪੁ ਨ ਰੇਖਿਆ ਮਿਤਿ ਨਹੀ ਕੀਮਤਿ ਸਬਦਿ ਭੇਦਿ ਪਤੀਆਇਦਾ ॥੯॥

Through the Divine Shabad, one unlocks the mystery of the Divine -that He has no form or shape or bounds and is immeasurable.

First Guru GGS p. 944, line 13

ਨਦਰਿ ਕਰੇ ਸਬਦੁ ਘਟ ਮਹਿ ਵਸੈ ਵਿਚਹੁ ਭਰਮੁ ਗਵਾਏ ॥

When He bestows His Glance of Grace, the Shabad comes to abide within the heart, and all skepticism is eradicated from within.

Shabad, when audible, is very melodious and pleasing.

Once the seeker grasps the Cosmic Sound, the journey becomes easier as one begins to sense the Divine landscape with specific pointers. Additionally, this sound frequency is very absorbing and pleasing and once you catch hold of it, the problem of forcibly concentrating the mind goes away. The unstruck celestial melody captivates the mind; the experience of it is unbelievable. Once found, the mind relishes it, and the seeker can follow the sound, which will eventually lead to the unfolding of the Reality.

The Shabad is not only a sound frequency to listen to and follow but is also the one that merges one's consciousness into the Divine Consciousness. The Shabad is the sound wave energy of the Divine that caused the Creation in the first place, and it is also the Sound wave energy that will eventually pull back everything with a form unto the Formless Divine

Energy. It is the Divine Shabad that will one day cause everything to be subsumed into the Divine and extinct in its form. It is through the Shabad that Creation will happen again.

As one gets in tune with the Shabad, one becomes aware of the Divine Energy and starts to shed ego, greed, anger, lust, and attachments. It is the Shabad that dispels ignorance, illusion, and darkness and liberates a person from the Karma-driven cycle of birth and death. The Divine, which is always there and present, can only be seen/experienced by practicing to get attuned to the Shabad.

The Divine Shabad burns away attachments and the veil of ignorance and illuminates the heart. By catching hold of the Shabad, one can behold the Divine. The Shabad reveals for us to see that invisible to us, the Divine is pervading each one of us including the waters, the lands, and the skies. Following the Divine Shabad, you learn that the Immaculate Divine, whose Unstruck Sound resonates constantly, has no physical form, is neither male nor female but has a mesmerizingly unique and indescribable presence and the source of all life and consciousness.

In their own words:

First Guru GGS P, 21, line 2
ਅਨਹਦ ਸਬਦਿ ਸੁਹਾਵਣੇ ਪਾਈਐ ਗੁਰ ਵੀਚਾਰਿ ॥੨॥
The pleasant Celestial Sound of the Shabad is obtained by contemplating on the Eternal Guru, Almighty God.

First Guru GGS p. 1187, line 19
ਗੁਰ ਸਬਦੁ ਬੀਚਾਰੇ ਸਹਜ ਭਾਇ ॥੧॥

Contemplates on the Divine Shabad slowly and steadily (without forcibly opening energy channels through Hatha Yoga).

First Guru GGS p. 839, line 14

ਅਨਹਦ ਸਬਦੁ ਨਿਰਾਲਾ ਵਾਜੇ ॥

The unique Celestial musical sound current of the Shabad vibrates of itself.

First Guru GGS p.436, line 13

ਅਨਹਦੋ ਅਨਹਦੁ ਵਾਜੈ ਰੁਣ ਝੁਣਕਾਰੇ ਰਾਮ ॥ ਮੇਰਾ ਮਨੋ ਮੇਰਾ ਮਨੁ ਰਾਤਾ ਲਾਲ ਪਿਆਰੇ ਰਾਮ ॥

The melodious Celestial Sound current resounds and creates pleasant vibrations. My mind, my mind is imbued with the love of my Beloved Divine.

First Guru GGS p. 1042, line 9

ਧੁਨਿ ਅਨੰਦ ਅਨਾਹਦੁ ਵਾਜੈ ਗੁਰ ਸਬਦਿ ਨਿਰੰਜਨੁ ਪਾਇਆ ॥੧੧॥

The blissful music of the Celestial Sound current vibrates and resounds; the Immaculate Divine is witnessed through the Divine Shabad.

First Guru GGS p. 1291, line 2

ਦੀਪ ਲੋਅ ਪਾਤਾਲ ਤਹ ਖੰਡ ਮੰਡਲ ਹੈਰਾਨੁ ॥ ਤਾਰ ਘੋਰ ਬਾਜਿੰਤ੍ਰ ਤਹ ਸਾਚਿ ਤਖਤਿ ਸੁਲਤਾਨੁ ॥

Worlds and realms, nether regions, solar systems and galaxies are then wondrously revealed. The strings and the harps vibrate and resound where the Divine ruler's throne is.

First Guru GGS p. 1038, line 17

ਨਿਰਮਲ ਜੋਤਿ ਸਰਬ ਜਗਜੀਵਨੁ ਗੁਰਿ ਅਨਹਦ ਸਬਦਿ ਦਿਖਾਇਆ ॥੪॥

The Immaculate Light Energy that is the lifeline of everything is revealed through the Divine unstruck sound.

First Guru GGS p. 1040, line 4

ਪੰਚ ਸਬਦ ਝੁਣਕਾਰੁ ਨਿਰਾਲਮੁ ਪ੍ਰਭਿ ਆਪੇ ਵਾਇ ਸੁਣਾਇਆ ॥੮॥

The Divine Himself has put out the pure music of the Panch Shabad, the five primal sounds for one to hear.

Third Guru GGS p. 1089, line 2

ਗੁਰ ਸਬਦੀ ਕਮਲੁ ਬਿਗਾਸਿਆ ਇਵ ਹਰਿ ਰਸੁ ਪੀਜੈ ॥

The Divine Shabad opens up the inner self like a lotus with one sipping the sublime essence of the Divine.

First Guru GGS p. 62, line 4

ਸਬਦ ਸੁਰਤਿ ਸੁਖੁ ਊਪਜੈ ਪ੍ਰਭ ਰਾਤਉ ਸੁਖ ਸਾਰੁ ॥

When consciousness is tuned into the Divine Shabad, happiness wells up. Attuned to God, one finds true peace.

Fourth Guru GGS p. 1114, line 9

ਅਦ੍ਰਿਸਟੁ ਅਗੋਚਰੁ ਪਕੜਿਆ ਗੁਰ ਸਬਦੀ ਹਉ ਸਤਿਗੁਰ ਕੈ ਬਲਿਹਾਰੀਐ॥

I have gotten hold of the Invisible, Unfathomable Divine through the Divine Shabad. I can give my life for the Divine, the eternal Guru.

First Guru GGS p. 226, line 11

ਤਿਸ ਕਉ ਵਾਹੁ ਵਾਹੁ ਜਿ ਸਬਦੁ ਸੁਣਾਵੈ ॥

Hail, hail, to the one who enables you to hear the Divine Shabad.

Third Guru GGS p. 120, line 2

ਗੁਰ ਕੈ ਸਬਦਿ ਰਿਦੈ ਦਿਖਾਇਆ ॥

The Divine Shabad showed me the Divine's presence within my own heart.

Third Guru GGS p. 37, line 4

ਗੁਰ ਸਬਦੀ ਮਨੁ ਬੇਧਿਆ ਪ੍ਰਭੁ ਮਿਲਿਆ ਆਪਿ ਹਦੂਰਿ ॥੨॥

With the mind pierced through by the Divine Shabad, God Himself ushers you into His Presence.

Chapter 9: The Experience of Enlightenment

> *Process of Revelation of the Divine through the Tenth Gate.*
> *The Experience of Enlightenment – What it is like.*

Process of Revelation of the Divine through the Tenth Gate

The vehicle for experiencing the Divine while living, is Naam which is to remember the existence of God by contemplating on the attributes of God. Naam is the starting point. As one's mind becomes quieter and single-minded focus develops, one starts to hear the Divine Sound that has always been there but was not audible. When one's meditation practice gets better and better, one can slowly and steadily tune in to the Divine Sound-the Shabad. The Divine Shabad eventually opens the Tenth Gate.

In India, it was a common practice among ascetics in pursuit of the Divine to use various physical postures or Hatha Yoga to energize and move the spiritual life-force called Kundalini from the base of the spine up towards the brain to ultimately open the Tenth gate. To jump start their pursuit, some were also using psychedelic substances to get to an altered consciousness state The Sikh Gurus and other enlightened saints whose statements are recorded in Guru Granth Sahib, preached that instead of forcibly energizing the Kundalini, one should use the slow and steady approach of contemplation and loving devotion to do the same. They explained that forcibly energizing the Kundalini does not transform the mind and does not make one a better person. In fact, it can harm people around them when those ascetics attain some occult powers using Hatha Yoga techniques and try to control other people with their powers.

One can attain some super-natural powers using Hatha Yoga but it won't by itself open the Tenth Gate. Divine Grace is an important element in the opening of the Tenth Gate and witnessing the Divine. Meditation and a longing to see the Divine makes one eligible for the Divine Grace.

As the following quotations explain, by practicing the slow and steady method of Sehaj Yog and by remembering God, the energy channels in the body open up, leading to actual physical and chemical changes in the body and mind. This ultimately leads to the opening up of the Tenth Gate. Explaining the eventual process of opening the Tenth Gate, some of the things mentioned in the Sikh scripture are that one hears the melodious musical sounds which are so captivating that the mind gets totally immersed in that and gets ecstatic. Listening to these musical sounds, the heart opens up like a lotus flower. The Tenth Gate wells up and trickles down ambrosial nectar. With the breath resounding, there is a thud on top of the Tenth Gate. With the Tenth Gate opening, there is a loud thud as if there is a battle drum beating and the strike reaching the target inflicting a wound to the Tenth Gate (saint Kabir).

It is as if a string has been broken, and the top of the Tenth Gate has been blown away. The chakras of the coiled Kundalini energy open up and one meets the Sovereign Master in plain sight. As one witnesses the Divine, one feels as if there is nothing to put in words at that point.

In their own words:

Third Guru GGS p. 110, line 5
ਨਉ ਦਰਵਾਜੇ ਦਸਵੈ ਮੁਕਤਾ ਅਨਹਦ ਸਬਦੁ ਵਜਾਵਣਿਆ ॥
Beyond the nine gates is the Tenth Gate where the Celestial Divine Shabad resounds and liberates one (from the cycle of birth and death).

First Guru GGS p. 1033, line 10
ਬਜਰ ਕਪਾਟ ਜੜੇ ਜੜਿ ਜਾਣੈ ਗੁਰ ਸਬਦੀ ਖੋਲਾਇਦਾ ॥੨॥

The hard and heavy doors of the Tenth Gate are closed and locked. They are flung open through the Divine Shabad.

First Guru GGS p. 839, line 14
ਅਨਹਦ ਸਬਦੁ ਨਿਰਾਲਾ ਵਾਜੇ ॥

The unique Celestial musical sound current of the Shabad vibrates of itself.

First Guru GGS p.436, line 13
ਅਨਹਦੋ ਅਨਹਦੁ ਵਾਜੈ ਰੁਣ ਝੁਣਕਾਰੇ ਰਾਮ ॥ ਮੇਰਾ ਮਨੋ ਮੇਰਾ ਮਨੁ ਰਾਤਾ ਲਾਲ ਪਿਆਰੇ ਰਾਮ ॥

The melodious Celestial Sound current resounds and creates pleasant vibrations. My mind, my mind is imbued with the love of my Beloved Divine.

First Guru GGS p. 1042, line 9
ਧੁਨਿ ਅਨੰਦ ਅਨਾਹਦੁ ਵਾਜੈ ਗੁਰ ਸਬਦਿ ਨਿਰੰਜਨੁ ਪਾਇਆ ॥੧੧॥

The blissful music of the Celestial Sound current vibrates and resounds; the Immaculate Divine is witnessed through the Divine Shabad.

First Guru GGS p. 1291, line 2
ਦੀਪ ਲੋਅ ਪਾਤਾਲ ਤਹ ਖੰਡ ਮੰਡਲ ਹੈਰਾਨੁ ॥ ਤਾਰ ਘੋਰ ਬਾਜਿੰਤ੍ਰ ਤਹ ਸਾਚਿ ਤਖਤਿ ਸੁਲਤਾਨੁ ॥

Worlds and realms, nether regions, solar systems and galaxies are then wondrously revealed. The strings and the harps vibrate and resound where the Divine ruler's throne is.

First Guru GGS p. 1291, line 3
ਸੁਖਮਨ ਕੈ ਘਰਿ ਰਾਗੁ ਸੁਨਿ ਸੁੰਨਿ ਮੰਡਲਿ ਲਿਵ ਲਾਇ ॥ ਅਕਥ ਕਥਾ ਬੀਚਾਰੀਐ ਮਨਸਾ ਮਨਹਿ ਸਮਾਇ ॥

Listening to the music of the Shabad in the Sukhmna energy channel, one enters the realm which is free of any thoughts other than the Shabad. Contemplating on the indescribable Divine, the desires of the mind are dissolved.

First Guru GGS p. 1291, line 4

ਉਲਟਿ ਕਮਲੁ ਅੰਮ੍ਰਿਤਿ ਭਰਿਆ ਇਹੁ ਮਨੁ ਕਤਹੁ ਨ ਜਾਇ ॥ ਅਜਪਾ ਜਾਪੁ ਨ ਵੀਸਰੈ ਆਦਿ ਜੁਗਾਦਿ ਸਮਾਇ ॥

With the heart-lotus turned downside up, and filled with Ambrosial Nectar, this mind never gets distracted. The mind then never forgets to unspokenly chant the Divine Name and is immersed in the Primal Divine who is forever there.

First Guru GGS p. 1291, line 5

ਸਭਿ ਸਖੀਆ ਪੰਚੇ ਮਿਲੇ ਗੁਰਮੁਖਿ ਨਿਜ ਘਰਿ ਵਾਸੁ ॥ ਸਬਦੁ ਖੋਜਿ ਇਹੁ ਘਰੁ ਲਹੈ ਨਾਨਕੁ ਤਾ ਕਾ ਦਾਸੁ ॥੧॥

All the senses enjoy the five primal sounds like a group of friends and the seeker of the Divine finds the true home deep within to dwell. Say Nanak, those who find this home through the Shabad, I am (willing to be) their slave.

Third Guru GGS p. 91, line 12

ਅਨਹਦ ਧੁਨੀ ਸਦ ਵਜਦੇ ਉਨਮਨਿ ਹਰਿ ਲਿਵ ਲਾਇ ॥

When the Celestial Melody constantly vibrates within, mind is exalted and lovingly absorbed in the Divine.

Fifth Guru GGS p. 105, line 15

ਅੰਮ੍ਰਿਤੁ ਵਰਖੈ ਅਨਹਦ ਬਾਣੀ ॥

Tuned into the Celestial musical sound, the Ambrosial Nectar rains down.

First Guru GGS p. 21, line 3

ਅਨਹਦ ਬਾਣੀ ਪਾਈਐ ਤਹ ਹਉਮੈ ਹੋਇ ਬਿਨਾਸੁ ॥

Egotism goes away after getting hold of the Celestial musical sound.

172

Saint Baini Ji GGS p. 974, line 18
ਪੰਚ ਸਬਦ ਨਿਰਮਾਇਲ ਬਾਜੇ ॥

The Panch Shabad, the music of five primal sounds, resounds there in its pure essence.

Fifth Guru GGS p. 1002, line 6
ਅਨਹਦ ਸਬਦੁ ਦਸਮ ਦੁਆਰਿ ਵਜਿਓ ਤਹ ਅੰਮ੍ਰਿਤ ਨਾਮੁ ਚੁਆਇਆ ਥਾ॥੨॥

When the Celestial melodious Shabad resounds in the Tenth Gate, the Ambrosial nectar of Divine Naam trickles down.

Fifth Guru GGS p. 263, line 14
ਪ੍ਰਭ ਕੈ ਸਿਮਰਨਿ ਅਨਹਦ ਝੁਨਕਾਰ ॥

Immersed in remembrance of God, the Celestial melody vibrates.

Saint Kabir GGS p. 334. Line 19
ਥਿਰੁ ਭਈ ਤੰਤੀ ਤੂਟਸਿ ਨਾਹੀ ਅਨਹਦ ਕਿੰਗੁਰੀ ਬਾਜੀ ॥੩॥

The string of music becomes steady, and does not break; the inner guitar vibrates with the Celestial musical Shabad.

Saint Baini Ji GGS p. 974, line 8
ਤਹ ਬਾਜੇ ਸਬਦ ਅਨਾਹਦ ਬਾਣੀ ॥

The Celestial melodious sound current of the Shabad vibrates there.

Saint Kabir GGS p. 344, line 3
ਅਹਿਨਿਸਿ ਬਾਜੇ ਅਨਹਦ ਤੂਰ ॥

Day and night, the symphony of the celestial melody resounds.

Fifth Guru GGS p. 393, line 16
ਵਾਜੇ ਤਾ ਕੈ ਅਨਹਦ ਤੂਰਾ ॥੫॥੪੦॥੫੧॥

The celestial symphony of Divine Sound resounds in them.

Fifth Guru GGS p. 545, line 3

ਤਹ ਅਨਦ ਬਿਨੋਦ ਸਦਾ ਅਨਹਦ ਝੁਣਕਾਰੇ ਰਾਮ ॥

There is always bliss and ecstasy, with the celestial melody resounding.

Third Guru GGS p. 602, line 14

ਕਮਲੁ ਪ੍ਰਗਾਸਿ ਸਦਾ ਰੰਗਿ ਰਾਤਾ ਅਨਹਦ ਸਬਦੁ ਵਜਾਇਆ ॥

Ever imbued with Divine love, the inner self opens up like a lotus flower and the celestial melody of the Shabad resounds within.

Fifth Guru GGS p. 621, line 11

ਤਹ ਅਨਹਦ ਸਬਦ ਅਗਾਜਾ ॥

The celestial melody of the Divine Shabad resounds there.

Saint Kabir GGS p. 656, line 11

ਬਾਜੀਅਲੇ ਅਨਹਦ ਬਾਜੇ ॥੧॥

The celestial melody of the Divine Sound starts to resound.

Saint Naam Dev GGS p. 657, line 2

ਤਹ ਅਨਹਦ ਸਬਦ ਬਜੰਤਾ ॥

The celestial music of the Divine Shabad resounds there.

First Guru GGS p. 879, line 8

ਧੁਨਿ ਵਾਜੇ ਅਨਹਦ ਘੋਰਾ ॥

The Celestial melody of the Divine Sound resonates and resounds.

Fifth Guru GGS p. 888, line 17

ਅਨਹਦ ਬਾਜੇ ਅਚਰਜ ਬਿਸਮਾਦ ॥

One is wondrously ecstatic hearing the Celestial Musical Sound.

First Guru GGS p. 903, line 18

ਵਾਜੈ ਅਨਹਦੁ ਮੇਰਾ ਮਨੁ ਲੀਣਾ ॥

My mind is immersed into the Celestial symphony of the Divine sound resounding within.

First Guru GGS p. 904, line 7

ਅਨਹਦ ਸਬਦੁ ਵਜੈ ਦਿਨੁ ਰਾਤੀ ॥

The Celestial Musical Sound current vibrates inside day and night.

Saint Kabir GGS p. 972, line 4

ਤਹ ਬਾਜੇ ਅਨਹਦ ਬੀਣਾ ॥੩॥

There the flute of the Celestial Musical Sound resonates.

First Guru GGS p. 1034, line 1

ਅਨਹਦੁ ਵਾਜੈ ਭ੍ਰਮੁ ਭਉ ਭਾਜੈ ॥

When the Celestial Musical Sound current resounds within, doubt and fear run away.

First Guru GGS p. 1040 line 5

ਹਉਮੈ ਤਿਆਗੀ ਅਨਹਦਿ ਰਾਤਾ ॥

Immersed in the Celestial Musical sound, one sheds the ego.

Fifth Guru GGS p. 1226, line 17

ਅਨਹਦ ਧੁਨੀ ਮੇਰਾ ਮਨੁ ਮੋਹਿਓ ਅਚਰਜ ਤਾ ਕੇ ਸ੍ਵਾਦ ॥੧॥ ਰਹਾਉ ॥

The Celestial Melody has captivated my mind; the experience of it is unbelievable.

First Guru GGS p. 1291, line 3

ਸੁਖਮਨ ਕੈ ਘਰਿ ਰਾਗੁ ਸੁਨਿ ਸੁੰਨਿ ਮੰਡਲਿ ਲਿਵ ਲਾਇ ॥

Listening to the music of the Divine Shabad in the Sukhmana energy channel, practice connecting with the realm of Absolute Stillness (Suun).

First Guru GGS p. 944, line 18

ਸੁਖਮਨਾ ਇੜਾ ਪਿੰਗੁਲਾ ਬੂਝੈ ਜਾ ਆਪੇ ਅਲਖੁ ਲਖਾਏ ॥ ਨਾਨਕ ਤਿਹੁ ਤੇ
ਉਪਰਿ ਸਾਚਾ ਸਤਿਗੁਰ ਸਬਦਿ ਸਮਾਏ ॥੬੦॥

When the unseen Divine reveals Himself, one
spontaneously understands the Sushmana, Ida and Pingala
energy channels. Says Nanak, after merging in the Divine
Sound, one finds that the Eternal Divine's abode is beyond
the three energy channels (Ida, Pingula and Sukhmana).

First Guru GGS p. 953, line 2

ਗਗਨ ਮੰਡਲ ਮਹਿ ਰੋਪੈ ਥੰਮੁ ॥

Anchoring the mind at the Tenth Gate, the high sky of the
mind.

First Guru GGS p. 1331, line 19

ਉਪਰਿ ਕੂਪੁ ਗਗਨ ਪਨਿਹਾਰੀ ਅੰਮ੍ਰਿਤੁ ਪੀਵਣਹਾਰਾ ॥.

The apex Tenth Gate wells up and trickles down Ambrosial
Nectar to drink.

First Guru GGS p. 943, line 14

ਬੋਲੈ ਪਵਨਾ ਗਗਨੁ ਗਰਜੈ ॥ ਨਾਨਕ ਨਿਹਚਲੁ ਮਿਲਣੁ ਸਹਜੈ ॥੫੦॥

With the breath resounding, there is a thunder on top of
the Tenth Gate. Says Nanak, then one spontaneously meets
the Eternal, Unchanging Divine.

First Guru GGS p. 153, line 9

ਅੰਮ੍ਰਿਤ ਧਾਰ ਗਗਨਿ ਦਸ ਦੁਆਰਿ ॥

From the apex Tenth Gate, the Ambrosial Nectar trickles
down.

First Guru GGS p. 153, line 15

ਗਰਬੁ ਨਿਵਾਰਿ ਗਗਨ ਪੁਰੁ ਪਾਏ ॥੧॥

The apex Tenth Gate is found only after getting rid of
(preconceptions that cause) egotistical pride.

Saint Kabir GGS p. 334, line 11

ਤਾਗਾ ਤੂਟਾ ਗਗਨੁ ਬਿਨਸਿ ਗਇਆ ਤੇਰਾ ਬੋਲਤੁ ਕਹਾ ਸਮਾਈ ॥

The string has been broken, and the top of the Tenth Gate has been blown away. There is nothing to put in words now.

Saint Kabir GGS p. 972, line 3

ਬੇਧੀਅਲੇ ਚਕ੍ਰ ਭੁਅੰਗਾ ॥ ਭੇਟੀਅਲੇ ਰਾਇ ਨਿਸੰਗਾ ॥੨॥

The chakras of the coiled Kundalini energy open up and one meets the Sovereign Master in plain sight.

Saint Baini GGS p. 974 line 10

ਅੰਮ੍ਰਿਤ ਰਸਿ ਗਗਨੰਤਰਿ ਭੀਜੈ ॥

The ambrosial nectar trickles down from the apex Tenth Gate.

Saint Kabir GGS p. 1105, line 4

ਗਗਨ ਦਮਾਮਾ ਬਾਜਿਓ ਪਰਿਓ ਨੀਸਾਨੈ ਘਾਉ ॥

With the apex of the Tenth Gate opening, there is a loud sound as if there is a battle drum beating and the strike reaching the target inflicting a wound to the Tenth Gate.

The Experience of Enlightenment - What it is Like

When the Tenth Gate opens up and the veil of ignorance is lifted, you see the Reality as it is. You see that it is all a manifestation of God in various roles. You find out that you are not the fragile body vulnerable to pain and suffering, but manifestation of God Himself. You see everything as interconnected and a manifestation of God in various roles. You come to know that the soul does not die and nobody comes and leaves the world (as we see it). You see that it is all a Play set in motion by God and God is you and you are God.

The pleasure, pain and disenchantment are all part of His Play. Beholding the Divine, you are in a total blissful state. You see your own real Divine origin and real destination, and the fear of birth/death goes away.

There is no enmity or fear left. All fears, doubts and attachments are gone; one sees none other than God. One attains the state of fearlessness. Darkness and ignorance is dispelled from within the body when illuminated by the Divine Shabad. The Divine Shabad illuminates the inner self and opens it up like a lotus flower. One feels as if illuminated from millions of suns.

One is no longer subject to a Karma-driven cycle of birth and death and transcends the limits of the physical body. It is a state of pure bliss where instead of reading somewhere or hearing from others, you see the Divine Reality unfolding before your very eyes, and all you can say is Wow! Wow! Because there are no words available to fully describe what you see.

In their own words:

Fifth Guru GGS p. 176, line 9
ਸਭ ਨਦਰੀ ਆਇਆ ਬ੍ਰਹਮੁ ਪਰਗਾਸਾ ॥
Everywhere I look, I see God manifested.

Fifth Guru, GGS p. 782, line 8
ਬ੍ਰਹਮੇ ਪਸਾਰਾ ਬ੍ਰਹਮੁ ਪਸਰਿਆ ਸਭੁ ਬ੍ਰਹਮੁ ਦ੍ਰਿਸਟੀ ਆਇਆ ॥
You see that it is all a manifestation of the Creator (which followers of Hindu religion believe to be the legendary personality Brahma) and the Creator is pervading everywhere. You see that everything is the Creator Himself.

First Guru GGS p. 765, line 9

ਹਉ ਬਿਸਮ ਭਈ ਦੇਖਿ ਗੁਣਾ ਅਨਹਦ ਸਬਦ ਅਗਾਜਾ ਰਾਮ ॥

I am ecstatic beholding His glorious excellence, with the Celestial Divine sound resounding.

Fifth Guru GGS p. 209 line 11

ਨਾ ਕਿਛੁ ਆਵਤ ਨਾ ਕਿਛੁ ਜਾਵਤ ਸਭੁ ਖੇਲੁ ਕੀਓ ਹਰਿ ਰਾਇਓ ॥

Nobody comes and leaves the world (as we see it); It is all a Play set in motion by God, the Sovereign ruler.

Fifth Guru, GGS p.409, line 3

ਹਰਖ ਸੋਗ ਬੈਰਾਗ ਅਨੰਦੀ ਖੇਲੁ ਰੀ ਦਿਖਾਇਓ ॥੧॥ ਰਹਾਉ ॥

As the Blissful God has revealed to me, pleasure, sorrow and (finally) the longing to go back home are all part of His Play.

Fifth Guru GGS p. 1074, line 12

ਨਾ ਕੋ ਆਵੈ ਨਾ ਕੋ ਜਾਵੈ ਗੁਰਿ ਦੂਰਿ ਕੀਆ ਭਰਮੀਜਾ ਹੇ ॥੧੪॥

Nobody comes (to this world) and nobody leaves (as we see it). The Guru has driven out my ignorance.

Fifth Guru GGS p. 890, line 15

ਸਰਬ ਅਨੰਦ ਜਬ ਦਰਸਨੁ ਪਾਈਐ ॥

Beholding the Divine, you are in a total blissful state.

Fifth Guru GGS p. 401, line 3

ਭੈ ਬਿਨਸੇ ਭ੍ਰਮ ਮੋਹ ਗਏ ਕੋ ਦਿਸੈ ਨ ਬੀਆ ॥

All fears are removed, and doubts and attachments are gone; one sees none other than God.

Fifth Guru GGS p. 621, line 17

ਜਨਮ ਮਰਣ ਭੈ ਲਾਥੇ ॥੪॥੨॥੫੨॥

Fears of birth and death are gone.

Fifth Guru GGS p. 1184, line 1

ਭੈ ਬਿਨਸੇ ਨਿਰਭੈ ਪਦੁ ਪਾਇਆ ॥

Fears are dispelled and one attains the state of fearlessness.

Saint Kabir GGS p. 334, line 11

ਤਾਗਾ ਤੂਟਾ ਗਗਨੁ ਬਿਨਸਿ ਗਇਆ ਤੇਰਾ ਬੋਲਤੁ ਕਹਾ ਸਮਾਈ ॥

The string has been broken, and the top of the Tenth Gate has been blown away. There is nothing to put in words now.

Fifth Guru GGS p. 682, line 6

ਜਹ ਜਹ ਪੇਖਉ ਤਹ ਨਾਰਾਇਣ ਸਗਲ ਘਟਾ ਮਹਿ ਤਾਗਾ ॥

Wherever I look, the Divine is there as a string running through everyone.

Fifth Guru GGS p. 1096, line 14

ਗੁਝੜਾ ਲਧਮੁ ਲਾਲੁ ਮਥੈ ਹੀ ਪਰਗਟੁ ਥਿਆ ॥

The hidden jewel has been found; revealed through my own forehead.

Fifth Guru GGS p.612, line 13

ਦੇਖਹੁ ਅਚਰਜੁ ਭਇਆ ॥ ਜਿਹ ਠਾਕੁਰ ਕਉ ਸੁਨਤ ਅਗਾਧਿ ਬੋਧਿ ਸੋ ਰਿਦੈ ਗੁਰਿ ਦਇਆ ॥

Behold, a wondrous miracle has happened! That Divine Master, who is said to be unfathomable and Incomprehensible, by His Grace, I see is enshrined within my heart.

Saint Kabir GGS p. 1374, line 10

ਦਿਲ ਮਹਿ ਸਾਂਈ ਪਰਗਟੈ ਬੁਝੈ ਬਲੰਤੀ ਨਾਂਇ ॥੧੮੬॥

When the Divine is revealed within your heart, the burning fire of desires inside is extinguished. ||186||

Fifth Guru GGS p. 700, line 17

ਨਾਮੁ ਜਪਤ ਕੋਟਿ ਸੂਰ ਉਜਾਰਾ ਬਿਨਸੈ ਭਰਮੁ ਅੰਧੇਰਾ ॥੧॥

Chanting the Naam, (the Name of the Divine), the darkness from ignorance and skepticism is dispelled as if by the light of millions of suns.

Fifth Guru GGS p. 208, line 9

ਅੰਧਕਾਰੁ ਮਿਟਿਓ ਤਿਹ ਤਨ ਤੇ ਗੁਰਿ ਸਬਦਿ ਦੀਪਕੁ ਪਰਗਾਸਾ ॥

Darkness is dispelled from within the body when illuminated by the Divine Shabad.

First Guru GGS p. 224, line 3

ਗੁਰ ਕੈ ਸਬਦਿ ਕਮਲੁ ਪਰਗਾਸਾ ॥੭॥

The Divine Shabad illuminates the inner self and opens it up like a lotus flower.

Fifth Guru GGS p. 249, line 18

ਭ੍ਰਮੁ ਖੋਇਓ ਸਾਂਤਿ ਸਹਜਿ ਸੁਆਮੀ ਪਰਗਾਸੁ ਭਇਆ ਕਉਲੁ ਖਿਲਿਆ ॥

My doubts have been dispelled, the Divine Master has bestowed peace and tranquility; my inner self has opened up like a lotus flower and illuminated me.

First Guru GGS p. 412, line 4

ਅੰਤਰਿ ਨਾਮੁ ਕਮਲੁ ਪਰਗਾਸਾ ॥

With Divine Naam within, your inner self blossoms and opens up like a lotus flower.

Fifth Guru GGS p. 639, line 19

ਮਿਟੈ ਅੰਧੇਰਾ ਅਗਿਆਨਤਾ ਭਾਈ ਕਮਲ ਹੋਵੈ ਪਰਗਾਸੁ ॥

Brethren, the darkness of ignorance is dispelled and your inner self opens up like a blossoming lotus flower.

First Guru GGS p. 661, line 12

ਸਚਿ ਸਿਮਰਿਐ ਹੋਵੈ ਪਰਗਾਸੁ ॥

Meditating on the (Divine) Reality, one gets enlightened.

Fifth Guru GGS P. 293, line 18

ਤਿਨਿ ਦੇਖਿਆ ਜਿਸੁ ਆਪਿ ਦਿਖਾਏ ॥ ਨਾਨਕ ਤਿਸੁ ਜਨ ਸੋਝੀ ਪਾਏ ॥੧॥

He alone sees Him, unto whom God Himself reveals. Says
Nanak, that humble being then comes to comprehend it.

Fifth Guru GGS p. 717, line 1

ਸਾਂਤਿ ਸਹਜ ਸੁਖ ਮਨਿ ਉਪਜਿਓ ਕੋਟਿ ਸੂਰ ਨਾਨਕ ਪਰਗਾਸ
॥੨॥੫॥੨੪॥

Peace, poise and comfort have welled up within my mind;
says Nanak, it is like millions of suns illuminating me.

Saint Ravidas GGS p. 875, line 9

ਉਪਜਿਓ ਗਿਆਨੁ ਹੂਆ ਪਰਗਾਸ ॥

One gets enlightened when the inner self has been
illuminated.

Fifth Guru GGS p. 901, line 3

ਗੁਣ ਗਾਵਤ ਹੋਵਤ ਪਰਗਾਸੁ ॥

Singing the glorious attributes of the Divine leads to
enlightenment.

First Guru GGS p. 907, line 10

ਦੀਪਕ ਤੇ ਦੀਪਕੁ ਪਰਗਾਸਿਆ ਤ੍ਰਿਭਵਣ ਜੋਤਿ ਦਿਖਾਈ ॥੭॥

From the lamp of God, the lamp within is lit; one sees the
Divine Light illuminating this world and the worlds
beyond.

First Guru GGS p. 1021, line 11

ਆਪੇ ਸਾਚੇ ਗੁਣ ਪਰਗਾਸੰ ॥

The Divine Reality Himself reveals His glorious attributes.

Saint Kabir GGS p. 1123, line 6

ਜਿਹ ਮੰਦਰਿ ਦੀਪਕੁ ਪਰਗਾਸਿਆ ਅੰਧਕਾਰੁ ਤਹ ਨਾਸਾ ॥

Darkness (ignorance) is destroyed for the person whose temple (body) is illuminated by the Divine lamp.

Saint Kabir GGS p. 1162, line 17

ਕੋਟਿ ਸੂਰ ਜਾ ਕੈ ਪਰਗਾਸ ॥

They (those achieving enlightenment) are illuminated as if from millions of suns.

First Guru GGS p. 1329, line 5

ਆਪਾ ਮਧੇ ਆਪੁ ਪਰਗਾਸਿਆ ਪਾਇਆ ਅੰਮ੍ਰਿਤੁ ਨਾਮੁ ॥੧॥

Within the self, the Divine is revealed, when one is blessed with the Ambrosial Naam of the Divine.

Third Guru GGS p. 772, line 7

ਆਵਣ ਜਾਣ ਰਹੇ ਸੁਖੁ ਪਾਇਆ ਘਰਿ ਅਨਹਦ ਸੁਰਤਿ ਸਮਾਣੀ ॥

When one's consciousness merges in the Celestial musical Sound, one is freed from the cycle of coming and going (cycle of birth and death).

Fifth Guru GGS p. 781, line 7

ਮਹਾ ਬਿਕਾਰ ਗਏ ਸੁਖ ਉਪਜੇ ਬਾਜੇ ਅਨਹਦ ਤੂਰੇ ॥

Even the most evil thoughts vanish and peace wells up as the Celestial harmony vibrates and resounds.

Chapter 10: Consistency with Modern Science

➢ *One Divine Command set the Creation into motion - Big Bang.*

➢ *Creation and Extinction has happened many times.*

➢ *There are countless planets, suns and moons, held in place orbiting precisely per Divine Design.*

➢ *God has strung the entire creation upon His Thread.*

➢ *Total of Mass and Energy remains the same even though the composition of it may change.*

➢ *At the outset of Creation, nothing was visible. Dense gaseous fog prevailed for a long time.*

➢ *From His state of no manifestation, God started the process of Creation with five elements.*

➢ *The statements that God's energy pervades not only in living beings but also in inanimate things.*

➢ *The process of creation may have involved splitting two disks or splitting a cosmic egg.*

➢ *The body is a microcosm of the universe.*

➢ *Air, water, and earth are sacred and should be taken care of like a Guru, father, and mother.*

Description of the creation and operation of the universe described by those who had experienced the Divine is consistent with modern science.

Written in the 15th and 16th century by successive Sikh Gurus and some non-Sikh saints, Guru Granth Sahib's description of the creation and operation of the universe is being borne out by advances in modern science, including the Big Bang Theory and elements of the Quantum Field Theory. Hopefully, as physicists continue their research on Quantum Field Theory, Unified Field Theory, Dark Matter, and Dark Energy, they will uncover more that aligns with the Guru Granth Sahib's description. Such research might help explain how the Divine can be both beyond and within creation at the same time and how energy and matter constantly interact and transform into one another. Written at a time when Western scholars were debating whether the earth was round or flat and whether the sun revolved around the earth or vice versa, the Guru Granth Sahib stated in clear terms that there are countless planets, suns, and moons with each held in place orbiting precisely according to the Divine system set up by the Creator.

As recorded in Guru Granth Sahib, the Creation is not accidental or random but created by the all-knowing, ever-present Divine, which manifests in various forms for periods of time as part of the magnificent Divine Play. After the period of manifestation is over, all forms, animate and inanimate, are subsumed in the Divine's state of formlessness (called Suun state of no form). In the Suun state, the Divine is One Absolute Conscious Pure Energy with no manifested form and absorbed in a primordial trance-like state. In the Suun state, there are no oceans, suns or moons, wind or fire, life or vegetation in any form.

With these descriptions, those who experienced the Divine are trying to tell us to think about how little we know about what is out there and how it all works. They are trying to teach us to not only rely on what we see and are inviting us to contemplate and introspect on the Divine and the Divine system.

For so long, the Divine was in His Primal Void (Suun state) with no form or manifestation. There was no earth or Akash (the empty gravitational space over the earth commonly called sky). There was no day or night, no moon or sun. The Divine was in His primal state of invisibility with nothing in any form existing. There was no air, water or fire; no oceans or lands. There was no birth or death.

The universe began with a single pronouncement or command (sound) of the Divine. There was utter fogginess for long periods of time. After periods of utter fogginess with no visibility, the Creator started to manifest Himself in forms.

From the Absolute state of formlessness, He manifested in the form of the five elements. From the Eternal Divine came the air and from the air came water. He started the planets and solar systems and brought to manifestation what was invisible before. He set up days and nights. From the Absolute state of formlessness (His state of no manifest form or Suun), He created the moon, the sun, and the earth. Creating the planets, suns, and moons, He infused His Light into them. The whole Creation is the Expanse of One Creator who is Infinite and Unfathomable.

There are millions of lands and realms of the world and countless suns, moons, and planets. There are (countless) planets, solar systems, and galaxies. One cannot describe how many because they are so limitless. The planetary bodies such as the sun, moon, and earth all have a finite lifespan and will eventually cease to exist. The Only One that stays forever is the Divine Himself.

The Divine Energy runs through everything and everyone like a string holding the beads and keeps everything running. The sun and the moon keep orbiting, holding their place perfectly. The sun is in His discipline; the moon is in His discipline. He created the sun and the moon, setting them in motion to mark night and day as He intended. Just like a bucket tied to a rope in a well to draw water, He is holding the worlds above and below in place with His design as if the worlds above and below were all tethered in place. His (own) Naam Energy is what holds the planets in place. Without any pillars, He supports the earth and the Akash. The earth has water locked in it; the wood has fire locked in it.

Back in those days, more than 500 years ago, it would have been impossible to explain to people how one Divine thread runs through everything. However, in the present-day world of satellites controlling communications, remote control operations, and cyber surveillance systems, it may be easier to explain how Almighty God could remotely monitor the whole creation and how using a string (signal?) could remotely sustain or remotely take life out of it all.

The Eternal Divine created the universe, joining the elements together, splitting the cosmic egg and separating it. He created the earth and Akash (the empty gravitational space over the earth) by joining the two disks and then splitting them. It is likely that the referenced disks are energetic disks, not physical. He supports the planets without any pillars, solely by Divine Energy.

Everything (that is outside), including the continents and worlds, is also within the human body. Just as the drop of water is in the ocean, the ocean is in the drop of water, indicating that the information of the whole universe is contained in each of its parts. The body and, in fact, every particle or building block of the Creation is a microcosm of the universe. Everything seemingly inanimate has life, and mass and energy are interchangeable.

God is distinct but, at the same time, infused in the entire creation. It is His Energy that keeps everything and everyone together. He has strung the entire creation upon His thread. His Divine string runs through the entire creation. When He pulls out this thread, all manifested forms of the Creator are subsumed in the Creator. Then, the One Creator alone remains. The cycle of creation and expansion from His formless state, and all forms being subsumed back into His formless state, has occurred multiple times. When He brings His play to its close, then only the One Divine remains.

According to statements in Guru Granth Sahib, the Divine set in motion the process of creation by creating the five elements (earth, water, air, fire and Akash) necessary for life[19]. As there is no statement that human beings or other forms of life came into being directly from the Big Bang, the concept of Creation starting with the five elements necessary for life to exist, seems to be more in line with the theory of evolution of life. It also seems consistent with modern cosmology which addresses the formation of the early universe and what we see today as galaxies and planets followed by the eventual evolution of life on our planet.

---

[19] Charles Darwin: "I have never denied the existence of God. I think the theory of evolution is fully compatible with faith in God.

One Divine Command set the Creation into motion – the Big Bang.

In their own words:

Fifth Guru GGS p. 1003, line 18
ਖੰਡ ਦੀਪ ਸਭਿ ਲੋਆ ॥ ਏਕ ਕਵਾਵੈ ਤੇ ਸਭਿ ਹੋਆ ॥੧॥

All the land mass, the continents and the worlds- One command of the Divine set it all in motion.

First Guru GGS p. 3, line 16
ਕੀਤਾ ਪਸਾਉ ਏਕੋ ਕਵਾਉ ॥

He created the vast expanse of the Universe with One Word!

Third Guru GGS p. 117, line 8
ਉਤਪਤਿ ਪਰਲਉ ਸਬਦੇ ਹੋਵੈ ॥ ਸਬਦੇ ਹੀ ਫਿਰਿ ਓਪਤਿ ਹੋਵੈ ॥

Creation and extinction happens through the Divine Shabad (Sound). It is through the Shabad that Creation happens again.

Creation and Extinction has happened many times.

In their own words:

Fifth Guru GGS p. 276, line 13
ਕਈ ਬਾਰ ਪਸਰਿਓ ਪਾਸਾਰ ॥ ਸਦਾ ਸਦਾ ਇਕੁ ਏਕੰਕਾਰ ॥

So many times, He has caused the Expansion (from His formless state). Only the One Creator is there for ever and ever.

Fifth Guru GGS p. 999, line 19

ਭਣਤਿ ਨਾਨਕੁ ਜਬ ਖੇਲੁ ਉਝਾਰੈ ਤਬ ਏਕੈ ਏਕੰਕਾਰਾ ॥੪॥੪॥

Says Nanak, when He brings His play to its close, then only the One, the One Divine remains.

Fifth Guru, GGS p. 292, line 2
ਆਪਨ ਖੇਲੁ ਆਪਿ ਕਰਿ ਦੇਖੈ ॥ ਖੇਲੁ ਸੰਕੋਚੈ ਤਉ ਨਾਨਕ ਏਕੈ ॥੭॥

He Himself is beholding the Drama He created. When He winds up the Drama, says Nanak, then He alone remains.

First Guru GGS p. 144, line 2
ਨ ਸੂਰ ਸਸਿ ਮੰਡਲੋ ॥ ਨ ਸਪਤ ਦੀਪ ਨਹ ਜਲੋ ॥
ਅੰਨ ਪਉਣ ਥਿਰੁ ਨ ਕੁਈ ॥ ਏਕੁ ਤੁਈ ਏਕੁ ਤੁਈ ॥੪॥

Neither the sun, nor the moon, nor the planets, nor the seven continents, nor the oceans, nor food, nor wind are forever. Only You (God) and You are forever.

Fifth Guru GGS p. 1076, line 1
ਖੰਡ ਪਤਾਲ ਦੀਪ ਸਭਿ ਲੋਆ ॥ ਸਭਿ ਕਾਲੈ ਵਸਿ ਆਪਿ ਪ੍ਰਭਿ ਕੀਆ ॥

All the continents, worlds below our world, islands and worlds - God Himself made them all subject to time (and death).

Fifth Guru GGS p. 1354, line 13
ਘਟੰਤ ਰੂਪੰ ਘਟੰਤ ਦੀਪੰ ਘਟੰਤ ਰਵਿ ਸਸੀਅਰ <u>ਨਖੵਤ੍ਰ ਗਗਨੰ</u> ॥

Beauty diminishes, continents diminish, the sun, moon, stars and Akash or Gagan all diminish.

Fifth Guru GGS p.108, line 12
ਖਿਨ ਮਹਿ ਥਾਪਿ ਉਥਾਪਨਹਾਰਾ ॥ ਆਪਿ ਇਕੰਤੀ ਆਪਿ ਪਸਾਰਾ ॥

He can do and undo anything in an instant. He Himself is the One, and He Himself is the expanse into various forms.

Fifth Guru GGS p. 237, line 12

ਸਗਲ ਪਾਸਾਰੁ ਦੀਸੈ ਪਾਸਾਰਾ ॥ ਬਿਨਸਿ ਜਾਇਗੋ ਸਗਲ ਆਕਾਰਾ ॥੫॥

The entire world and the visible universe - all forms of existence shall come to an end.

First Guru GGS p. 352, line 6

ਜੋ ਦੀਸੈ ਸੋ ਉਪਜੈ ਬਿਨਸੈ ॥

Whatever/whoever we see is subject to a beginning and an end.

Fifth Guru GGS P. 277, line 1

ਹੁਕਮੇ ਧਾਰਿ ਅਧਰ ਰਹਾਵੈ ॥ ਹੁਕਮੇ ਉਪਜੈ ਹੁਕਮਿ ਸਮਾਵੈ ॥

By His Divine Design, He established the planets and He maintains them unsupported. By His Order, the Creation came into being and by His Order, it shall merge again into Him.

Tenth Guru, Benti Chaupai, stanza 389

ਜਬ ਉਦਕਰਖ ਕਰਾ ਕਰਤਾਰਾ ॥ ਪ੍ਰਜਾ ਧਰਤ ਤਬ ਦੇਹ ਅਪਾਰਾ ॥
ਜਬ ਆਕਰਖ ਕਰਤ ਹੋ ਕਬਹੂੰ ॥ ਤੁਮ ਮੈ ਮਿਲਤ ਦੇਹ ਧਰ ਸਭਹੂੰ ॥੩੮੯॥

Almighty God, when you projected yourself (from formlessness to manifesting in various forms), so many beings and lands came into existence. At the time you draw everything back unto you, your Creation manifested in innumerable forms immerses back in you.

There are countless planets, suns, moons, and earth. They are all held in place orbiting precisely per Divine Design.

At the time the scripture was written and compiled, many thinkers, philosophers and religious writers around the world believed that the sun was revolving around the earth. In India, some Hindu scriptures maintained that the earth's weight was supported from underneath by a 1000-headed snake called Sheshnaag. There was also the belief that the weight of the earth was being held on the horns of a mythic bull. In one of his first compositions, Guru Nanak Dev explained that there were countless planets, suns, moons, and earths, and rhetorically asked that if the mythic bull was carrying the weight of our earth, then who was supporting the weight of the other countless planets.

In their own words:

First Guru GGS p. 3, line 14
ਧਰਤੀ ਹੋਰੁ ਪਰੈ ਹੋਰੁ ਹੋਰੁ ॥ ਤਿਸ ਤੇ ਭਾਰੁ ਤਲੈ ਕਵਣੁ ਜੋਰੁ ॥
So many earths beyond this earth-so very many! What power holds them, and supports their weight?

First Guru GGS p. 3, line 14
ਜੇ ਕੋ ਬੁਝੈ ਹੋਵੈ ਸਚਿਆਰੁ ॥ ਧਵਲੈ ਉਪਰਿ ਕੇਤਾ ਭਾਰੁ ॥
(Referring to a belief in Hinduism that a bull is carrying the weight of the earth on its horns) A bull carrying the weight of the earth? Anyone understanding the Reality will know that it is not the mythic bull carrying the weight of the earth.

First Guru GGS p. 1021, line 11
ਆਪੇ ਧਰਤੀ ਧਉਲੁ ਅਕਾਸੰ ॥
He Himself is the earth and the mythical bull which supports it and the Akash.

First Guru GGS p. 1037, line 3
ਹੁਕਮੇ ਧਰਤੀ ਧਉਲ ਸਿਰਿ ਭਾਰੰ ॥
The Divine Order or System is the mythical bull which supports the burden of the earth on its head.

First Guru GGS p. 8, line 6
ਤਿਥੈ ਖੰਡ ਮੰਡਲ ਵਰਭੰਡ ॥ ਜੇ ਕੋ ਕਥੈ ਤ ਅੰਤ ਨ ਅੰਤ ॥

There are (countless) planets, solar systems and galaxies. One cannot describe how many because they are so limitless.

First Guru GGS p. 5, line 2
ਪਾਤਾਲਾ ਪਾਤਾਲ ਲਖ ਆਗਾਸਾ ਆਗਾਸ ॥

There are worlds beneath worlds, and hundreds of thousands of skies over them .

First Guru GGS, p. 4, line 7
ਅਗੰਮ ਅਗੰਮ ਅਸੰਖ ਲੋਅ ॥ਅਸੰਖ ਕਹਹਿ ਸਿਰਿ ਭਾਰੁ ਹੋਇ ॥

Out of our reach, really inaccessible countless celestial realms. Even to call them countless, one has to wonder if that appropriately captures the reality.

First Guru GGS p. 1291, line 2
ਦੀਪ ਲੋਅ ਪਾਤਾਲ ਤਹ ਖੰਡ ਮੰਡਲ ਹੈਰਾਨੁ ॥

Worlds and realms, worlds below our world , solar systems and galaxies are wondrously revealed.

First Guru GGS p. 1283, line 14
ਖੰਡ ਪਤਾਲ ਅਸੰਖ ਮੈ ਗਣਤ ਨ ਹੋਈ ॥

There are countless planets and worlds below our world; I cannot count their number.

Fifth Guru GGS p. 275, line 19
ਕਈ ਕੋਟਿ ਦੇਸ ਭੂ ਮੰਡਲ ॥

There are millions of lands and realms of the world.

Fifth Guru GGS p. 275, line 19
ਕਈ ਕੋਟਿ ਸਸੀਅਰ ਸੂਰ ਨਖੵਤੁ ॥

Millions of moons, suns and planets.

193

Fifth Guru GGS p. 276, line 1
ਕਈ ਕੋਟਿ ਦੇਵ ਦਾਨਵ ਇੰਦ੍ਰ ਸਿਰਿ ਛਤੁ ॥

(Referring to certain deities mentioned in Hindu scriptures), Millions of demi-gods, demons and Indras, with regal canopies over their heads.

Fifth Guru GGS p. 276, line 3
ਕਈ ਕੋਟਿ ਕੀਏ ਰਤਨ ਸਮੁਦ ॥

Millions of oceans with pearls.

Fifth Guru GGS p. 276, line 3
ਕਈ ਕੋਟਿ ਨਾਨਾ ਪ੍ਰਕਾਰ ਜੰਤ ॥

Millions of beings of so many kinds.

Fifth Guru GGS p. 276, line 3
ਕਈ ਕੋਟਿ ਕੀਏ ਚਿਰ ਜੀਵੇ ॥

Millions with very long lives.

First Guru GGS p. 142, line 2
ਚੰਦੁ ਸੂਰਜੁ ਦੁਇ ਫਿਰਦੇ ਰਖੀਅਹਿ ਨਿਹਚਲੁ ਹੋਵੈ ਥਾਉ ॥

The sun and the moon keep orbiting holding their place perfectly.

First Guru GGS p. 464, line 14
ਭੈ ਵਿਚਿ ਸੂਰਜੁ ਭੈ ਵਿਚਿ ਚੰਦੁ ॥

Sun is in His discipline; the moon is in His discipline.

First Guru GGS p. 580, line 8
ਸੂਰਜੁ ਚੰਦੁ ਸਿਰਜਿਅਨੁ ਅਹਿਨਿਸਿ ਚਲਤੁ ਵੀਚਾਰੋ ॥੧॥

He created the sun and the moon; night and day, they move as he willed.

Fifth Guru GGS p. 884, line 16
ਚੰਦੁ ਸੂਰਜੁ ਦੁਇ ਜਰੇ ਚਰਾਗਾ ਚਹੁ ਕੁੰਟ ਭੀਤਰਿ ਰਾਖੇ ॥

The sun and the moon are the two lamps which shine, with the four corners of the world placed between them.

First Guru GGS p. 228, line 18

ਡੋਲੁ ਬਧਾ ਕਸਿ ਜੇਵਰੀ ਆਕਾਸਿ ਪਤਾਲਾ ॥੬॥

Like a bucket tied to the rope in a well to draw water, He has tethered the worlds in place above and below.

Fifth Guru GGS p. 1071, line 11

ਗਗਨੁ ਰਹਾਇਆ ਹੁਕਮੇ ਚਰਣਾ ॥

He has spread (empty gravitational space) Gagan or Akash, over the earth supported by His Command.

First Guru GGS p. 1188, line 13

ਬਾਝੁ ਕਲਾ ਧਰਿ ਗਗਨੁ ਧਰੀਆ ॥੨॥

Without any pillars, He supports the earth and the Akash commonly called sky.

First Guru GGS p. 1279, line 6

ਵਿਣੁ ਥੰਮ੍ਹਾ ਗਗਨੁ ਰਹਾਇ ਸਬਦੁ ਨੀਸਾਣਿਆ ॥

Without any pillars, He supports the Akash (also called gagan), through the insignia of His Shabad (Divine Sound).

First Guru GGS p. 464, line 12

ਭੈ ਵਿਚਿ ਪਵਣੁ ਵਹੈ ਸਦਵਾਉ ॥

The ever-blowing winds and breezes are under His discipline.

First Guru GGS p. 1037, line 4

ਹੁਕਮੇ ਆਡਾਣੇ ਆਗਾਸੀ ॥

Per His Order, (the empty gravitational space) Akash is spread over the earth.

Fourth Guru GGS p. 605, line 16

ਆਪੇ ਧਰਤੀ ਸਾਜੀਅਨੁ ਪਿਆਰੈ ਪਿਛੈ ਟੰਕੁ ਚੜਾਇਆ ॥੧॥

Dear Almighty God designed the earth and fine-tuned its balancing attaching a counter-weight.

God has strung the entire creation upon His Thread.

Various verses in Guru Granth Sahib describe that like a string holding hundreds and thousands of beads, He has woven himself into His Creation. The One thread of the Divine runs through the world. When He pulls out this thread, everything collapses, and the One Creator alone remains. His Divine power holds the thread. When He withdraws the thread, the beads scatter into nothing. This Divine thread could be a sort of unified field which physicists are currently searching for via the Unified Field Theory.

Back in those days, more than 500 years ago, it would have been impossible to explain to people how one Divine thread runs through everything. However, in the present-day world of satellites controlling communications, remote control operations, and cyber surveillance systems, it may be easier to explain how Almighty God could remotely monitor the whole creation and how using a string (signal?) could remotely sustain or remotely take life out of it all.

In their own words:

Fifth Guru GGS p. 250, line 12

ਏਕਹਿ ਸੂਤਿ ਪਰੋਵਨਹਾਰਾ ॥

He strung it all upon His One thread.

Fifth Guru GGS p. 276, line 1

ਸਗਲ ਸਮਗ੍ਰੀ ਅਪਨੈ ਸੂਤਿ ਧਾਰੈ ॥

He has strung the entire creation upon His thread.

Fifth Guru GGS p. 284, line 6
ਸਗਲ ਪਰੋਈ ਅਪੁਨੈ ਸੂਤਿ ॥

All are strung upon His string.

Bhagat (Saint) Naam Dev Ji, GGS p. 485, line 3
ਸੂਤੁ ਏਕੁ ਮਣਿ ਸਤ ਸਹੰਸ ਜੈਸੇ ਓਤਿ ਪੋਤਿ ਪ੍ਰਭੁ ਸੋਈ ॥੧॥

Like a string holding hundreds and thousands of beads, He has woven himself into His creation.

Fifth Guru GGS p. 292, line 2
ਖੇਲੁ ਸੰਕੋਚੈ ਤਉ ਨਾਨਕ ਏਕੈ ॥੨॥

Says Nanak, when He winds up the drama, He alone remains.

Fifth Guru GGS p. 292, line 9
ਆਪਨ ਸੂਤਿ ਸਭੁ ਜਗਤੁ ਪਰੋਇ ॥

You have strung the whole world upon your thread.

Fifth Guru GGS p. 886, line 7
ਏਕੈ ਸੂਤਿ ਪਰੋਏ ਮਣੀਏ ॥ ਗਾਠੀ ਭਿਨਿ ਭਿਨਿ ਭਿਨਿ ਭਿਨਿ ਤਣੀਏ ॥

One Divine thread has all the beads strung on it. By means of many, various, diverse knots, they are tied, and kept separate on the string.

Fifth Guru GGS p. 387, line 2
ਸਗਲ ਸਮਗ੍ਰੀ ਜਾ ਕੈ ਸੂਤਿ ਪਰੋਈ ॥

Everything is strung on His string.

Fifth Guru GGS p. 1150, line 15
ਜਾ ਕੈ ਸੂਤਿ ਪਰੋਇਆ ਸੰਸਾਰੁ ॥

Whose thread has strung the universe.

Fourth Guru GGS p. 507, line 7

ਏਹੁ ਪਰਪੰਚੁ ਖੇਲੁ ਕੀਆ ਸਭੁ ਕਰਤੈ ਹਰਿ ਕਰਤੈ ਸਭ ਕਲ ਧਾਰੀ ॥ ਹਰਿ
ਏਕੋ ਸੂਤੁ ਵਰਤੈ ਜੁਗ ਅੰਤਰਿ ਸੂਤੁ ਖਿੰਚੈ ਏਕੰਕਾਰੀ ॥੭॥

All this worldly drama is set in motion by the Divine Creator. He has infused His Divine power into all. The One thread of the Divine runs through the world; when He pulls out this thread, the One Creator alone remains.

Fifth Guru GGS p. 518, line 2

ਇਕਤੁ ਸੂਤਿ ਪਰੋਇ ਜੋਤਿ ਸੰਜਾਰੀਐ ॥

Stringing all with One thread, He has infused His Light in them.

Fourth Guru GGS p. 604, line 19

ਆਪੇ ਸੂਤੁ ਆਪੇ ਬਹੁ ਮਣੀਆ ਕਰਿ ਸਕਤੀ ਜਗਤੁ ਪਰੋਇ ॥

He Himself is the thread, and He Himself is the many beads; through His Almighty Power, He has strung the worlds.

Fourth Guru GGS p. 605, line 1

ਆਪੇ ਹੀ ਸੂਤਧਾਰੁ ਹੈ ਪਿਆਰਾ ਸੂਤੁ ਖਿੰਚੇ ਢਹਿ ਢੇਰੀ ਹੋਇ ॥੧॥

The Loving Divine Himself is the holder of the thread; when He withdraws the thread, the beads scatter into nothing.

Fifth Guru GGS p. 609, line 13

ਤੁਟਿ ਜਾਇਗੋ ਸੂਤੁ ਬਾਪੁਰੇ ਫਿਰਿ ਪਾਛੈ ਪਛੁਤੋਹੀ ॥੩॥

The string (sustaining you) shall break, o' ignorant, and then, you shall repent and regret.

Mass and Energy are interchangeable, but the total of mass and energy remains the same.

There are numerous verses in Guru Granth Sahib which state that when the physical body ceases to exist upon death, all the elements change their composition and merge in their elements, such as water, earth, and air, and concludes that nothing really dies. This seems to be in line with our modern understanding of Physics that the total of mass and energy remains constant even if it may change form.

In their own words:

Fifth Guru GGS p.885, line 16
ਨਹ ਕੋ ਮੂਆ ਨ ਮਰਣੈ ਜੋਗੁ ॥ ਨਹ ਬਿਨਸੈ ਅਬਿਨਾਸੀ ਹੋਗੁ ॥੩॥

No one dies; no one is capable of dying. No one perishes because of imperishability.

Fifth Guru GGS p. 885, line 12
ਪਵਨੈ ਮਹਿ ਪਵਨੁ ਸਮਾਇਆ ॥ ਜੋਤੀ ਮਹਿ ਜੋਤਿ ਰਲਿ ਜਾਇਆ ॥

ਮਾਟੀ ਮਾਟੀ ਹੋਈ ਏਕ ॥ ਰੋਵਨਹਾਰੇ ਕੀ ਕਵਨ ਟੇਕ ॥੧॥

(When someone dies), the wind merges into the wind. The light blends into the light. The dust becomes one with the dust. The one lamenting the death has nothing to hold on to.

Fifth Guru GGS p.885, line 13
ਕਉਨੁ ਮੂਆ ਰੇ ਕਉਨੁ ਮੂਆ ॥ ਬ੍ਰਹਮ ਗਿਆਨੀ ਮਿਲਿ ਕਰਹੁ ਬੀਚਾਰਾ ਇਹੁ ਤਉ ਚਲਤੁ ਭਇਆ ॥੧॥ ਰਹਾਉ ॥

Who has died? O' who has died? O' knowledgeable ones, meet together and think about how this is part of the great Divine Play.

Tenth Guru composition Akal Ustat Stanza 17

ਜੈਸੇ ਏਕ ਆਗ ਤੇ ਕਨੂਕਾ ਕੋਟਿ ਆਗਿ ਉਠੇ ਨਿਆਰੇ ਨਿਆਰੇ ਹੁਇ ਕੈ
ਫੇਰਿ ਆਗ ਮੈ ਮਿਲਾਹਿੰਗੇ ॥

ਜੈਸੇ ਏਕ ਧੂਰਿ ਤੇ ਅਨੇਕ ਧੂਰਿ ਪੂਰਤ ਹੈ ਧੂਰਿ ਕੇ ਕਨੂਕਾ ਫੇਰ ਧੂਰਿ ਹੀ
ਸਮਾਹਿੰਗੇ ॥

ਜੈਸੇ ਏਕ ਨਦ ਤੇ ਤਰੰਗ ਕੋਟਿ ਉਪਜਤ ਹੈ ਪਾਨਿ ਕੇ ਤਰੰਗ ਸਬੈ ਪਾਨਿ ਹੀ
ਕਹਾਹਿੰਗੇ ॥

ਤੈਸੇ ਬਿਸ੍ਵ ਰੂਪ ਤੇ ਅਭੂਤ ਭੂਤ ਪ੍ਰਗਾਟ ਹੋਇ ਤਾਹੀ ਤੇ ਉਪਜਿ ਸਬੈ ਤਾਹੀ ਮੇ
ਸਮਾਹਿੰਗੇ ॥੧੧॥੮੧॥

*Just as countless sparks fly off a fire in distinct shapes and
are absorbed back in the fire. Just as countless dust particles
rise from dust and get back to dust. Just as countless waves
are formed in large bodies of water to be called as water
again.   In the same way, animate and inanimate forms
coming out of the Almighty God get absorbed back in Him.*

At the outset of Creation, dense gaseous fog prevailed for a long time.

Before the Creation, God was there in His primal void in
a state of absolute formlessness. There were no planets, no
suns, moons or stars and no life in any manifest form.
Nothing existed in any form until God manifested Himself in
various forms. The state of formlessness is described as the
Suun state. When God started the Creation, dense gaseous fog
prevailed for a long time and there was no visibility.

In their own words:

First Guru GGS p. 940, line 11
ਆਦਿ ਕਉ ਬਿਸਮਾਦੁ ਬੀਚਾਰੁ ਕਥੀਅਲੇ ਸੁੰਨ ਨਿਰੰਤਰਿ ਵਾਸੁ ਲੀਆ ॥
*(Guru Nanak's response to questions from ascetics as to
where the Absolute Formless God dwells before Creation
and after the Creation is wound up) We can only express a*

sense of ecstatic wonder about the beginning. The Absolute formless continuously abided deep within Himself in the Primal Void then.

Fifth Guru GGS p. 1081, line 18

ਕੇਤੜਿਆ ਦਿਨ ਸੁੰਨਿ ਸਮਾਇਆ ॥

For so long, the Divine was in His Primal Void with no form or manifestation.

First Guru GGS p. 1035, line 9

ਅਰਬਦ ਨਰਬਦ ਧੁੰਧੂਕਾਰਾ ॥ ਧਰਣਿ ਨ ਗਗਨਾ ਹੁਕਮੁ ਅਪਾਰਾ ॥

For endless eons, there was no visibility as if in utter fogginess. There was no earth or gagan (also called Akash); there was no Divine system (or Hukam) in operation (because there was only the Divine).

First Guru GGS p. 1026, line 14

ਕੇਤੇ ਜੁਗ ਵਰਤੇ ਗੁਬਾਰੈ ॥ ਤਾੜੀ ਲਾਈ ਅਪਰ ਅਪਾਰੈ ॥ ਧੁੰਧੂਕਾਰਿ ਨਿਰਾਲਮੁ ਬੈਠਾ ਨਾ ਤਦਿ ਧੰਧੁ ਪਸਾਰਾ ਹੇ ॥੧॥

For many ages, there was nothing visible. The Infinite, Unfathomable Divine was absorbed in the primal void. He was by Himself with nothing visible to anyone and with no expanse.

Fifth Guru GGS p. 1215, line 3

ਏਕੈ ਪਰਗਟੁ ਏਕੈ ਗੁਪਤਾ ਏਕੈ ਧੁੰਧੂਕਾਰੋ ॥

The same One Divine is Manifest in form and Invisible and formless; the same One Divine dwells in utter fogginess where nothing is visible.

Fourth Guru GGS p. 555, line 17

ਜੁਗ ਛਤੀਹ ਗੁਬਾਰੁ ਕਰਿ ਵਰਤਿਆ ਸੁੰਨਾਹਰਿ ॥

For ages (using thirty six ages commonly mentioned in
Hinduism as an example), He created dense atmosphere
with no visibility and invisibly abided in His void.

First Guru GGS p. 1035, line 10
ਨਾ ਦਿਨੁ ਰੈਨਿ ਨ ਚੰਦੁ ਨ ਸੂਰਜੁ ਸੁੰਨ ਸਮਾਧਿ ਲਗਾਇਦਾ ॥੧॥

There was no day or night, no moon or sun while God was
in His Primal Void with no manifest form.

First Guru GGS p. 1035, line 11
ਖਾਣੀ ਨ ਬਾਣੀ ਪਉਣ ਨ ਪਾਣੀ ॥ ਉਪਤਿ ਖਪਤਿ ਨ ਆਵਣ ਜਾਣੀ ॥
ਖੰਡ ਪਤਾਲ ਸਪਤ ਨਹੀ ਸਾਗਰ ਨਦੀ ਨ ਨੀਰੁ ਵਹਾਇਦਾ ॥੨॥

There were no root sources of creation or the sound of
speech, no air or water. There was no Creation or
Destruction, no coming or going. There were no continents,
no worlds below our world, seven seas, rivers or flowing
water.

First Guru GGS p. 1035, line 12
ਨਾ ਤਦਿ ਸੁਰਗੁ ਮਛੁ ਪਇਆਲਾ ॥ ਦੋਜਕੁ ਭਿਸਤੁ ਨਹੀ ਖੈ ਕਾਲਾ ॥
ਨਰਕੁ ਸੁਰਗੁ ਨਹੀ ਜੰਮਣੁ ਮਰਣਾ ਨਾ ਕੋ ਆਇ ਨ ਜਾਇਦਾ ॥੩॥

There were no heavenly realms, earth or worlds below the
earth. There was no heaven or hell, no death or time. No
hell or heaven, no birth or death, no coming or going into
and out of the world.

First Guru GGS p. 1037, line 10
ਸੁੰਨ ਕਲਾ ਅਪਰੰਪਰਿ ਧਾਰੀ ॥

The Divine from the Absolute state of formlessness, assumed
His power (to start Creation).

Fifth Guru GGS p. 1081, line 19
ਕੇਤੜਿਆ ਦਿਨ ਧੁੰਧੂਕਾਰਾ ਆਪੇ ਕਰਤਾ ਪਰਗਟੜਾ ॥੧੨॥

After a period of utter fogginess with no visibility, the Creator manifested Himself (in forms).

From His state of no manifestation, God started the process of Creation with five elements.

Before the start of Creation, God was not manifest in any form and was formless. From His state of no manifestation, He started the process of Creation with five elements: earth, water, air, fire, and Akash ((the empty gravitational space over the earth) also commonly called the sky.

In their own words:

First Guru GGS p. 1038, line 7

ਪੰਚ ਤਤੁ ਸੁੰਨਹੁ ਪਰਗਾਸਾ ॥

From the Absolute state of formlessness, He created the five elements.

First Guru GGS p. 1037, line 11

ਪਉਣੁ ਪਾਣੀ ਸੁੰਨੈ ਤੇ ਸਾਜੇ ॥

From the Absolute state of formlessness, He fashioned air and water.

First Guru GGS p.1033, line 12

ਪਉਣ ਪਾਣੀ ਅਗਨੀ ਇਕ ਵਾਸਾ ॥ ਆਪੇ ਕੀਤੋ ਖੇਲੁ ਤਮਾਸਾ ॥

By making air, water and fire coexist, he himself staged His wondrous Play.

Fourth Guru GGS p. 735, line 5

ਵਿਚੇ ਧਰਤੀ ਵਿਚੇ ਪਾਣੀ ਵਿਚਿ ਕਾਸਟ ਅਗਨਿ ਧਰੀਜੈ ॥

Earth has water locked in it; wood has fire locked in it.

Fourth Guru GGS p. 605, line 18

ਆਪੇ ਧਰਤੀ ਆਪਿ ਜਲੁ ਪਿਆਰਾ ਆਪੇ ਕਰੇ ਕਰਾਇਆ ॥

The Beloved Himself is the earth, and He Himself is the water; He Himself is the operator who acts and causes others to act.

First Guru GGS p. 877, line 11

ਪਾਣੀ ਪ੍ਰਾਣ ਪਵਣਿ ਬੰਧਿ ਰਾਖੇ ਚੰਦੁ ਸੂਰਜੁ ਮੁਖਿ ਦੀਏ ॥

Binding together water and air, He infused the breath to create life into beings and provided the sun and the moon as lamps.

Fifth Guru GGS p. 1003, line 17

ਓਅੰਕਾਰਿ ਉਤਪਾਤੀ ॥ ਕੀਆ ਦਿਨਸੁ ਸਭ ਰਾਤੀ ॥

The One Universal Creator created the creation. He set up days and the nights.

Fourth Guru GGS p. 302, line 13

ਆਪੇ ਧਰਤੀ ਸਾਜੀਅਨੁ ਆਪੇ ਆਕਾਸੁ ॥

He Himself formed the earth and the Akash (the empty gravitational space over the earth).

First Guru GGS p.19, line 18

ਸਾਚੇ ਤੇ ਪਵਨਾ ਭਇਆ ਪਵਨੈ ਤੇ ਜਲੁ ਹੋਇ ॥

From the Eternal Divine came the air and from the air came water.

Third Guru GGS p. 162. Line 6

ਜੈਸੇ ਧਰਤੀ ਮਧੇ ਪਾਣੀ ਪਰਗਾਸਿਆ ਬਿਨੁ ਪਗਾ ਵਰਸਤ ਫਿਰਾਹੀ ॥੧॥

Just as He provided water within the earth, the clouds run around without any feet and shower down water.

First Guru GGS p. 350, line 15

ਪਉਣੁ ਉਪਾਇ ਧਰੀ ਸਭ ਧਰਤੀ ਜਲ ਅਗਨੀ ਕਾ ਬੰਧੁ ਕੀਆ ॥

He created the air and established the earth binding water and fire together.

First Guru GGS p. 1026, line 18
ਪਉਣੁ ਪਾਣੀ ਅਗਨੀ ਮਿਲਿ ਜੀਆ ॥
Life is created from the union of air, water and fire.

First Guru GGS p. 1031, line 9
ਪਵਣੈ ਪਾਣੀ ਅਗਨੀ ਜੀਉ ਪਾਇਆ ॥
He placed the soul in the body made of air, water and fire.

First Guru GGS p. 1036, line 11
ਪਉਣ ਪਾਣੀ ਅਗਨੀ ਕਾ ਬੰਧਨੁ ਕਾਇਆ ਕੋਟੁ ਰਚਾਇਦਾ ॥੧॥
Binding together air, water and fire, He created the fortress of the body.

First Guru GGS p. 1030, line 10
ਪੰਚ ਤਤੁ ਮਿਲਿ ਕਾਇਆ ਕੀਨੀ ॥
Five elements coming together formed the body.

First Guru GGS p. 1113, line 2
ਪਉਣੁ ਪਾਣੀ ਅਗਨਿ ਬਾਧੇ ਗੁਰਿ ਖੇਲੁ ਜਗਤਿ ਦਿਖਾਇਆ ॥
By binding the air, water and fire together, the Divine staged the drama of the world.

First Guru GGS p. 1257, line 10
ਪਉਣੈ ਪਾਣੀ ਅਗਨੀ ਕਾ ਸਨਬੰਧ ॥
It is a fusion of air, water and fire.

First Guru GGS p.1036 line 8
ਖੰਡ ਬ੍ਰਹਮੰਡ ਪਾਤਾਲ ਅਰੰਭੇ ਗੁਪਤਹੁ ਪਰਗਟੀ ਆਇਦਾ ॥੧੫॥
He started the planets, solar systems and regions below earths, and brought to manifestation what was invisible before.

205

First Guru GGS p. 1037, line 16

ਸੁੰਨਹੁ ਧਰਤਿ ਅਕਾਸੁ ਉਪਾਏ ॥

From the Absolute state of formlessness, the earth and the Akash were created.

First Guru GGS p. 1037, line 15

ਸੁੰਨਹੁ ਚੰਦੁ ਸੂਰਜੁ ਗੈਣਾਰੇ ॥

From the Absolute state of formlessness, came the moon, the sun and the Akash.

First Guru GGS p. 1037, line 17

ਸੁੰਨਹੁ ਖਾਣੀ ਸੁੰਨਹੁ ਬਾਣੀ ॥ ਸੁੰਨਹੁ ਉਪਜੀ ਸੁੰਨਿ ਸਮਾਣੀ ॥

From the Absolute state of formlessness, came the sources of creation, and the sound of speech. Created from the Absolute state of formlessness, they will merge back into the Absolute state of formlessness (Primal Void).

First Guru GGS p. 1037, line 19

ਸੁੰਨਹੁ ਰਾਤਿ ਦਿਨਸੁ ਦੁਇ ਕੀਏ ॥

From the Absolute state of formlessness, both night and day were created.

First Guru GGS p. 1279, line 6

ਸੂਰਜੁ ਚੰਦੁ ਉਪਾਇ ਜੋਤਿ ਸਮਾਇਆ ॥

Creating the sun and the moon, He infused His Light into them.

First Guru GGS p. 1038, line 2

ਸੁੰਨਹੁ ਸਪਤ ਪਾਤਾਲ ਉਪਾਏ ॥

(Referring to the seven regions below our earth called sapat pataal in Hindu scriptures, in his dialogue with Hindu ascetics, Guru Nanak says) All the seven pataals were created from the same Absolute state of formlessness.

First Guru GGS p. 1038, line 2

ਸੁੰਨਹੁ ਭਵਣ ਰਖੇ ਲਿਵ ਲਾਏ ॥

From the Absolute state of formlessness, the ever-revolving heavenly bodies supported by His Energy were created.

The statements that God's energy pervades not only in living beings but also in inanimate things.

Various verses in Guru Granth Sahib describe how God is within us (immanent) as well as outside of us (transcendent) with God's Energy being beamed into everyone and everything. God's energy pervades not only in living beings, but also in seemingly inanimate things. It must have been very difficult to explain this to people at a time when they were thinking of God in human terms, rather than as Conscious Energy that can be everywhere at the same time. In Guru Granth Sahib, God is described as without any form but Super-Conscious and All-knowing.

In recent history, scientists have shown that all matter (including seemingly inanimate things) is made up of the same energetic particles which are constantly in motion held together by electromagnetic and nuclear forces. Various verses in Guru Granth Sahib seem to be conveying this concept when stating that Divine conscious energy is pervading even in inanimate things.

In their own words:

Fourth Guru GGS p. 775, line 12

ਸਭ ਮਹਿ ਰਵਿ ਰਹਿਆ ਸੋ ਪ੍ਰਭੁ ਅੰਤਰਜਾਮੀ ਰਾਮ ॥

The Almighty God who even knows what goes on in our hearts and minds resides in all.

First Guru GGS p. 728, line 13
ਜਲਿ ਥਲਿ ਮਹੀਅਲਿ ਰਵਿ ਰਹਿਆ ਸੋਇ ॥੩॥

Almighty God is pervading and permeating the waters, the lands and the skies.

Third Guru GGS p. 124, line 16
ਗੁਪਤੁ ਪਰਗਟੁ ਤੂੰ ਸਭਨੀ ਥਾਈ ॥

You are everywhere, (in some) visibly and (in others) invisibly.

First Guru GGS p. 943, line 15
ਅੰਤਰਿ ਸੁੰਨੰ ਬਾਹਰਿ ਸੁੰਨੰ ਤ੍ਰਿਭਵਣ ਸੁੰਨ ਮਸੁੰਨੰ ॥

The Divine invisibly is deep within as well as outside of us and totally fills this world and the worlds beyond.

Fifth Guru, GGS p. 1095, line 14
ਸਭੁ ਬ੍ਰਹਮ ਪਸਾਰੁ ਪਸਾਰਿਓ ਆਪੇ ਖੇਲੰਤਾ ॥

The Creator spread out to create the expanse for the entire universe, and He Himself plays in it.

The process of creation may have involved splitting two disks or splitting a cosmic egg.

Some verses in Guru Granth Sahib seem to indicate that the process of creation may have involved splitting two disks. There is also a reference to something like splitting a cosmic egg.

In their own words:

First Guru GGS p. 839, line 4
ਆਪੇ ਸਚੁ ਕੀਆ ਕਰ ਜੋੜਿ ॥ ਅੰਡਜ ਫੋੜਿ ਜੋੜਿ ਵਿਛੋੜਿ ॥

The Eternal Divine Himself created the universe, joining the elements together. Splitting the cosmic egg, uniting it and separating it.

First Guru GGS p. 580, line 8

ਦੁਇ ਪੁੜ ਜੋੜਿ ਵਿਛੋੜਿਅਨੁ ਗੁਰ ਬਿਨੁ ਘੋਰੁ ਅੰਧਾਰੋ ॥

The two disks were joined and then split (creating the surface of the planet and its surrounding gravitational space-its Akash or sky). Without the Divine (revealing this), there is only pitch darkness (total ignorance).

Third Guru GGS p. 949, line 7

ਅੰਬਰੁ ਧਰਤਿ ਵਿਛੋੜਿਅਨੁ ਵਿਚਿ ਸਚਾ ਅਸਰਾਉ ॥

Splitting the earth and its sky, the Eternal Divine supported them from within.

The body is a microcosm of the universe.

The body and, in fact, every particle or building block of the Creation is a microcosm of the universe. The body has information about the universe. The droplet of water from the ocean understands the ocean, just as the ocean understands the droplet of water. Everything (that is outside) is also within the human body - the continents, worlds, and all that is not visible to us. The body is the microcosm of the universe.

In their own words:

First Guru GGS p. 878, line 18

ਸਾਗਰ ਮਹਿ ਬੂੰਦ ਬੂੰਦ ਮਹਿ ਸਾਗਰੁ ਕਵਣੁ ਬੁਝੈ ਬਿਧਿ ਜਾਣੈ ॥

The droplet of water is in the ocean, and the ocean is in the droplet of water, whoever can unravel this mystery and comprehend.

Fifth Guru GGS p. 287, line 3

ਬ੍ਰਹਮ ਮਹਿ ਜਨੁ ਜਨ ਮਹਿ ਪਾਰਬ੍ਰਹਮੁ ॥

God is in His created beings and the created beings are in God.

Third Guru GGS p. 754, line 7

ਕਾਇਆ ਅੰਦਰਿ ਸਭੁ ਕਿਛੁ ਵਸੈ ਖੰਡ ਮੰਡਲ ਪਾਤਾਲਾ ॥

Everything (that is outside) is also within the human body - the continents, worlds and worlds below worlds.

Third Guru GGS p. 112, line 12

ਇਸੁ ਕਾਇਆ ਅੰਦਰਿ ਬਹੁਤੁ ਪਸਾਰਾ ॥

Within this body are countless vast vistas.

Saint Pipa GGS p. 695, line 15

ਜੋ ਬ੍ਰਹਮੰਡੇ ਸੋਈ ਪਿੰਡੇ ਜੋ ਖੋਜੈ ਸੋ ਪਾਵੈ ॥

All that is in the universe is also in the body. Whoever explores it, will find out.

Air, water, and earth are sacred and should be taken care of like a Guru, father, and mother.

In many places, the scripture describes our natural environment - air, water, and earth as sacred and exhorts us to take care of it and revere it like a Guru, father, and mother.

God gave us all that is needed to sustain life in one fell swoop. The Divine design includes no provision for replenishment other than the built-in ability to repair and renew itself. So, we need to be very meticulous in protecting the air, water, and the earth for life to go on.

In their own words:

First Guru GGS p. 1037, line 3

ਹੁਕਮੇ ਪਉਣੁ ਪਾਣੀ ਗੈਣਾਰੰ ॥

By His Divine Order, air, water and the Akash came into being.

First Guru GGS p. 1021, line 2

ਪਉਣੁ ਗੁਰੂ ਪਾਣੀ ਪਿਤ ਜਾਤਾ ॥ ਉਦਰ ਸੰਜੋਗੀ ਧਰਤੀ ਮਾਤਾ ॥

Air is the agent of the Divine (like a Guru) which sustains life. Water is like a father where life originates. The Mother Earth produces for us like a mother's womb produces a child.

Second Guru GGS p. 8, line 10

ਪਵਣੁ ਗੁਰੂ ਪਾਣੀ ਪਿਤਾ ਮਾਤਾ ਧਰਤਿ ਮਹਤੁ ॥

Air is the agent of the Divine (like a Guru), Water is like Father, and Earth is the Great Mother of all.

First Guru GGS p. 1021, line 2

ਪਉਣੁ ਗੁਰੂ ਪਾਣੀ ਪਿਤ ਜਾਤਾ ॥

Air is the agent of the Divine (like a Guru and water is the originator of life like a father.

First Guru GGS p. 7, line 5

ਜੋ ਕਿਛੁ ਪਾਇਆ ਸੁ ਏਕਾ ਵਾਰ ॥

He has provided what is needed (to sustain life) in one fell swoop.

211

Chapter 11: Navigating life in this world

➢ *This world is a challenging place to navigate.*
➢ *God wants us to win the challenging game of life.*
➢ *We should earn our living in honest ways and have compassion for the needy.*
➢ *Only Almighty God liberates from the Karma record.*
➢ *Religious garb and rituals alone do not advance anyone on the path to the Divine.*

This world is a challenging place to navigate

The world is a tough place. Per Divine design, living in the world has a lot of challenges. In this Divine drama of life, actors are made to be ignorant of the Divine design, where they come from, and what their real home is. They are afflicted with ego, lust, greed, and attachment to themselves and their families. There is competitiveness and aggressiveness. The fact that people are not rewarded or punished for their actions immediately leads them to believe that nobody is watching and there is no accountability. So, over time, things can go from good to bad to worse and cause more pain and suffering than pleasure. There are a lot of evil actors and a lot of impediments to conquer which can exhaust people.

A total lack of transparency about what the future holds can be nerve-wrecking. Not knowing why we are here, where we came from, and where we go after death adds to the anxiety. Even though humans have developed law enforcement and justice systems to catch the offenders, so much goes unpunished because the Divine system, which only is capable of catching every offense, does not deliver prompt punishment that we can actually see.

Because we are caught in the cycle of birth and death based on our own Karma, there are many times when we feel as if we are in the middle of a terrifying ocean. The Sikh scripture reminds us that our real purpose in life is to break free from the Karma-driven cycle of birth and death, and to return to our true home with the Divine. This seems to be similar to the concept of eternal life in Christianity. Until people realize that there is God and their innate nature is divine, they suffer through the cycle of birth and death and are not liberated.[20]

Due to our ignorance of the Reality and the trappings of greed, ego, anger, lust, and attachments, it is difficult to absolutely stay on the right path such that we can be free of the automated cycle of birth and death on our own and go back home to the Divine. We are always on the slippery slope of doing something wrong. The only way to avoid bad karma and cross the frightening ocean of this world to return home is to stay aware of the Divine and the Divine System. Such realization will help us connect with God and enable us to refrain from hurting others. Remembrance and contemplation of God, refraining from hurting others, tempering our greed, anger, ego, and lust, and seeing past our attachment to worldly things and relationships are ways that will prepare us to go across the world ocean successfully.

In their own words:

Fifth Guru GGS p. 12, line 7

ਸਰੰਜਾਮਿ ਲਾਗੁ ਭਵਜਲ ਤਰਨ ਕੈ ॥

Put your efforts into crossing over this terrifying world-ocean (and to go back home).

First Guru GGS p. 59, line 11

ਭਵਜਲੁ ਬਿਖਮੁ ਡਰਾਵਣੋ ਨਾ ਕੰਧੀ ਨਾ ਪਾਰੁ ॥

The terrifying world-ocean is difficult and dreadful, not seeing the shore on this side or the one beyond.

Fourth Guru GGS p. 645, line 9

---

[20] John 5:24 "Very truly I tell you, whoever hears my word and believes him who sent me has eternal life and will not be judged but has crossed over from death to life." (Bible NIV)

ਜੋ ਸੇਵਹਿ ਸਤਿ ਮੁਰਾਰਿ ਸੇ ਭਵਜਲ ਤਰਿ ਗਇਆ ॥

Those who serve the True Divine, (who shows the Reality beyond our own self), cross over the terrifying world-ocean.

First Guru GGS p. 942, line 19
ਭਵਜਲੁ ਸਬਦਿ ਲੰਘਾਵਣਹਾਰੁ ॥੪੩॥

It is the Shabad that can carry us across the terrifying world-ocean.

First Guru GGS p. 1030, line 15
ਹਉਮੈ ਕਰਤਾ ਭਵਜਲਿ ਪਰਿਆ ॥

Believing own self to be all in all, one falls into the terrifying world-ocean.

First Guru GGS p. 1040, line 14
ਜੀਵਤ ਮਰਹੁ ਭਵਜਲੁ ਜਗੁ ਤਰਣਾ ॥

Annihilate your ego while living this life to cross over the terrifying world-ocean.

First Guru GGS p.1041, line 1
ਸਚ ਬਿਨੁ ਭਵਜਲੁ ਜਾਇ ਨ ਤਰਿਆ ॥

Without the Eternal Divine (as your support), the terrifying world-ocean cannot be crossed.

First Guru GGS p. 1042, line 6
ਇਹੁ ਭਵਜਲੁ ਜਗਤੁ ਸਬਦਿ ਗੁਰ ਤਰੀਐ ॥

Shabad is the vehicle to cross over this terrifying world-ocean.

God wants us to win the challenging game of life

We came to this world as actors in the grand Divine drama which is purposely designed to be a challenge. We must remember that God wants us to go back home victorious by getting over the various hurdles and not be caught in the endless Karma-driven cycle of birth and death. The key to winning this game is to develop awareness of God and temper the undesirable instincts that are part of this game.

In their own words:

Fifth Guru GGS p. 1185, line 12

ਕਾਮੁ ਕ੍ਰੋਧੁ ਲੋਭੁ ਮੋਹੁ ਜੀਤਹੁ ਐਸੀ ਖੇਲ ਹਰਿ ਪਿਆਰੀ ॥੨॥

Conquer lust, anger, greed and worldly attachment. (Having thrown these instincts into the game), conquering these instincts is a game dear to God.

First Guru GGS p. 23, line 15

ਇਹੁ ਤਨੁ ਧਰਤੀ ਬੀਜੁ ਕਰਮਾ ਕਰੋ ਸਲਿਲ ਆਪਾਉ ਸਾਰਿੰਗਪਾਣੀ ॥

Think of this body as a field and plant the seeds of good actions. Water it with the Name of the Divine.

Fifth Guru GGS p. 241, line 11

ਕਾਮ ਕ੍ਰੋਧ ਲੋਭੁ ਮੋਹੁ ਤਜੋ ॥

Abandon lust, anger, greed and attachment to this world.

Fifth Guru GGS p. 408, line 19

ਕਾਮੁ ਕ੍ਰੋਧੁ ਲੋਭੁ ਤਿਆਗੁ ॥

Abandon lust, anger and greed.

First Guru GGS p. 228, line 15

ਜਗੁ ਬਿਨਸਤ ਹਮ ਦੇਖਿਆ ਲੋਭੇ ਅਹੰਕਾਰਾ ॥

I have seen the world being destroyed by greed and egotism.

First Guru GGS p. 147, line 14

ਹੰਸੁ ਹੇਤੁ ਲੋਭੁ ਕੋਪੁ ਚਾਰੇ ਨਦੀਆ ਅਗਿ ॥

Cruelty, material attachment, greed and anger are the four rivers of fire.

Third Guru GGS p. 600, line 6
ਇਸੁ ਦੇਹੀ ਅੰਦਰਿ ਪੰਚ ਚੋਰ ਵਸਹਿ ਕਾਮੁ ਕ੍ਰੋਧੁ ਲੋਭੁ ਮੋਹੁ ਅਹੰਕਾਰਾ ॥
Within this body dwell the five thieves (which rob you of your opportunities to do good deeds) -lust, anger, greed, emotional attachment and egotism.

We should earn our living in honest ways and have compassion for the needy.

We need to temper our greed and earn our living in honest ways. We should practice contentment and not be overly greedy. We should show compassion for those who are less fortunate and offer our help. Serving those in need is more rewarding in the Divine Court compared to just practicing religious rituals and making pilgrimages to holy places. We will be rewarded for helping someone in need and reducing their pain and suffering.

In their own words:

First Guru GGS p. 472, line 8
ਨਾਨਕ ਅਗੈ ਸੋ ਮਿਲੈ ਜਿ ਖਟੇ ਘਾਲੇ ਦੇਇ ॥੧॥
Says Nanak, in the world hereafter, what you get is based on what you give (to the needy) from your own earnings and labor.

First Guru GGS p. 469, line 18
ਜੇਹਾ ਘਾਲੇ ਘਾਲਣਾ ਤੇਵੇਹੋ ਨਾਉ ਪਚਾਰੀਐ ॥ ਐਸੀ ਕਲਾ ਨ ਖੇਡੀਐ ਜਿਤੁ ਦਰਗਹ ਗਇਆ ਹਾਰੀਐ ॥

(In the world hereafter), you are known by your deeds. So do not play such a game that you will be judged a loser in the Divine Court.

First Guru GGS p. 1245, line 19

ਘਾਲਿ ਖਾਇ ਕਿਛੁ ਹਥਹੁ ਦੇਇ ॥ ਨਾਨਕ ਰਾਹੁ ਪਛਾਣਹਿ ਸੇਇ ॥੧॥

One who earns honest living and helps (the needy) with some of the earnings, recognizes the true path.

First Guru GGS p. 468, line 11

ਦਇਆ ਜਾਣੈ ਜੀਅ ਕੀ ਕਿਛੁ ਪੁੰਨੁ ਦਾਨੁ ਕਰੇਇ ॥

Showing mercy to other beings, sharing some part of your earnings with the needy.

First Guru GGS p. 1411, line 18

ਖੇਤੁ ਪਛਾਣੈ ਬੀਜੈ ਦਾਨੁ ॥

One who understands that the body is like a farm (to sow good karma) and plants the seeds of generosity.

Fifth Guru GGS p. 51, line 10

ਸਤੁ ਸੰਤੋਖੁ ਦਇਆ ਕਮਾਵੈ ਏਹ ਕਰਣੀ ਸਾਰ ॥

Practicing chastity, contentment and kindness which is the essence of conduct (in this human life).

Fifth Guru GGS p. 812, line 5

ਸਤੁ ਸੰਤੋਖੁ ਦਇਆ ਧਰਮੁ ਸੀਗਾਰੁ ਬਨਾਵਉ ॥

Adorn yourself with chastity, contentment, compassion and righteousness.

Fifth Guru GGS p. 213, line 11

ਕੋਟਿ ਜੋਰੇ ਲਾਖ ਕ੍ਰੋਰੇ ਮਨੁ ਨ ਹੋਰੇ ॥

People may accumulate hundreds of thousands, millions, tens of millions in wealth, and yet the mind is not content.

Fifth Guru GGS p. 379, line 3

ਕਾਮ ਕ੍ਰੋਧ ਮਾਇਆ ਮਦ ਮਤਸਰ ਏ ਖੇਲਤ ਸਭਿ ਜੂਐ ਹਾਰੇ ॥ ਸਤੁ ਸੰਤੋਖੁ
ਦਇਆ ਧਰਮੁ ਸਚੁ ਇਹ ਅਪੁਨੈ ਗ੍ਰਿਹ ਭੀਤਰਿ ਵਾਰੇ ॥੧॥ ਜਨਮ ਮਰਨ
ਚੁਕੇ ਸਭਿ ਭਾਰੇ ॥

Intoxicated by lust, anger, delusion of the Reality, ego and
jealousy, people gamble away the game of life. Usher in
chastity, contentment, compassion, righteousness and
truthfulness into yourself. That gets rid of the load of
Karma and liberates one from the cycle of birth and death.

Only Almighty God liberates from the Karma record.

Seeing the widespread practice of worshipping various
gods and goddesses as part of the Hindu religion, the Sikh
Gurus and other saints whose writings are included in the
Sikh scripture stressed to worship only One God. According
to them, only God can erase one's Karma record and liberate
from the Karma-driven cycle of birth and death. They
explained that if there are any gods and goddesses or deities,
they are under the command of One Almighty God. They
preached that the powers which were erroneously being
associated with many gods and goddesses were, in fact, the
powers of God. Because people were accustomed to reciting
names of certain deities (e.g., Ram, Vishnu, Brahma, Shiva),
the Sikh scripture exhorted them to start associating those
names with God instead of the mythical or fictional characters
associated with those names in ancient literature with too
fantastical stories about them. To teach worshippers of
various deities to focus on one God, the Sikh scripture uses
the names of those deities for God extensively and freely.

Those who experienced the Divine also stressed that one
should not succumb to worshipping deities, gods, and
goddesses out of fear and greed. Any deities or other gods one

worships will transform the worshipper's mind based on their own attributes. Those deities would affect and guide the mind of the worshipper, who will end up imbibing the characteristics of those deities. We should not let anybody prey on our fears of disease and death. Contemplating God and praying is a better way of allaying our fears. Rains, fires, and other natural calamities are physical phenomena, and there are no gods of fire and water to appease. Worshipping One Almighty God will make a person kind, fearless, and without enmity.

In their own words:

Fifth Guru GGS p. 455, line 19
ਕੋਟਿ ਦੇਵੀ ਜਾ ਕਉ ਸੇਵਹਿ ਲਖਿਮੀ ਅਨਿਕ ਭਾਤਿ ॥

Millions of gods including Luxmi (the Hindu goddess of wealth) worship God in so many ways.

Fifth Guru GGS p. 740, line 1
ਰਹਣੁ ਨ ਪਾਵਹਿ ਸੁਰਿ ਨਰ ਦੇਵਾ ॥

The angelic beings and demi-gods do not live for ever- they have to face death too.

First Guru GGS p 227, line 4
ਮਾਇਆ ਮੋਹੇ ਦੇਵੀ ਸਭਿ ਦੇਵਾ ॥

All the gods and goddesses are caught in the delusion (Maya) too.

Fifth Guru GGS p. 258, line 14
ਭਰਮੇ ਸੁਰਿ ਨਰ ਦੇਵੀ ਦੇਵਾ ॥

The angelic beings, goddesses and gods are in delusion too (not knowing their origin and destination).

First Guru GGS p. 223, line 19
ਜੈਸਾ ਸੇਵੈ ਤੈਸੋ ਹੋਇ ॥੪॥

You become like the one you worship.

Third Guru GGS p. 755, line 8
ਏ ਮਨ ਜੈਸਾ ਸੇਵਹਿ ਤੈਸਾ ਹੋਵਹਿ ਤੇਹੇ ਕਰਮ ਕਮਾਇ ॥

O' mind, who you worship, so do you become, and so are the deeds that you do.

Religious garb and rituals alone do not advance anyone on the path to the Divine.

When Sikhism came into being in India, people were engaged in many rituals in their daily lives. There was a significant emphasis on pilgrimages and purifying the body by taking baths at holy places. Despite the Hindu scriptures, such as the Vedas, pointing to the existence of one God and the importance of remembering God, the priestly class engaged the masses in various rituals for their own benefit. The kings and rich people were engaged in elaborate fire ceremonies and sacrificial offerings to the gods. The priestly class performed various rituals at birth, marriage, and death and enriched itself at the expense of the poor and ignorant. People were lured into paying for the welfare of their deceased relatives and praying for the good fortune of the living. The priestly class distinguished itself by its garb and exercised its superiority and access to the Divine.

The Sikh Gurus explained that unless various rituals helped in the understanding and remembrance of one Almighty God and resulted in steady transformation of the mind to do good deeds, those rituals were futile. They asserted that the priestly class did not have special access to the Divine. Instead, they advised everyone to remember one

God who has created the world and sustains it. They stressed that after death, it is only one's good and bad deeds and remembrance of God that will decide one's fate.

Guru Nanak, the founder of the Sikh religion traveled far and wide within India as well as outside of India. He made it his mission to clear the confusion around various gods and goddesses and to convince people about the existence of One God. He tried to show the futility of so many rituals that the priestly class had engaged people in for their personal gain. He went to various places of pilgrimage to engage in dialogue with those who could use their positions to guide people about God and how the Divine system works.

Sikh Gurus and saints from other faiths whose statements are included in Guru Granth Sahib also questioned how somebody professing to be a religious person could engage in the cruel practice of sacrificial killing of animals as was being practiced by some Hindu sects at the time. They advocated the devotional transformational approach over Hatha Yoga and renunciation. They firmly believed that spiritually evolved individuals should stay in society and benefit it with their knowledge rather than staying away from it.

In their own words:

First Guru GGS p. 75, line 17

ਤੀਰਥ ਵਰਤ ਸੁਚਿ ਸੰਜਮੁ ਨਾਹੀ ਕਰਮੁ ਧਰਮੁ ਨਹੀ ਪੂਜਾ ॥ ਨਾਨਕ ਭਾਇ ਭਗਤਿ ਨਿਸਤਾਰਾ ਦੁਬਿਧਾ ਵਿਆਪੈ ਦੂਜਾ ॥੨॥

Neither pilgrimages, nor fasts, nor refusing to touch this or that to assert purity nor ritual ceremonies or worship. Says Nanak, only loving devotional meditation can liberate you from the cycle of birth and death. All else keeps one in duality (instead of oneness with God).

First Guru GGS p. 1245, line 10

ਸਚੁ ਵਰਤੁ ਸੰਤੋਖੁ ਤੀਰਥੁ ਗਿਆਨੁ ਧਿਆਨੁ ਇਸਨਾਨੁ ॥ ਦਇਆ ਦੇਵਤਾ
ਖਿਮਾ ਜਪਮਾਲੀ ਤੇ ਮਾਣਸ ਪਰਧਾਨ ॥

(Speaking of ritualistic fasting and pilgrimages) Those who observe truth as their fast, contentment as their sacred pilgrimage, spiritual wisdom and meditation as their cleansing bath, consider kindness as their deity and forgiveness as their rosary-are the ones who will get Divine approval.

Saint Parmanand GGS p. 1253, line 5

ਤੈ ਨਰ ਕਿਆ ਪੁਰਾਨੁ ਸੁਨਿ ਕੀਨਾ ॥ਅਨਪਾਵਨੀ ਭਗਤਿ ਨਹੀ ਉਪਜੀ ਭੂਖੈ
ਦਾਨੁ ਨ ਦੀਨਾ ॥੧॥ ਰਹਾਉ ॥ਕਾਮੁ ਨ ਬਿਸਰਿਓ ਕ੍ਰੋਧੁ ਨ ਬਿਸਰਿਓ ਲੋਭੁ ਨ
ਛੁਟਿਓ ਦੇਵਾ ॥ਪਰ ਨਿੰਦਾ ਮੁਖ ਤੇ ਨਹੀ ਛੂਟੀ ਨਿਫਲ ਭਈ ਸਭ ਸੇਵਾ ॥੧॥

So think of what you have accomplished by listening to the Puraanas (a category of Hindu scriptures). If lasting devotion has not welled up within you, and you do not give food to the hungry. If you have not tamed your lust and anger and you are still driven by greed. If you have not stopped slandering others. Your service (time spent in the name of God) has all gone in vain.

Saint Kabir, GGS p. 324, line 10

ਕਾਇਆ ਰਤਿ ਬਹੁ ਰੂਪ ਰਚਾਹੀ ॥ ਤਿਨ ਕਉ ਦਇਆ ਸੁਪਨੈ ਭੀ ਨਾਹੀ
॥੨॥

There are those who are more into how (religious) they look and they adorn various garbs. They do not feel compassion even in their dreams.

Saint Kabir GGS p. 970, line 18

ਕਹਤੁ ਕਬੀਰੁ ਸੁਨਹੁ ਰੇ ਸੰਤਹੁ ਧਰਮੁ ਦਇਆ ਕਰਿ ਬਾੜੀ ॥੩॥੭॥

Says Kabir, listen, O' Saints: cultivate righteousness and compassion.

Chapter 12: Takeaways

Awareness of the Divine and the Divine System can make the world a better place.

Over time, too many people have lost touch with the Divine and think that this world is all there is. They want to accumulate as much wealth and power as they can to ensure their own security and control over others. Thinkers and wise leaders have come up with justice systems and political and social structures that force people to behave in a way that is conducive to maintaining a semblance of equality, justice, and order. However, these systems are not capable of catching all the offenses. Additionally, these systems are being challenged worldwide by individuals seeking power, who utilize disinformation and various tactics to fulfill their own agendas while suppressing dissent with impunity.

History is replete with rulers and leaders who have used religion as a tool to consolidate their power and to unleash hate, bigotry, and persecution of those who stand in the way. In our own time now, we are witnessing the destruction of life, livelihoods, and liberty by ruthless rulers on a scale that nobody ever imagined could occur after countries had come up with an international order to protect people.

In many parts of the world today, religion is frequently used as a tool to consolidate power, even by those who have no genuine allegiance to the faith they claim to follow. They simply use religion as a tool to gain and retain power. While atrocities by some autocratic rulers are visible for people to see, in so many other countries, repression and brutality are being perpetrated against religious and other minorities under the radar to achieve similar goals.

Prophets of major religions and enlightened people from time to time have given the world messages that there indeed is God whose consciousness has designed the Divine system and governs it. They tell us that God is loving, merciful, and forgiving, but there is accountability for our actions.

However, over time, the spiritual aspects of all religions have been relegated to the background. Instead, their primary focus has been on strengthening religious establishments and institutions with objectives that diverge from the original goals of the prophets who founded those faiths. So much so that it is not inconceivable that religious scriptures written long after a prophet's time might have fallen prey to the machinations of those who wanted to use religion as a tool to gain and maintain power.

Various religious establishments have strayed very far from their prophets' messages about the Divine and the Divine system. They are partnering with politicians and rulers who want to divide and rule. They share the same desire to control as the rulers and would dig up anything aside from their main holy scriptures that they could use to create a wedge among people to serve their own interests.

Those who had direct experiences of the Divine provide a clear and simple roadmap of how we should conduct ourselves in this world. Here are some reflections on how the revelations of those who have experienced the Divine can inspire personal growth and contribute to creating a more just and harmonious world.

Let us connect with the same God that the prophet we revere was connected to.

All those who have personally experienced the Divine testify that God is conscious, compassionate, and in control and holds everyone accountable. Prophets of all major religions proclaimed the same Divine message. No prophets ever gave us a message that God hates some and loves some simply because of who they are. Their messages reinforce God as the supreme Father who is loving, kind, forgiving, and compassionate. There is no "other" for God. We all came from the same God. All of us are subject to the same Divine rules of conduct and justice.

God sent our prophets to this world to give us God's message in various nooks and corners of the world and to speak to us in languages that we could understand. God wants us to understand that this world is not all there is, and we are not meant to live in misery. God wants us to know that even though there is accountability for our actions, there is a pathway to forgiveness and redemption by realizing the error of our ways and by keeping the Divine in our minds. By connecting with the Divine, we can make the most of this life and go back home to the Divine, which is pure bliss.

We must disregard any insinuations or messages about our God vs. other people's God. We are children of the same God and subject to the same Divine rules. We should try to understand the motivations and intentions of those who try to use us to engender hate and enmity towards others by distracting us from the One Almighty God that our prophet spoke of.

Let us not smear our own Men of God (Prophets).

Power-hungry people have found that religion has the most sway over people's minds and can be used as the most potent tool to consolidate their own power and for domination over others. These people attribute statements to their prophets that are not consistent with the prophet's description of the Divine. In the process of creating self-serving divisions based on religion, the rulers and religious establishments who stand to benefit from that do not care that they are distorting the Divine truth and smearing their own prophets. It is entirely possible that those seeking to consolidate their power by creating self-serving divisions based on religion, may have introduced the idea of exclusive access to God.

We should not smear our own prophets by attributing messages to them that lack compassion, kindness and justice and result in spreading hate and division. We should not accept branding and re-branding of our prophet's message by some for their own ulterior motives. To re-focus on the Divine and the Divine System, a good way is to take your own prophet's key messages about God and the Divine System and see if what you are told to do by the religious establishment is consistent with those key messages.

We need to reclaim our prophets' messages about the Divine and the Divine system. God's doors are open for anyone, and there is no preferential or exclusive access. The Divine system of accountability, justice, forgiveness, and redemption applies equally to all. As various prophets have proclaimed, there is only One God, no other. We are all children of the same God.

We should experience the joy of life and not live in misery.

God has staged a magnificent Divine Play with immensely diverse and rich life and natural phenomena for us to enjoy and wants us to win the game of life. Just as we design games and sports by incorporating some hurdles to make the game more challenging and interesting, God has incorporated some built-in challenges in the Divine game that we are part of.

Playful and Blissful God wants us to have joy in living and wants us to live life to the fullest. God wants us to enjoy the world with all of our senses and not be miserable accumulating riches and making enemies. We are here to have a good time participating in the magnificent Divine Play in this world. The formless Divine created life forms with various senses of perception and feeling for us to experience and enjoy the world.

Instead of experiencing joy, we are caught up in excessive greed and unhealthy attachments to this world. Let us try to temper the built-in instincts of greed, anger, ego, lust, and unhealthy attachment to this world. Remembering that we are here as actors in a play and will be judged based on how well we overcame the various afflictions can give us a goal for this life.

But one might ask: How would a society focused on the world beyond this life flourish? Wouldn't all progress come to a halt with us living in kind of a stone age?

When put in the perspective of why the Divine created this world in the first place, one can see that it is not an either/or choice where you either enjoy this world or have a blissful existence in the life beyond. We are here to enjoy life as well. The problems arise when we lose sight of the life beyond the transient life in this world. Life here is a delicate balancing act. What is problematic is the excessive greed, ego, and unhealthy attachments to this world.

Additionally, we need to answer this question in terms of the human spirit, which is endlessly creative and fun-loving. We have been led to believe that greed, ego, and attachment to this world are essential for humans to keep on exploring, inventing, and discovering new frontiers. But is excessive greed, ego and unhealthy attachment to this world necessary for enhancing the quality of life in this world? Excessive greed just leads people to accumulate wealth for the sake of wealth and not to serve any purpose. Knowing the distinction between healthy and unhealthy attachment in this world will result in more equitable sharing and service to others. The human spirit has drivers other than excessive greed to build a flourishing society where the total happiness level for all would be better. What we need is a paradigm shift of the mind, which knowledge of the Divine and the Divine system can help create. It cannot be done well by regulation and over-regulation alone.

The human body, in particular, is a prized life form because of the enormous intellect, intuition, and control that it can exert over the rest of the species. All other species crave this opportunity to have human life. Humans have the unique capability to understand and connect with God and get out of the Karma-driven cycle of birth and death based on our actions.

The goal of human life is to enjoy and win the game of life, get out of the Karma-driven cycle of birth and death, and go back home, which is all bliss. Enjoy participating in the Divine drama. You chose to be part of it to enjoy. Don't sweat too much accumulating wealth that you do not need.

We need to conduct ourselves with the awareness of the existence of the Divine.

All those who experienced the Divine personally, including prophets, saints, and gurus, have a simple message for us. They say that we should conduct ourselves in life with the awareness of the existence of the Divine and the Divine system of governance and redemption. It is the same Divine for all of us who is conscious, compassionate and in-control and holds everyone accountable. We should refrain from bad actions and should add to our count of good actions. Imagine what our world would be like if everyone acted with the awareness that the Divine system is watching all that we do and that we would be held accountable.

Because of the absence of prompt punishment or reward from the Divine for our actions, we often believe that nobody is watching. Those in power, in particular, become the worst actors. They think they can escape accountability because of their grip on power, by disinformation campaigns and by repression. Those who experienced the Divine caution us against fooling ourselves. They say we will be held accountable for everything we do.

As God is merciful and forgiving, a key feature of the Divine design is that remembrance of God and prayer will put aside any bad Karma. God knows that we are purposely afflicted with instincts such as greed and attachments as part of the Divine Play, and we are always on a slippery slope of making mistakes in spite of our best efforts. When we become aware of the existence of God, realize the error of our ways, and develop a longing to connect with God, the record of our actions is set aside, and we become free of the automated Karma-driven cycle of birth and death and go back to our eternal home to the Divine.

Connecting with God is the only means for us to get out of the Karma-driven cycle of birth and death and go back home. Remembrance of God is the currency that will help us erase our bad actions. We need to prioritize remembrance of God in our daily life above everything else because liberation from the Karma-driven cycle of birth and death is only possible with His remembrance and Grace.

However, we must keep in mind that nothing in the Divine design is subject to manipulation. There is no room for lying, disinformation, and influence-pedaling in the Divine court. So, we cannot count on a plan to remember

God at the end of life while continuing bad behavior throughout life. Remembrance of God is not a switch that we or our loved ones can turn on for us at the time of death. We cannot have God in our minds while dying if we do not have God in mind while living.

It is not our role to judge people.

Beyond the established legal system and ethical standards of society for it to function smoothly, it is not our role to judge people. While being aware that God holds us accountable for our actions, one thing that we must never do is to look at somebody's suffering and walk past thinking this person must have done something horrible in a past life. Life in this world is complex, and we do not know precisely why things happen in people's lives. There are good reasons why the Divine has unfolded only a tiny part of our life to us in this world. We must be helpful and try to reduce the suffering of those around us.

Imagine a world where all are focused on good Karma, help those in need, and fight disease, hunger, and evil together. We can create a heaven on earth if we focus on our actions and avoid bad Karma.

Our actions should be guided by the ultimate fact that life is short and we have an eternal home to return to.

It is important to remember that we are here on earth for a short time and must go back home. Although people may live to 100 years or more which seems very long and forever, in the journey of the soul, life in this world is like a blip or a one-night dream. Death is certain, although the time of death is uncertain.

No one can take any belongings or property with them when they die. The only thing that accompanies a person is a record of their deeds during their lifetime. One should not use dishonest ways to accumulate wealth and riches because none of that wealth will go along after death. We should not be fooled and carried away by the desire to leave our heirs big fortunes using corrupt ways of gathering wealth. Our heirs are actors in the drama and will not be answerable for us in the Divine court.

So let us earn our living in honest ways and share with the needy. Let us not be overly greedy and let us temper other instincts as well (you cannot totally overcome them because they are built-in and necessary to carry out tasks in life) for peaceful coexistence and enjoyment of life

Knowing that we must leave everything behind upon death is not saddening but truly liberating.

The realization that we do not die but go back home is a liberating feeling that creates a blissful state of mind (Anand). It is only the body that dies and the soul lives on. The person who truly realizes that it is only the record of our deeds in this world that will go with us will work on creating a good record and not waste time accumulating what must be left behind. If we truly remember God and understand that we are here for a short time and cannot take anything along after death, we will avoid doing anything hurtful or bad to others.

The soul does not die. One should be fearless and stand up for what is right.

Our life essence, inner being, or soul does not die because its origin is Divine. It is only the body that dies. The soul can manifest in various life forms throughout the cycle of birth and death. In the continuum of life of our soul, this whole life is like a blip or a one-night dream. Like a good or bad dream, it will soon pass even though it seems very long to us. We should maintain our focus on God and the divine design and continue to do good even when facing difficult situations.

Those who experience the Divine come to see that this world is a magnificent Divine Play, and nobody dies as the soul is immortal. Their fears of death are dispelled, and they become fearless. Such enlightened people do not intimidate or strike fear in anyone, but they are not intimidated by anyone else either. That is the reason that truly spiritual people stood up to injustices and tyrannical rulers in the past and gave their lives for humanity. History is replete with examples such as of Jesus Christ, Sikh Gurus and other holy ones who sacrificed their lives to help others.

The enlightened ones say that God can even transform the sinners and erase their sins; He is the one who can rid one of fear. He is the support of those who have no support.

One should be vigilant in spiritual pursuit as many bad actors are trying to exploit.

The touchstone in the journey to the Divine is to connect with One Almighty God. We need to be vigilant of those whose only goal is to secure our connection to them personally. There are a lot of actors in this space for their own interests. We should only follow in the footsteps of those whose conduct and actions in life match their words and teachings. Anybody preaching to others to part with their wealth but accumulating it themselves is obviously not spiritual.

One should not succumb to worshipping deities out of fear or greed. If the deities and gods and goddesses with power do exist, they are under the command of the One God. Additionally, any deity or gods and goddesses who are described as not having control of lust, greed, anger, and ego cannot be good role models to shape our moral values and behavior. It is important to be aware that any deities or other gods we worship will affect and transform our minds based on their own attributes. We will end up being guided by the personalities of those deities that we hear about over and over and can imbibe their own characteristics.

Connecting with One Almighty God who will make us kind, fearless, and without enmity and will redeem us of any bad Karma should be our goal.

Let us not blame God for all the evil we see. Our apathy and self-interest helps evil grow.

God put a magnificent Divine play into motion for all of us to enjoy. It is us who have made it a mess. Let us not blame God for all the evil we see. Evil only grows when we think we do not need to bother or are afraid to confront it. We are God's eyes and ears. We can stop evil in its tracks, but we do not because it does not affect us or may actually benefit us. Evil cannot survive if we stand up to it when it hurts others. Indifference helps evil grow to the point that we all get affected. But it may be too late by that time. We should never succumb to fear or intimidation by others or strike fear in anyone else.

Don't be disheartened if you are not able to change the outcome by your actions.

We only have the duty and the ability to act righteously. The outcome of our actions is not in our hands. How things turn out depends on how the Divine System ordained it. The

Divine System holds us accountable for our actions, not whether we were able to change the outcome. Sometimes, we take some actions and do not get the result we want to see and get discouraged. We get disheartened and start to believe that maybe there is no God, which would be a mistake.

Many times, we refrain from taking action because it seems futile. We think we are too small and inadequate to make a difference and decide not to bother. Remembering that the result is not in our hands and we are not judged by the result but by our actions can make us more willing and ready to help.

Let us do our part to mitigate natural disasters by not upsetting the delicate balance of nature.

We are here to enjoy the beauty of the natural environment that we have been blessed with. God gave us everything we need in abundance in one fell swoop. Let us take care of the environment because God is not coming to replenish what he gave us in this cycle of creation. We are the custodians of the natural environment, and we can shape it for the better or for the worse.

Take care of this earth as you would take care of your mother. Treat water as you would treat your father and take care of it. Treat air with the same reverence as you would for your Guru.

Let us start connecting with the Divine Creator.

Let us start connecting with the Divine Creator and experience the awe and wonder of life around us. Wow! Wow!

is the only expression we will find ourselves capable of when we explore and witness the Divine!

In their own words:

First Guru GGS p. 788, line 15
ਵਾਹੁ ਖਸਮ ਤੂ ਵਾਹੁ ਜਿਨਿ ਰਚਿ ਰਚਨਾ ਹਮ ਕੀਏ ॥
Wow! My Master! Wow! You engineered the Creation and made us.

Third Guru GGS p. 755, line 2
ਵਾਹੁ ਮੇਰੇ ਸਾਹਿਬਾ ਵਾਹੁ ॥
Wow! My Master! Wow!

Bottomline

Prophets, saints, gurus, and sages from all religions who personally experienced the Divine state that there is One God for all of us who is conscious, compassionate, and in control and has a justice system that holds everyone accountable. We are all children of the same God. Imagine a world where everybody truly believed this and acted as if the Divine system was watching all of our actions!

God has staged a magnificent Divine Play with immensely diverse and rich life and natural phenomena for us to enjoy and wants us to win the game of life. We are all actors in this Play and have been given the challenge to act justly in spite of some built-in instincts such as lust, greed, ego, anger, etc. We have been purposely kept in the dark about our origin and our destination.

Merciful God knows that we have a tough challenge to win the game of life and can get caught up in the Karma-driven cycle of birth and death based on our actions alone. A feature of the Divine design is that whoever becomes aware of the existence of God and connects with God is redeemed and freed of the Karma record. The goal of human life is to solve this puzzle, connect with God, and go back to our eternal home.

However, we have been led astray by those who want to gain and retain power using religion as a divisive tool. It is time for us to connect with the same God that our prophet was connected to. There is more common between various prophets' messages for us than what we are often led to believe. When we hear various people talk about their God versus other people's God and exclusive or preferential access to God, we need to be skeptical about the religiosity of the statement.

The goal of human life is to enjoy and win the game of life, get out of the Karma-driven cycle of birth and death, and go back home, which is all bliss. Enjoy participating in the Divine drama. You chose to be part of it. Don't sweat too much accumulating wealth that you do not need.

Let us start connecting with the Divine Creator and experience the awe and wonder of life around us. Wow! Wow! is the only expression we will find ourselves capable of when we witness the Divine!

End

Acknowledgements

The descriptions of the Divine and the Divine system in the Sikh scripture Guru Granth Sahib are written in the common spoken language of the people and for the common people, so they are quite easy to understand. However, there are descriptions of some mystical experiences, and references to some phenomena that are not visible to us, where help of those who have deeper knowledge in that area is useful. Various interpretative books called *steeks* have been written to help understand those areas.

I am deeply indebted to Professor Sahib Singh Ji and Bhai Vir Singh Ji for their *steeks* and the authors of every other *steek* who have performed the labor of love to make these descriptions easier to understand.

I owe an immense debt of gratitude to Dr. Sant Singh Khalsa whose English translation is the latest. Seeing various translations, I see that each successive translation has benefitted from the ones before. Built on the translation by Bhai Manmohan Singh, I found Dr Khalsa's translation very helpful and have used it as my starting point.

I am so very thankful to Dr. Kulbir Singh Thind of *Srigranth.org* for his invaluable contribution to make not only the Guru Granth Sahib electronically accessible, but also various *steeks* and English translations with all the needed search capabilities. He is indeed a visionary and a pioneer who understood the need for this years ago and started this project when nobody was thinking about it.